THE THIRTY-FOURTH DIVISION
1915-1919

MAJOR-GENERAL E. C. INGOUVILLE-WILLIAMS, C.B., D.S.O.
Who made the 34th Division

[Frontispiece]

THE
THIRTY FOURTH
DIVISION

The Story of its Career from
Ripon to the Rhine

1915 – 1919

By
LIEUT.-COLONEL J. SHAKESPEAR,
C.M.G., C.I.E., D.S.O.

PUBLISHED BY
THE NAVAL & MILITARY PRESS

PREFACE

DEAR COMRADES OF THE 34TH DIVISION,—I am very sorry this is such an inadequate account of what you did, and I am also sorry that I have been so long writing it. Although it is far from being the sort of book that the 34th Division deserves, yet I hope that some of you will find it interesting, and if some of you think that what you yourselves did has not been sufficiently described you are probably right, but I've done my best with the material and the space at my disposal, and I have honestly tried to give everyone a fair show, so please don't shoot the Author —he's done his best.

My thanks are due to our late G.O.C. for so kindly wading through the typescript, for giving me many useful hints and much very valuable information, and also for the loan of his diaries and maps, without which the book could not have been written. I have also to thank many others for help and loans of maps, diaries, etc.; among these are Colonel Simpson, Lieutenant-Colonel Vignoles, Majors Pery-Knox-Gore, Glendenning, Anderson, and Rought; Captains Grieg, Willis and Wilson; Lieutenant Robson, and Corporal Brierley.

If some of the space has been occupied with the trivialities of war I hope you will not feel that it has been wasted. I want to bring back to you the good times as well as the days of stress and trial. I don't know what you think, but personally I consider the three years I spent in the 34th Division as the happiest time in my life.

Wishing you all the best of luck, and asking your pardon for the inadequacy of my story, I remain, yours ever.

JOHN SHAKESPEAR

CONTENTS

LIST OF ILLUSTRATIONS

MAPS

THE THIRTY-FOURTH
DIVISION 1915-1919

CHAPTER I

THE RAISING OF THE DIVISION

IT was my original intention to give full particulars
of the raising of the different units of the Division, for
every detail connected with the raising and equipment
of the immense force, which was called into being to
meet the German onslaught, is of interest, and the
names of all those who found the money, and gave
their labour gratuitously and unsparingly, to create
the force, and to supply their units with comforts and
assist the dependents through the weary years of
war, should certainly be placed on record. But I
have had to abandon the idea on account of the
necessity of keeping the record within the limits of
space allowed me, and therefore, I can only in the
name of the Division thank our numerous " Raisers "
for their very great kindness and liberality to us and
our dependents, and assure them that we are grateful
and shall never forget.

The 34th was a typical New Army Division. By
the time it came to be raised most of the old hands,
whether in the commissioned or non-commissioned
ranks, had joined up, and our units were composed
almost entirely of new men, with little, if any,

military training, and very few indeed had ever been on active service. Prior to our embarkation, however, some senior officers from the B.E.F. joined various units.

The composition of the Division is shown below :

DIVISIONAL ARTILLERY.

152nd Brigade R.F.A.—Raised by the Mayor of Nottingham's Recruiting Committee.

160th Brigade R.F.A.—Raised early in 1915 by Alderman Stanefield Richardson, the Mayor of Sunderland, and Recruiting Committee. First Commanding Officer, Colonel C. W. P. Barker, R.G.A. (T.).

175th Brigade R.F.A.—Raised in Staffordshire by Colonel E. C. Meisey Thompson.

176th Brigade R.F.A. (Howitzers).—Raised in June, 1915, by a Committee in Leicester, presided over by the Duke of Rutland and Alderman J. North, Mayor of Leicester. First Commanding Officer, Colonel L. E. Coker, R.F.A.

Divisional Ammunition Column.—Raised in Nottingham during the summer of 1915, and later moved to Codford. The personnel had but little experience of horsemastership, and when Lieutenant-Colonel C. A. Simpson took over command in November, 1915, he found much to be done, but all ranks were keen, and by the time came for embarkation the Column was fit to take the field. Lieutenant-Colonel Simpson held command until the 34th Division gave place to the Eastern Division.

ROYAL ENGINEERS.

207th Field Company.	All the Companies were raised in Norwich, by the Mayor (Gordon Munn, Esq.) and a Committee. Colonel A. C. MacDonnell, R.E., took command, and organised the units, becoming the first C.R.E. of 34th Division.
208th Field Company.	
209th Field Company.	
Signal Company.	

INFANTRY.

101st Brigade.—Brigadier-General H. G. Fitton, C.B., D.S.O. A.D.C. The Brigade was first brought together at Ripon, in June, 1915.

15th Royal Scots.—Raised in September, 1914, half in Edinburgh, by the Lord Provost, and half in Manchester, by the Lord Mayor. First Commanding Officer, Sir R. Cranston, K.C.V.O., C.B.

16th Royal Scots,—Raised in Edinburgh in November, 1914, by Sir George McCrae and a Committee. First Commanding Officer, Sir George McCrae.

10th Lincoln Regiment.—Raised at Grimsby in September, 1914, by the Mayor and a Committee. First Commanding Officer, Lieutenant-Colonel the Honourable G. E. Heneage.

11th Suffolk Regiment.—Raised at Cambridge during September, 1914, and following months by Cambridgeshire and Isle of Ely Territorial Force Association. First Commanding Officer, Colonel C. W. Somerset, M.V.O.

102nd *Brigade* (*The Tyneside Scottish Brigade*).—Brigadier Trevor Ternan, C.M.G., D.S.O. The Brigade was concentrated in hutments at Alnwick by end of March, 1915. The Brigade was raised by Mr Johnstone Wallace (now Sir Johnstone Wallace, K.B.E.), Lord Mayor of Newcastle, and a representative Committee of Scotsmen.

20th Northumberland Fusiliers (1st Tyneside Scottish).— First Commanding Officer, Lieutenant-Colonel C. H. Innes Hopkins (late Scottish Rifles).

21st Northumberland Fusiliers (2nd Tyneside Scottish).— First Commanding Officer, Colonel V. M. Stockley (late Indian Cavalry).

22nd Northumberland Fusiliers (3rd Tyneside Scottish).— First Commanding Officer, Lieutenant-Colonel A. P. A. Elphinstone (late Indian Army).

23rd Northumberland Fusiliers (4th Tyneside Scottish).— First Commanding Officer, Captain J. C. Campbell (Militia).

103rd *Brigade* (*The Tyneside Irish Brigade*).—Brigadier-General Collings, who was shortly succeeded by Brigadier-General O'Leary, who held command till September 1915, when he received another appointment, and Brigadier-General Malcolm took command, but was succeeded by Brigadier-General N. J. G. Cameron, C.M.G., before the Brigade left England. The Brigade was trained at Woolsington Camp. The Brigade was raised by a representative Committee of Irishmen, under the Presidency of Sir Charles Parsons. Both the Irish and Scottish Brigades were at first financed by Colonel Joseph Cowen, of Stella Hall, Blaydon-on-Tyne.

24th Northumberland Fusiliers (1st Tyneside Irish).—First Commanding Officer, Colonel V. M. Stockley (late Indian Cavalry).

25th Northumberland Fusiliers (2nd Tyneside Irish).—First Commanding Officer, Lieutenant-Colonel H. M. Hatchell, D.S.O. (late 18th Royal Irish).

26th Northumberland Fusiliers (3rd Tyneside Irish).—First Commanding Officer, Lieutenant-Colonel Hussey-Walsh (late 1st Cheshire Regiment).

27th Northumberland Fusiliers (4th Tyneside Irish).—First Commanding Officer, Lieutenant-Colonel L. Grattan Esmonde (late Waterford R.F.A.).

Pioneer Battalion (18th Northumberland Fusiliers).—Raised by the Military Committee of Newcastle and Gateshead Chamber of Commerce. First Commanding Officer, Major R. Temperly, T.D. (late 6th Northumberland Fusiliers and Chairman of Military Committee Chamber of Commerce).

The raising and equipment of the different units was entrusted by the War Office to various local bodies, who found all the money necessary, and made all arrangements for clothing, housing, and equipping the troops, and later recovered from the War Office as much as they could of the cost. Units raised in this way fared better than those raised by the War Office direct, for the " Raisers " were unhampered by any of the rules and regulations which control a government department, and as they conducted their own recruiting campaigns, in some cases in opposition to a rival body in the same town or area, they were anxious to do their recruits as well as possible, and every want was promptly supplied, without any thought as to how much was going to be recovered. In almost every case a great many business men were to be found amongst the " Raisers," and these formed sub-committees, each of which dealt with the details of that portion of the task with which its members were most conversant.

The system worked well, in so far as the rapid raising and equipping of the force was concerned, and there is no doubt that these various local bodies saved the situation; without their aid the task could not have been completed, and they certainly deserve well of their country.

Whether the country is justified in expecting individuals voluntarily, for no remuneration, to undertake such difficult tasks, and incur such heavy liabilities, is very doubtful.

What these local bodies were out of pocket, after recovering all they could from Government, it is impossible to say. The amounts probably varied considerably. The net cost to one such body, which raised about five thousand five hundred men, worked out to just over £50,000, of which about one-tenth is represented by the amounts paid in connection with the raising, which were not recovered from Government. Nearly four-fifths of the sum was expended on dependents and discharged men.

How was the force raised ? How were the officers and non-commissioned officers obtained ? Very simply. Once permission to recruit had been obtained from the War Office, which in some cases was not so simple, advertisements in the local press and a few posters, brought together groups of men of all classes, who lined up in some by-road, under the supervision of some local celebrity with a certain amount of military training. If a young fellow had O.T.C. training, he was at once haled out, invested with authority, and turned on to drill the remainder. Commissions in those days were easily got. Generally some elderly retired officer of the Regular, Militia, Territorial, or Volunteer forces would be given command on the recommendation of the Mayor, Provost, or other head of the " Raisers." Before him would be paraded various aspirants for commissions, callow youths, young men, middle-aged men, nay, even old men. A few minutes' conversation, a few searching questions, and the applicant would withdraw. If he had met with approval, he would receive an order to join as soon as possible, with an intimation that his name had been submitted by the Mayor to the War Office for a commission as Second-Lieutenant in the ――. That was all. No competitive exams, no worrying delay. A casual system, no doubt, but how well it worked! There were, of course, cases in which the selections did not turn out satisfactory, but they were surprisingly few.

As numbers increased, sections, platoons, and companies were formed. Command of these was given without any regard for seniority. What was seniority worth when all were such recent recruits? Men with the necessary qualities of leaders and administrators were picked, and pushed on from rank to rank with a celerity which shocked some of the old regime.

Clothing and equipment, being in the hands of the " Raisers," came along fairly quickly, though khaki was not obtainable for some time. Arms, however, were scarce; the Infantry did not receive their final issue of rifles till very shortly before embarking. The Gunners were even worse off. The 176th Brigade, for instance, did not receive its first Howitzer till 13th August, 1915, and the full complement was not received till 24th November. The Brigade had only three days' gun practice before it embarked, and two of the Battery Commanders took over command less than ten days prior to embarkation.

In spite of all difficulties, however, training went on vigorously; the keenness of all ranks was wonderful. Esprit de corps was quickly evolved; platoon rivalled platoon; section rivalled section. The progress of other units was closely watched. Officers were sent off on courses of all sorts, and returned full of knowledge. Wounded officers soon appeared; not yet fit for active service, but fit to teach us. How eagerly we listened to them! So it went on, and rapidly the recruits of the autumn grew into soldiers, and by the summer of 1915 there were murmurings at the delay in despatching us overseas.

The 34th Division did not come into being till June, 1915.

In the beginning was

LOCK

On the 15th or 16th June there arrived at Ripon Major R. F. Lock, R.A., to take up his appointment as D.A.A. and Q.M.G. 34th Division. On his inquiring at Headquarters, 4th New Army, the whereabouts of the 34th Division, he was informed that he was IT, or words to that effect. Losing no time, Major Lock took two houses, and started getting together furniture and clerks. Officers of " G " arrived a few days later, and about a week later, came to train the new Division Major-General E. C. Ingouville-Williams, C.B., D.S.O., who had been brought from France, where, since the beginning of the War, he had been commanding the 16th Brigade.

The 34th Division was lucky in its first Commander. A thorough soldier, as much at home on the " Q " as on the " G " side. He knew what his men were entitled to, and he saw that they got it. Absolutely fearless, and apparently never tired, all ranks trusted and loved him, and there were few dry eyes among the crowd of mourners when he was laid to rest in Warloy cemetery on the 23rd July, 1916.

The rest of the Divisional Staff Officers soon arrived, and got busy collecting " other ranks " from various units to complete their office establishments.

The 101st Brigade collected at Fountains Abbey. The 102nd and 103rd remained at their training camps. The Divisional troops were encamped at Kirkby Malzeard, some six miles away.

The arrival of the first batch of mules merits a paragraph. Major Lock one morning received a telegram to the effect that three hundred mules for the Division would reach Ripon next morning. On inquiring at the station, he was informed that the animals would be there within twenty minutes, and must be detrained at once. The nearest troops from whom help could be got were too far off to be of use, so with the help of the G.S.O.3 and 6 Mounted Military Policemen, Major Lock somehow or other got the creatures out of the train. Just when this was completed, and the station yard was a seething mass of squealing, kicking mules, another train arrived, and was found to contain three hundred mules for 34th Division. The gallant D.A. and Q.M.G. and his perspiring assistants had detrained the mules intended for the 31st Division!

It was originally intended that the training of the Division should be completed in the Ripon training area, but before a real start had been made, fresh orders were issued, and the various component parts proceeded by various routes to Salisbury Plain, and after brief halts elsewhere they were assembled at, or near, Sutton Veny by the end of September. An unfortunate motor-car accident put the G.O.C. on the sick list for about a month, and it was near the end of October before he was fit to resume command. This undoubtedly caused the training to get into arrears, for though all were working hard at useful jobs, and perfecting themselves as units, Divisional training was practically in abeyance during his absence, which necessitated work being carried on at very high pressure after his return.

The weather at this time showed pro-Boche tendencies, and the appearance of orders for any extensive operations was sufficient to ensure a soaking wet day, but, with truly Boche devilry, it remained doubtful, or promised fair, until the troops were well on their way to their respective stations, and then it came down with a vengeance. Endless were the arguments at the conclusion of these days between the defenders and their assailants, as to what would really have been the result had bullets been flying, fraught with trouble was the post of umpire, but these

[To face p. 9]

A Cook's Touring Party in 1915
Somewhere in France

experiences are common to all peace manœuvres and need not be dwelt on.

There was about this time some uncertainty as to our destination. In December we were all equipped with sun helmets, and thought we were off to India; but in fact we were detailed for East Africa, the day of our departure had, unknown to most of us, actually been fixed, and accommodation arranged for us in the transports which were waiting at Southampton. At the last moment the orders were cancelled, and our helmets returned to store, but a few days later fresh orders came to reissue them, which, in their turn, were cancelled before they could be carried out, and so France was ultimately our destination.

Besides the field days and much route marching, we dug trenches and practised occupying them. We completed a course of musketry. The R.E. and Pioneers made bridges and varieties of obstacles. There was one particular production of the R.E. yard which pleased us. It was a motor horn, fitted under a board, and was to be placed in large numbers in front of our trenches, to give us warning by plaintive hootings when trodden on by a Boche. As far as we can recollect, it must be added to the many magnificent ideas of which a hidebound War Office refused to take advantage. To these last must be added the ingenious device to propel grapnels into the Boche's wire by means of rockets, and then with a long pull and a strong pull transfer the said wire to our side of No-Man's-Land. This promising idea for economising labour and material failed, owing to the erratic behaviour of the rockets in its early trials, which nearly set fire to a camp some distance in rear of the firing point.

A grand ceremonial parade was practised in anticipation of a visit from the King, but the unfortunate accident which occurred during His Majesty's tour of the front, prevented our having the honour of marching past our Sovereign, and an inspection by a detachment of Japanese officers hardly compensated us, especially as the day was one of the vilest. The rain came down in continuous torrents, but the programme was carried out in every detail, and the Japanese were reported to have been much impressed by what General Ternan has aptly described as a "distinctly amphibian performance."

At last embarkation leave was put in orders, and we began to really feel like going. But the work went on just the same right up to the last moment, and most units only got their orders to move twenty-four hours before the hour of departure.

On the final parade a message of kindly good wishes and farewell from the King was read to each unit. Then they departed silently and unobserved; no cheering crowds sped them on their way, no columns of bombastic description announced the sailing of their transports. Those who had sailed to Table Bay noted the change with satisfaction.

CHAPTER II

SETTLING DOWN IN FRANCE

THE officers of "Q" staff crossed on 4th January, a cold, rough day, and motored to G.H.Q., then in St Omer, in misty weather, over muddy roads, losing their way more than once. By the time the first units put in an appearance they had made things fairly straight as regards billets.

The following extracts from an officer's letters will recall many memories.

"S.I.F. (Havre),
"*Tuesday, 11th January, 1916.*

". . . I am quite well and fit, and had a good night last night under canvas. We have drawn three blankets for each officer, and I was as warm as a toast. . . . There is a café near by, where we had lunch and tea yesterday, and breakfast this morning —lovely rolls, delicious café au lait in bowls, splendid omelette, which I tackled bravely . . . and . . . apple jelly.

"The town is very quiet, not many people. All the gamins talk a few words of English, and beg cigarettes and biscuits, and sing 'Tipperary' for half-pennies.

"We had a good passage, very calm. . . . Nine of us in a stuffy cabin on our boat. . . . Colonel —— had a state-room, with two large four-post beds, and lavatory attached."

" Somewhere in France (Wallon-Cappel, near Hazebrouck),
    " *Nine p.m., Friday, 14th January,* 1916.

" We had a very tiring journey, leaving our camp there about one-thirty p.m. on Tuesday, and the train got away about six in the evening. The men were packed thirty-six in each cattle truck, and the officers a little better off in a second class carriage, but we could not lie down. . . . We did not leave the train till one p.m., the poor men having very little in the way of breakfast, and no lunch. We marched off at about two-thirty, and after we were clear of the town (Blendecque) we stopped and had a meal of bully beef and biscuit, and the men were quite ready for it! We reached this village at eight p.m., by which time the poor fellows were dead beat with the heavy load they were carrying (62½ lbs.), and, further than that, they had no rest the night before. . . .

" I was allotted three farms for my men, but, to my great disgust, found that another battalion had pinched one of them, while we had to crowd into the other two. We are very comfortable; four of us are sleeping in the biggest farm, on beds, the other two in the other farm, also on beds. Here, in the larger farm, we have a room in which we feed, and another room where —— and the other servants do the cooking. ' Madame ' makes coffee for us, so we get along very well, and don't mind how long we stay here."

The difficulty of finding one's friends, that so many of us experienced, is summarised thus : " We hope to see —— soon, but as he cannot say where he is, and we may not say where we are, it is rather like a game of Blind Man's Buff." Boys will be boys, and we read : " Of course the subs have found a nice café in the nearest town, and run in when they have time and get tea there!" Did the O.C. Company never go?

The Division was scattered over a considerable area south-east and east of St Omer, but only stayed there a short time, during which it was reviewed by General Joffre; that is to say, the Infantry of the Division was drawn up in line along a road, and the General passed by in his car at a good pace. We find that our kind friend who has lent us his letters, records that his battalion earned the special commendation of the great man. As far as we recollect the same was told to other units, and if the general commendation was, in repetition, converted into a special one, what harm. Troops that marched twenty miles to be gazed at for a few seconds would be none the worse for a pat on the back.

On the 19th January the Division suffered its first battle casualty. Brigadier-General Fitton, while on a visit of instruction to the 16th Brigade, near Ypres, in company with the G.O.C. the Brigade, was in the front line at night. Owing to a communication trench having been blown in, the party had to cross a bit of open, and the night being bright, they were spotted by a watchful sniper, who got the General through both thighs. Brigadier-General Nicholson, commanding the Brigade (later to become our Divisional Commander), and his Brigade-Major, Captain B. Tower, were the only ones present, and they had a difficult job getting the wounded General, who was a very big man, down the trench, though some stretcher-bearers of the K.S.L.I. came to their help. On the next day General Fitton died. One of his Staff records in his diary: "This was a great loss to the Brigade, as he was much liked and admired, and was a keen soldier." It was truly hard luck to be knocked over in this inglorious manner, before the troops which he had trained so well had even got into the line.

The command of the 101st Brigade went to

Lieutenant-Colonel R. C. Gore, C.M.G., Argyll and Sutherland Highlanders, who took over command on 28th January.

On the 23rd the Division moved into the 3rd Corps area, as Division in Corps reserve, being disposed approximately as follows : D.H.Q. at Blairingham; R.A. round Lynde, Wittes, Blairingham, and La Croquet; 101st Infantry Brigade round or in Morbecque; 102nd, round or in Steenbecque; 103rd at La Belle Hotesse and Sercus; Pioneer Battalion at Les Ciseaux; C.R.E. and 207th and 208th Field Companies, R.E., between Steenbecque and Morbecque; 209th F.C., Nouveau Monde. The Field Ambulances were disposed : 104th at Morbecque; 102nd and 103rd at Estaires; Divisional Ammunition Column was at Neuf Berquin, and Ammunition Sub Park at Vieux Berquin.

We had been engaged in route marching and being put through gas drill and other courses, and we now began to get practice of a more practical nature, units, or portions of them, being attached to the 23rd and 8th Divisions, which were holding the sector of the line allotted to the Corps. The marches from the billeting to the front area were good practice, and had apparently their pleasant intervals : "Very comfortable place (Vieux Berquin) last night. P—— found it, and also discovered a very pretty girl in the billet. It was screamingly funny to hear him talking to her in ' pidgin ' English. The girl was, of course, a great attraction to my subs (Only to the subs ?), and they were taking French lessons all the evening." During these periods of instruction the new-comers were attached to corresponding units of the Division in the line, and were most kindly received.

The records of those early days, and of the first experiences in the line, are interesting, the comments on various objects and events then so new, but soon to become so common as to pass unnoticed. The

" pretty little puffs of smoke against the lovely blue sky," amid which the planes floated calmly along. "It was wonderfully pretty to *watch*, but I don't know how the beggar in the plane felt about it." The novelty of the trench life : "It was really quite comfortable. One could not quite have a bath . . . one had to sleep in one's clothes." "We had a very quiet time, and I will say that the Boche behaved in a gentlemanly manner while we were in." But this was not always the Boche's way, for the records of another kind friend state that the 15th and 16th Royal Scots, during their tour, were very heavily bombarded. "They behaved splendidly, and were perfectly cool and steady." We had our first experience of being bombed from the air, but the only casualty recorded "was a bird killed by flying glass."

On the 24th February General Ingouville-Williams assumed command of the Left Division 3rd Corps front, 8th Division on right and 21st on left, his headquarters being at Croix du Bac, where also lived the C.R.A. and C.R.E. The 101st Infantry Brigade held the right sector, and the 103rd the left. General Gore's headquarters was at Rolanderie Farm, a pleasant, old-fashioned pile of buildings, in which a warm welcome and a good meal awaited all visitors in the cosy mess-room. General Cameron was not so lucky in his billet, which was in a medium-sized house in Rue Marle, on the outskirts of Armentières. The 102nd Brigade, which was in reserve, had its headquarters in Erquinghem, but it had previously been attached to the 8th Division and held the right sub-sector of that Division's front from 14th to 21st February. The gunners were, of course, considerably scattered. Lieutenant-Colonel Kincaid Smith, commanding 152nd Brigade, had his headquarters in a farm at the junction of the Rue De Lettrée and Rue des Charles. This farm escaped all unwelcome attention from the Boche, who, owing to all absence of movement near it, must have concluded that it was unoccupied. All ingress and egress was from the rear, under cover of hedges. A poor groom, who, in all innocence, tried to take his master's horse through the front gate, nearly had to be admitted to hospital suffering from " shock " after meeting the Brigade Commander. The batteries were : A at Le Crombalot ; B, La Toulette ; C, North of Bois Grenier ; D, Rue des Charles.

The Left Group Commander, Major W. Furnival, 175th Brigade, had his headquarters in Rue Marles, on the Chapelle d'Armentières road, the batteries being : A at Rue 'Allee ; B on Rue Fleurie ; C at l'Armée ; D at the brick-fields Chapelle d'Armentières. The 176th Brigade (Howitzers), Colonel G. R. Rundle, C.B., had its headquarters also in Rue Marles, the batteries being : A at Le Crombalot ; C, South of Rue Marles ; D, Grispot. The 160th Brigade, Lieutenant-Colonel W. H. Warburton, headquarters in Erquinghem ; batteries : 'A', B, and D in Rue Fleurie ; C, Rue des Charles.

The three Field Companies were billeted : 207th attached to 101st Infantry Brigade, commanded by Major McMahon, in Erquinghem ; 208th attached to 102nd Brigade, commanded by Captain J. Stephens, in Rue Marles ; 209th attached to 103rd Infantry Brigade, commanded by Major Hilder Daw, in Erquinghem. The Field Companies, however, did not move when the brigades left the line on relief, the continuity of the engineering policy in the trench system requiring them to be shifted as little as possible. 209th Field Company looked after all work behind the front line system, and the R.E. yard, which was in Erquinghem.

The Pioneer Battalion headquarters was in Rue Marles with one company in dug-outs in the B.G. line at the foot of Haystack 'Avenue, and one in Rue des Acquis. One company was attached to the 8th Division, which had no Pioneer Battalion, and one company was in the Forêt de Nieppe making fascines, etc. The three Field Ambulances were : 102nd, Lieutenant-Colonel A. E. S. Irvine, D.S.O., at Fort Rompu; 103rd, Lieutenant-Colonel Ligertwood, at Steenwerk; 104th, Major P. S. Stewart, at Erquinghem. The latter was attached to the 101st Infantry Brigade, the other two to the brigades bearing their numbers.

Lieutenant-Colonel R. H. Mangles joined the Divisional Staff as G.S.O. on 9th of February ; he had been Brigade-Major to the G.O.C. when he held command of the 16th Infantry Brigade. It was curious that the lines we were now occupying were originally constructed by that brigade when the race to the coast in 1914 ended in the temporary stale mate of trench warfare, and it was most interesting to accompany General Ingouville-Williams and Colonel Mangles and listen to their recollections of the period when these lines were being created, when sand-bags were doled out by twenty-fives, and three shells a day per gun was thought a good allowance.

The Divisional front extended from the Lille road on the left to just beyond Bridoux salient on the right. There was also another salient, the Rue du Bois, near the centre. Both were unhealthy spots, the former especially, being very near to the Boche line. The front line was a continuous breast work with a ditch in front and trench behind, the latter very shallow on account of the nearness of surface water.

Some one thousand yards in rear was the reserve line, generally known as the B.G. line, from the village of Bois Grenier (Boise Greneer), which was one of the main features of its defences. From this rather weak earth work, which ran along the whole front, led the communication trenches forward to the front line. For sake of auld lang syne let us put down some of them, commencing from the left : Haystack, Wellington, Park Row for the left Brigade, and Shaftesbury, Moat Farm, and, later, Greatwood for the right. On our arrival we found the trenches in

B

far from good order.   The winter had been a wet one, the land was low and almost level, so that drainage was a very difficult problem.   Before we left, the Pioneers had drained Greatwood and laid a tramway in it from the B.G. line to the support line at White City, and the Field Companies and infantry working parties had effected vast improvements by constant labour.   But though the weather improved during our stay it was a constant struggle to keep the lines dry.

The whole of our position was overlooked by the Boche from the top of Radinghem Ridge, and it did not make us any happier to know that our G.O.C. and his 16th Brigade had once held the top of that ridge, whence they had been obliged to retire " in accordance with plan."

It was during these early days that we got our Trench Mortar Batteries.   The days of jam-pot bombs hurled from catapults had passed, but the trench mortar was still in its infancy, and those who used it were still looked on with ill-disguised mistrust by the garrison of the front line, who felt doubtful as to the amount of damage they could do the Boche, but none whatever regarding the amount of retaliation the Boche would send over in reply.

Our Medium Batteries were originally numbered 60, 61, and 70, and were renumbered X, Y, and Z 34th, on 11th March.   The Light Trench Mortar Batteries, which were numbered according to the brigades of which they formed a part, were also formed about this time.   On the 13th March, Stokes' three inch mortars were used for the first time, and, judging from the language used by the Boche, the result was satisfactory.   X and Z Batteries were in the Rue du Bois and Bridoux salients, and fired a good deal, but had hardly got started before we were relieved.

For those not actually in the trenches our sector

had many advantages; the billets were generally excellent, though Chapelle d'Armentières, where lived a battalion of the left brigade, was at times extremely uncomfortable, but that it was possible to occupy it showed how well the Boche was behaved, for it was very far forward. Some of the best known billets were Charley's Farm, Streaky Bacon Farm, Canteen Farm, La Vesée, Grispot, the farms along Rue Fleurie and l'Armée, all of which were comfortable, and though often shelled, not unduly unhealthy. Farther back were Erquinghem, Jesus Farm, Fort Rompu, and "Hallobaloo." Erquinghem and Armentières were still going concerns, many shop's estaminets and pâtisseries being still open. The Au Bœuf and Lucienne's gave good dinners at moderate prices. A Staff Officer records : "March 1st. Had tea at the tea shop which everyone knows. It was crowded as usual. Wonder if the cakes or the pretty waitress is the chief attraction to the subs?" (The subs again, but what took our Red Tab there?)

The Boche generally was on his good behaviour, but lest it should be thought that life was all beer and skittles, the following extract from a once well-known periodical is repeated : "Summary, six a.m. 29th to six a.m. 1st March. The enemy's artillery fairly active during the day; Chapelle d'Armentières was shelled in the morning. Between ten-thirty a.m. and one-thirty p.m., the enemy shelled I.8.a.3.8 and I.13.c.3.7 with 4·2's, but did no damage. Roads in H.36.b received about sixty shells from 77 m.m. battery, about O.7.d.7.a. About fifty 77 m.m. shells fell near White City. Between two p.m. and five p.m. about fifty shells were fired in the direction of l'Armée and H.12.d, and about seventy-five 5·9's were fired between H.11.d and the railway. The estaminet I.14.b.4½ and Grispot Corner got their *usual* shelling."

Our friend the Red Tab, above quoted, records against the 12th March, "An auspicious day, fine and sunny, and the first day since we came into the line when we had no man killed or wounded (in the Brigade)." Our average daily battle casualties at this period was about ten.

The following extract shows that our gunners had learnt their job by this time : " I was up in another artillery observation post the other day. The officer was showing me two points on the enemy's parapet between which he had to fire. He was describing them to me, and suddenly said, ' Half a minute,' gave an order down the speaking tube, and in fifteen seconds a round hit the parapet fairly. ' That is the right point,' he remarked, gave another order, another round fired. ' That is the left point,' said he. It was just as if he had reached out a gigantic arm to touch the points he wished to show me on the enemy's parapet nearly a mile away."

The 102nd Infantry Brigade relieved the 103rd in the left section on 4th March, and on 14th the 103rd relieved 101st in the right section, and 101st on 23rd relieved the 116th Infantry Brigade of the 8th Division in the left section of that Division's front, which came under G.O.C. 34th Division, the 8th going off to " the Somme area," whither also went the headquarters of 3rd Corps, and the 34th Division became a portion of 2nd Corps, 2nd Army. A bad spell of snowy weather caused us all much discomfort about this time. It seemed to anger the Boche, for I find on record that in the new area " The Boches had an energetic fit one week, and knocked out seven of our batteries."

On the 7th April we were relieved by the 2nd Australian Division. Sir George McCrae tells an amusing tale of this relief. His opposite number paid him a visit in the morning, and was highly pleased to find how comfortable the farm was in which the headquarters was located. He left after a good lunch, expressing his opinion that he was in luck this time. Unfortunately for him, the Boche took a dislike

to the farm, and before the hour of relief it had ceased
to exist. In the midst of the hottest part of the
" straf," a signaller crawled from his sand-bagged
shelter to a similar edifice, in which Sir George was
pretending he liked it, and tendered him a message
from O.C. " B " Company, announcing " Battalion
Headquarters are being shelled."   What the
Australian C.O. said is better left unrecorded.

We proceeded by route march to the 2nd Army
Training area behind St Omer.   (Shortly before this
G.H.Q. had vacated that town for Montreuil.)   We
certainly had not had a very exciting time during our
first spell of the line, but we had done a lot of useful
work, and had got accustomed to be shelled, and had
found our feet.

The move to the training area was completed by
14th April. D.H.Q. was at Tilques, and the troops
in good billets in the neighbourhood. A thorough
brush up and polish was commenced at once, and there
was some grumbling among the war-tried warriors at
having to go back to " Right turn, left turn, take the
beggar's name down " sort of work. Apparently
there were relaxations, for I read in a diary of a
gunner, " Expended thirty-two francs on an American
cane rod, reel, line, casts, six flies, three worm hooks,
and a minnow."   I find also references of sports
being held, and to the delights of lying in the grass
among apple trees bursting into blossom, and listening to the birds singing instead of to the whistling
of the shells. Later, there were strenuous field days,
necessitating early rising.   " The ground was laid out
in trenches named and modelled on those we afterwards
took on the Somme."

Early in May we left those peaceful regions, and
partly by train, and partly on our own feet, we wended
our way back to the line, reaching it at Albert, where
we rejoined the 3rd Corps, and were again between
the 8th and 21st Divisions, but this time the former
was on our left, and the latter on our right.   We also

found our Pioneer Battalion, which had come on ahead to straighten out things for us, and had been here nearly a month, their rest and training having been compressed into four days.

D.H.Q. was now in the château at Basieux, and the G.O.C. took over command of right sector of 3rd Corps front on 10th May. The 103rd Infantry Brigade took over the line from 70th Infantry Brigade, 23rd Division, 101st Brigade was at Bresle, and 102nd at Franvillers. The C.R.A. established himself in Moulin Viviers, a comfortable billet. The C.R.E. headquarters and yard were at Dernacourt. The Field Ambulances were placed : 102nd at Franvillers, 103rd at Moulin Viviers, and 104th at La Houssoye. The two Field Companies detailed for duty in the front area were 207th and 209th. The Pioneers, having been early on the scene, had secured good billets in Albert, their headquarters being in a fine house belonging to Monsieur Bompart, a lawyer.

The headquarters of the Brigade in the line was in Bellevue Farm, which is described as the worst possible place for the purpose, being in the middle of a nest of batteries of all sorts, which were constantly getting shelled, and the Brigade Headquarters shared in the trouble, and disliked the constant noise made by our own guns.

The front here was much shorter than that at Armentières, about two thousand yards against over three thousand, so that at first it was held by one brigade, which had two battalions in the trenches, one in Albert, and one in Dernacourt. The two Infantry Brigades in the back area were occupied with training, and between 20th and 31st May carried out several practices with aircraft, communicating with flare lamps and ground sheet signals. The gunners had a very strenuous time preparing gun positions and O.P.'s, for instead of inheriting ready-made positions, as at Armentières, they had to make new ones, as the number of guns was vastly in excess of what it had been before. The Artillery Brigades went out in turn to train in the back area.

The country hereabouts was very different to the damp muddy flats we had come from, and it reminded us greatly of Salisbury Plain. Rolling downs with a chalk subsoil, few trees, and no hedges. The villages were old fashioned, clusters of houses with considerable distances between them. There were some fine châteaux, which made good billets for the Corps and Division, and sometimes Brigade Head-quarters, but the lesser folk missed the comfortable farms they had got accustomed to.

The town of Albert had been occupied by the Boche in the very early days, and the mark of the beast had been left on it, but it still contained some good billets, and some shops were open, and a *pâtisserie* carried on bravely. The town lies in the valley of the Ancre, the ground rising to east and west immediately outside, but very gradually, and to no great elevation, so that the top of the belfry of the basilica, with its statue of the Virgin holding up her child, was visible from the plateau east of La Boisselle, which accounted for the damage done it by the Boche. Eastward from the town ran three roads, one to Ovillers la Boisselle, one direct to Bapaume, just passing to the north of La Boisselle, and the most southerly to Becourt Château, and thence to Fricourt. The first was in the 8th Division area. The second ascended the slope, and for about one thousand yards from the outskirts of the town was in dead ground, but then it became necessary to enter either Perth or St Andrew's Avenue, which ran on the south and north of the road from The Barrier. This was the limit to which transport could go, and its name will recall many uncomfortable hours waiting with carrying parties for wagons that seemed never coming. Near it were the kitchens of the battalion in the line, whence the meals were carried in huge thermos flasks, slung on poles, to the hungry men on the other side of the slope, which was too much in view to allow of any cooking being done there. Not far beyond The Barrier, the road passed through a slight depression in the Usna-Tara Ridge, and descended somewhat abruptly to the Mash Valley, about four hundred yards wide, on far side of which the ground rose again, and on this slope was the village of La Boisselle, merely a collection of ruins, which, with immense labour, the Boche had converted into a strong fortress—a network of trenches and machine gun emplacements, with thick belts of barbed wire above ground, and a labyrinth of deep dug-outs and passages below.

The plateau, on the south-west edge of which lies Pozières, throws out three spurs, which are the chief features of the area over which the Division fought early in July. Of these three the most westerly, known as Chapes Spur, falls first south-west to La Boisselle, and then south to Becourt Château, a strongly built pile of buildings in a pleasant wood, but little damaged by shell fire. To the north of La Boisselle the valley was called Mash, and to the south Sausage. On the northern slope of the Mash Valley lies Ovillers la Boisselle, one thousand three hundred yards north of La Boisselle, and facing the 8th Division front.

The centre spur, which is broad and flat, falls in a southerly direction to between Fricourt and Becourt, and at its southern end is split by a ravine running north and south, at the head of which lies Round Wood. To the east of this ravine are the Crucifix and the Poodles.

At the northern end of the eastern spur is Contalmaison, thence the spur falls in a southerly direction to Railway Copse, which lies in the valley between the eastern and centre spurs. Higher up this valley lies Shelter Wood, and still higher up, close to Contalmaison, is Peake Wood. On the eastern spur are Bottom Wood and the Quadrangle.

The 34th Divisional front was, roughly, from the centre of the Mash to the centre of the Sausage Valleys. At its two extremities it was from four hundred to eight hundred yards from the Boche line, but in the centre, at La Boisselle, the two lines were practically touching. This was a region of mine craters of all sizes, a chalky waste, a perfect maze of trenches, many of them abandoned, and in a constant state of flux, into which it was unwise to venture without a guide, or you might find yourself suddenly confronted by the muzzle of a Boche rifle poking through a loop hole in a sand-bag wall, newly built across the trench. This portion of the line was held by isolated bombing posts, to which access by day was difficult, in each of which a few men, well supplied with bombs, kept ceaseless watch, through little loop-holes, on the Boches, often not more than fifteen yards away. This area was popularly known as " The Glory Hole "; behind it ran Tummel and Monifieth streets. The whole of our front line system was overlooked from the Boche's lines, for on their side the ground rose steadily, and each successive line of their defences had a better view. On our side the ground was less favourable; on the left the Usna-Tara Ridge rose so abruptly behind our front line that our defensive lines in this sector were much cramped, and the ridge itself was lower than the Boche front line, except a few yards just north of La Boisselle.

The Boche front line was strongly protected with massive lines of wire, and to the north of La Boisselle he had thrown out what we called, from its shape, the Y sap, a system of deep trenches, whence he troubled us constantly with " Oilcans " and " Minnies." We never had a chance of examining the Y sap, for at Zero two minutes, on the 1st July, it went to glory in a blaze, the 179th Tunnelling Company's accurately placed charge leaving nothing of it but a vast hole strewn with the debris of the deep dug-outs' timbers.

The method of propulsion of the "Oilcans" puzzled us, for the great cylindrical tins used to lob slowly over, with very little noise, but, on landing, burst with terrific force and noise. Later, we discovered that they were fired from wooden muzzle-loading guns, by means of fuzes from the muzzle. The Boche was in a worse temper here than at Armentières, and trench life was far from pleasant. Occasionally bombardments of La Boisselle and the Y sap were tried, all the heavies assisting, but generally not more than a quarter of an hour elapsed between the firing of the last round and the arrival of another "Oilcan" or "Minnie."

On 22nd May 101st Brigade relieved 103rd in the line, and on 4th June the 102nd Brigade relieved the 101st in the trenches at eight a.m., but the Boche had a word to say first. An intensive bombardment began at twelve-thirty a.m., and the Brigade Headquarters came in for a heavy dose, getting both H.E. and lachrymatory shells. The communications were considerably interfered with, and things were pretty warm. In the middle of it came a message from the right battalion in the line, saying the Boche had got into their trenches, and asking for reinforcements. General Gore's only comment was "Pushing beggars, these Germans." Before any reinforcements could get up, the enemy had been ejected, leaving behind one prisoner and one corpse. Our casualty list was small. The battalion concerned was the 21st Northumberland Fusiliers. The Divisional Commander records that the battalion did well, and it seems that the 15th Royal Scots, which was in process of being relieved, also deserve a word of praise. On the following night the "pushing Germans" repeated the experiment, some three hundred attacking the same spot, after a heavy bombardment of about an hour. They were beaten back by rifle fire and bombs, but another party of bombers effected an entrance through a breach which the guns had made in the parapet on

"Minnie" Thrower

Captured at La Boisselle by 207th Field Company R.E.

[To face p. 26]

the left, and took the defenders of the two trenches, attacked in rear. They were, however, ejected, but our bombers followed them into No-Man's-Land, and some fifteen of them were reported missing. The Boche left five dead behind.

During June we made several raids. The 24th and 26th Northumberland Fusiliers made two each. The party of the former battalion was held up on each occasion, and suffered casualties without being able to get in to the enemy's line. The latter on the first occasion bombed thirteen dug-outs, and on the second, after effecting an entry, was counter-attacked on both sides and across the open. A very fierce fight ensued, in which Captain Price was killed, and many wounded. General Ingouville-Williams, while regretting greatly Captain Price's death, expressed his satisfaction with the work done.

The 16th Royal Scots sent a party of two officers and thirty O.R.'s on the 29th to attempt an entry, but the wire was found uncut. A gallant attempt to cut it by hand had to be abandoned after two belts had been cut, the enemy's machine gun fire being too intense and accurate.

On the same night the 102nd Brigade made two raids. One was unsuccessful, but in the other the 23rd Northumberland Fusiliers effected an entry, and a savage bombing duel ensued. Having thrown all their bombs, the party returned, but Lieutenant Campbell and two men were left behind—" Missing, supposed dead."

The next night an effort was made to blow a gap in the wire which had escaped the gunners' attentions. Lieutenant Rought and nineteen other ranks of 207th Field Company formed the explosion party, and the covering party of 102nd Brigade was commanded by Lieutenant Hall, who was shot as he left our parapet. Lieutenant Rought took command of the whole party, and completed the job. Six ten foot gun-cotton torpedoes were laid carefully along the bars of the knife rest, and fired with most satisfactory results.

On 15th June the 101st Brigade was back again in the line, but only took over half the front, 102nd remaining in and taking the left sub-sector. General Ternan moved his headquarters to Villa Rochers, in the centre of the town, a palatial billet, which had somehow escaped notice till, with the sure instinct of an old campaigner, the G.O.C. 102nd Brigade spotted it. This move was preparatory to the great offensive, fixed for 29th June. The 103rd Brigade was in reserve, but daily sent up large working and carrying parties. The 19th Division, in Corps reserve, was also brought close up, and supplied working parties. Of work there was no lack. The digging of assembly trenches, and the stocking of the dumps with rations, water, bombs, S.A.A., tools, wire, etc., to be used during the "push" was an immense task, and fell entirely on the infantry. There were three divisional dumps : The main bomb store in the outskirts of Albert, the left dump to the north of the Bapaume road, in rear of St Andrew's Avenue, the right in Becourt Wood. In addition, each Infantry Brigade had a dump, that of the 101st being in the trenches on Chapes Spur, 102nd in St Andrew's, and 103rd in Kerriemuir Street.

The amount of stuff stored in these dumps was enormous, and the labour entailed in carrying it from the transport terminals, through the narrow trenches, taxed the infantry severely. For about a week prior to the commencement of the bombardment, the trenches were crowded all day and night with slow-moving lines of patient, heavily laden men. Fortunately the weather was good, and the Boche abstained from interfering, and by the 24th the dumps were reported complete, and handed over to the Pioneers, who were to be responsible for supplying the wants of the attacking infantry during the push.

A long line of deep dug-outs, called the Usna-

Tara-Becourt Avenue line, was constructed on the reverse slope of those hills by the R.E. and Pioneers. They were at a depth of about twenty feet, and were in two groups, one on each side of the Bapaume road. Each group was linked up by underground passages, and in rear the 19th Division dug a long assembly trench. The other works of the R.E. are too numerous and varied to be detailed. Two considerable tramway jobs fell to them : one up the side of the Becourt Château road, then through the wood to Panmure Street; the other up the Tara-Usna slope to the left divisional dump.

The Pioneers, in addition to much work on communication trenches, and the deep dug-outs referred to above, were employed on making trench mortar emplacements.

Our trench mortar folk had increased in number and skill. Three new Medium Batteries, named M, O, P, were formed out of men specially trained from the D.A.C., and in addition X 19 and Y and Z 38th joined us for the occasion. We also received three French guns, monsters which hurled two hundred pound shells one thousand yards. These formed V and W Batteries. All these batteries were under Captain D. T. James, who had commenced his career with the Division as Bombing Instructor. The sites for the emplacements were selected by him, and more thought was given as to their suitability for offence than for the comfort of the gun teams. Such unhealthy sites as Lochnagar, Scone, Kingsgate, and Athol Street found favour. On either side of the latter were the two guns of V Battery, under Captain Holmes. The emplacements were constructed by " B " Company, 18th Northumberland Fusiliers, assisted by the personnel of the battery. It was a considerable work. The guns were in mined chambers twenty-six feet below ground level, connected with other chambers at the same level for the teams and the ammunition. Very nearly all the rounds available were fired during the bombardment, and not a single casualty was incurred, though the Boche was very keen to find them, and blew in two out of the eight entrances to the system.

The last great work prior to the bombardment was the digging, in two nights, of an entirely new communication trench, called Northumberland Avenue, running back from Panmure Street, parallel to Berkshire Avenue. It was a very big job, well carried out by large working parties of tired but ever-willing infantry, under skilful supervision of the R.E. At last all preparations were completed. On the 24th June Albert was almost entirely vacated, in anticipation of the retaliation, which was expected when our bombardment started. One battalion of the 102nd Brigade stayed in the cavernous garden of the Villa des Rochers, and the French inhabitants refused to budge. The dressing station also remained in the Ecole Superieur, which was well supplied with cellars. The Boche, as a matter of fact, did not do very much damage to the town, but unfortunately there were several casualties among the medical officers.

On the afternoon of the 25th June aeroplanes from the sea to Switzerland attacked the Boche observation balloons. On our immediate front all that were up were burnt, and some twenty allied balloons were left in possession of the air.

On the night of 26-27th, gas was discharged from a very large number of cylinders, which had been placed in position in the front line on the nights of the 21st and 22nd. The result was that all trench mortars on the front attacked were silent for thirty-eight hours, and machine guns for a shorter period. This attack formed part of the preparatory bombardment.

The artillery of the Division had been augmented by the loan of two brigades (less one battery of Howitzers) from the 19th Division. The 27th

H.'A.G. also worked with the Division. It consisted of one 9·2 inches and three 6 inch Howitzer Batteries. At the last moment the French lent us a battery of their far-famed 75's, which did good work.

The bombardment began on 25th and was the heaviest, up to that date, which the British artillery had put up. All in the trenches were much " bucked " at the thought of the thin time the Boche was having. Many observers record that it really seemed impossible that anyone could be left alive in his trenches. We had not then experienced the protective value of the deep dug-out.

The strain on the artillery personnel and material was severe, as is shown by the following extract from a Battery Commander's diary :

" Saturday, June 26th, to June 30th, Friday. Wire cutting every day for an average of five hours per day. Also at least one special bombardment each day, and several abortive attempts to loose gas. The latter eventually went over one morning, about Wednesday. Shooting all night on approaches and wire cutting. Am living at the O.P. on sardines and bread. . . . The seven guns averaged nearly two thousand round per day, and are beginning to give buffer trouble; seldom more than five in action at the same time. Boche prisoners say they are finding great difficulty in getting up food and other supplies. The O.P. has had several shells right on top, but they have had absolutely no effect on it."

O.P.'s here were not in ruined houses as in Bois Grenier, but in underground chambers with concealed peep-holes on the forward slopes of the Usna-Tara Ridge.

Our feelings at the moment are aptly described in the following extract from an officer's letter : " When one thinks about it all, or stops to analyse it, it seems an extraordinary game—the awful waste— but the only thing to do is to go on and try to biff the Boche. We are all very cheerful, and confident that we shall do him in the end, and may it come soon.''

Thus ended our training, begun in the streets and lanes of England and Scotland, carried on in the mud of Flanders, and completed on the chalky downs of Picardy.

CHAPTER III

WHILE the guns are pounding away at the Boche lines, cutting his wire, searching his lines of communication and his billeting area, smashing up his elaborate system of trenches, and generally making his life one of discomfort and misery, let us take a look at the task before the Division.

As already described, the British and Boche lines were extremely close together at the western end of La Boisselle, and to the north of that village drew apart till a distance of about eight hundred yards separated them, oppposite the left extremity of the 34th Divisional front. The village of Ovillers la Boisselle lay to the north-east, and some one thousand five hundred yards from our line, so that any force advancing from the left of our line, to the north of La Boisselle, would have that village on its right flank, and Ovillers on its left front, and if the garrisons of these strongholds were not fully occupied it would have a poor time while making the passage of the wide expanse of No-Man's-Land.

From the western end of La Boisselle the two lines continued close together for about four hundred yards, and then the distance between them increased, till it reached about four hundred yards. On our right, on the southern slope of the Sausage Valley, there was on the Boche line a strong portion called Heligoland, connected with which were " The

Kipper " and " The Bloater " trenches.   From the the southern end of Heligoland the line turned south-east, and then south, passing into the 21st Division area.

At a distance of about two hundred and fifty yards in rear of the Boche front line ran the support line, and in rear of this, at distances varying from three hundred to four hundred yards, ran the first reserve line, with its flanks resting on Round Wood on the south, and The Quarry on the north, and the centre just touching the most easterly houses of La Boisselle.   The second reserve line also rested its flanks on Round Wood and The Quarry, but in the centre was bent back so that here about five hundred or six hundred yards separated the two trenches.   The intermediate line ran from the eastern end of Ovillers to Peake Wood, and the fourth skirted the western edge of Contal-maison Village and Wood, and extended northwards towards Pozières.   East of Contalmaison, at a distance of about two thousand yards, was a fifth line.

The task set the Division was to capture the Boche defences on its front, as far as the eastern edge of Contalmaison, beyond which it was to entrench itself with its left flank in touch with the 8th Division on the outskirts of Pozières, and its right thrown back to the south of Contalmaison to form a defensive flank towards Mametz Wood, and connecting with the 21st Division.

This meant an advance of about three thousand five hundred yards, on a front of about two thousand, capturing two fortified villages and six lines of trenches, which it was known were well provided with deep dug-outs, and made as strong as our industrious enemy could make them after two years of constant labour.   Truly might the representative of Army Headquarters, who came to address the officers, tell us that if we carried out the whole of the programme, we should do uncommonly well, and that we ought not to be disappointed if we only achieved a partial success.

The key of the position undoubtedly was La Boisselle, which stuck its ugly nose right into our ribs, and whence the wide stretches of No-Man's-Land, which lay to the north and south of it, were completely commanded.

The general scheme of the assault was as follows :

At six-thirty a.m. on Z day, the artillery were to increase their bombardment of the front lines, and under cover of this the 101st Brigade on the right, and the 102nd on the left, were to push their leading waves out into No-Man's-Land. At seven-twenty-five the guns were to do all they could. At seven-twenty-eight the mines were to go up, and at seven-thirty the assault was to start. The 101st had the 15th Royal Scots on the right, and the 10th Lincolns on the left. On their left came the 21st Northumberland Fusiliers of the 102nd Brigade, with its left just clear of La Boisselle. To the north of that village was the 20th Northumberlands. These front line troops were to seize and hold the Boche defences, up to and including the 1st reserve line. This constituted the first objective.

The second objective was the Boche intermediate line which was to be taken by the reserve battalions of the two leading Brigades, viz., from right to left, the 16th Royal Scots, 11th Suffolks of 101st Brigade, and 22nd Northumberlands of 102nd Brigade south of La Boisselle, and 23rd Northumberlands north of that horrid place.

The third objective, a line east of Contalmaison, was to be achieved by the 103rd Brigade, which was to follow the two others at a distance of five hundred yards. Its battalions in one line, the 25th Northumberlands were to pass to the north of La Boisselle; the rest of the Brigade to the south. This Brigade was called the Reserve Brigade, but it was scarcely a reserve, as it was to be launched to the attack along with the rest of the Division.

Each battalion was to advance in successive lines,

or waves, at one hundred and fifty paces distance. Special arrangements were made for " mopping up " the trenches captured, which proved to be inadequate, and for carrying parties to take up S.A.A., bombs and material for consolidation. The 103rd Brigade provided fully for patrols to be pushed out when it had reached its final position, east of Contalmaison, which it was timed to do at two-forty p.m.

La Boisselle was to be dealt with by a special force of bombers of the 102nd Brigade, under Lieutenants Rotherford and Connolly, each of whom had four bombing squads of eight men each. Rotherford's party was to follow the 21st Northumberland Fusiliers, and Connolly's the 20th, until they came opposite certain selected spots in the southern and northern faces of the La Boisselle salient, which it was estimated they would do at twelve minutes after zero. They were then to turn inwards, and enter the village. A special trench mortar barrage was to be kept on this portion of the village till the time of their entry, and it was hoped that they would find most of the defenders taking shelter in their deep dug-outs, and that, with the help of two platoons, from the 22nd and 23rd Northumberlands, which were to join them as those battalions passed, they would be able to clear the village and generally mop up the Brigade area. To prevent the Boche breaking out between the assaulting battalions, a company of the 18th Northumberland Fusiliers was lent to the Brigade, and held the " Glory Hole " from 25th June.

To assist in the operations, wind permitting, a smoke barrage was to be placed along each face of La Boisselle, by four inch Stoke's guns. The explosions of four mines, which had been prepared by the 179th Tunnelling Company, and which were to be fired at two minutes to zero, would, it was hoped, materially help Rotherford and Connolly. The largest mine, at a depth of fifty feet, reached to within a few yards of the Boche front line south of La

Boisselle, and was charged with eighty thousand pounds of ammonal; the second, which was under the Y sap, contained forty thousand pounds; and the two smaller ones, which started from Inch Street, had only eight thousand pounds each.

This Company had also constructed a tunnel from our front line, which extended nearly to the Boche line, in the vicinity of the spot under which was the eighty thousand pounds charge. We shall hear more of this later.

A most elaborate system of artillery barrage was arranged, calculated so that the front line of the assaulting infantry would always have as close before it, as was consistent with safety, a curtain of shrapnel and high explosive shells, which it was hoped would keep down the enemy's rifle and machine gun fire to such an extent as would allow of the advance being carried out without crushing losses. The heavy gun barrage lifted direct from one line to the next, but the field gun raked slowly back, just fast enough to keep a safe distance ahead of the infantry.

The medical arrangements were as follows : four regimental aid posts were established—(a) junction of Arbroath and Mcnymusk Streets, (b) junction of Mercier and Monifieth Streets, (c) junction of Gowrie and Methuen Streets, (d) junction of Kirkcaldy and Methuen Streets. Advance dressing stations were placed in Becourt Château, Charing Cross, the top of Northumberland Avenue, and on Perth Avenue. Collecting posts were established at Bapaume post, bottom of Northumberland Avenue, and at tram station near cemetery. Two main dressing stations were placed, one in Moulin Viviers, one in the Ecole Superieur.

Large scale maps were issued, showing the Boche trenches, which we, in anticipation of a change of ownership, renamed to suit our fancy, and some red-tabbed prophet, in the 101st Brigade, named a certain strong point Scots Redoubt, of which we shall hear

more later. On these maps each brigade marked a
forward dump, and the Pioneers made all arrangements for delivering the goods there as soon as the
Boche should have been evicted.

To ensure our knowing each other, we wore on
our backs huge yellow triangles, and lest anyone
should be ignorant of our destination, a huge
signboard was erected in Albert, bearing the words
" To Bapaume."

Reading over these elaborate orders, one thinks
sadly of the high hopes with which so many brave men
set out that sunshiny July morning, and of the small
part of the ambitious programme that they were able
to carry through.

At the last moment the assault was postponed
forty-eight hours. The weather had been atrocious,
and the trenches were hardly passable. Most of us
were glad of the postponement, but, opposite us, the
Boche took advantage of the delay to replace the
nerve-shattered garrisons of his front system by fresh
troops, and so the delay probably cost us dear.

On the night of the 30th June we all moved to our
battle posts : D.H.Q. to the Moulin Viviers ; the three
Brigadiers into deep dug-outs in the Usna-Tara-
Becourt line, where also were the troops of the 103rd
Brigade ; those of the two leading brigades being in
the trenches. The Pioneers were in Becourt Wood,
and the Field Companies with their brigades.

During the night Lieutenant Parkinson and a
small party of the 18th Northumberlands dug a
trench mortar emplacement out in No-Man's-Land,
opposite Heligoland, whence at daybreak Lieutenant
Kitton, of the 101st T.M. Battery, " strafed " that
strong point, with good effect, with two Stoke's guns.
He was wounded, and all his detachment were either
killed or wounded.

Lieutenant Nixon, with his platoon of the 18th
Northumberlands, spent the night in the tunnel above
referred to. The first information was to the effect

that the far end was only two feet below the surface, but it turned out to be ten, so that, instead of breaking through in a few minutes, it was not till ten a.m. that a practicable exit was achieved. The guns kept at it all night, and at six-thirty they quickened their rate, and for the last five minutes before zero the fire was awful.

At seven-twenty-eight the mines went off, and punctually at seven-thirty the assaulting troops moved forward. Owing to the wind, the smoke barrage was not entirely successful, which seriously increased our casualties. The Boche put down a terrific barrage on our front line directly the assault commenced, and opposite La Boisselle it was doubled. Chapes Spur and forward slopes of Tara and Usna were swept by machine gun fire. General Ingouville-Williams witnessed the first part of the assault from an advanced position, and describes the advance thus : " My Division did glorious deeds. Never have I seen men go through such a barrage of artillery. They advanced as on parade, and never flinched. I can't speak too highly of them."

The artillery fire was terrific, but more fatal was that of many machine guns, from the La Boisselle salient.

For sake of clearness we will deal with the doings of each Infantry Brigade separately, commencing with those of the 102nd Brigade.

The 20th and 23rd Northumberland Fusiliers, which attacked to the north of La Boisselle, were practically wiped out, but after the battle, the story of their gallant advance was made apparent, for their dead lay thickly across No-Man's-Land. Thinner and ever thinner the trail extended into the German lines, and among those who had penetrated farthest, General Ingouville-Williams found the bodies of Lieutenant-Colonels Lyle and Sillery, where they always wished to be at the head of their battalions.

The 21st and 22nd Northumberland Fusiliers

fared slightly better. To the south of La Boisselle, No-Man's-Land was narrower, and the explosion of the great mine shook the morale of the Boche.

The German second line was reached before any check was experienced, and a small party with a Lewis gun got some twenty yards farther forward, but, their gun jamming, a few survivors were obliged to retire. A little later, more men having come up, Major Acklom, 22nd Northumberland Fusiliers, managed to establish himself with a party of both battalions in the central portion of the third line.

In the meantime, Lieutenant Rotherford, though wounded, and though his bombing party was reduced from thirty-two to ten, had attempted to carry out his order, bombing up the communication trench towards La Boisselle, after leaving a "block" of two men behind him. The Boche rifle grenade fire proved very accurate, and his party was soon reduced to two men. Leaving these to establish a "block," Rotherford returned to his first block, and, with the two men left there, set out bombing towards the right, along the third line. For a time he was very successful, and inflicted severe losses on the flying enemy, but soon one of his men was killed, and the other, Private Johnson, 22nd Northumberland Fusiliers, was wounded. Taking him with him, Rotherford retraced his steps, and joined Major Acklom's party. As the Boche bombers continued to press on, and no further reinforcements seemed to be coming up, Major Acklom decided to evacuate the third line, and consolidate his position in the second. This he achieved by about eight p.m.

Another party of British troops had established itself in the New Crater, about one hundred yards south of Major Acklom's position. In this party were men of the Lincolns, under Second-Lieutenant Turnbull, who, though severely wounded, refused to give up his command, some of the 102nd, and some of the 103rd Brigade; among the latter Lieutenant-Colonel

Howard, 24th Northumberlands, who died there of his wounds.

Both these parties held their positions all day. No less than six attacks were beaten off by Major Acklom's men, Lieutenant McClusky, at the left flank barricade, doing grand work. By three p.m. telephone communication with Major Acklom was established by the Brigade Signal Staff. His strength then was seven officers and about two hundred other ranks.

After dark the two parties got in touch with each other, and the position was improved.

About this time General Ternan sent an order to " C " Company, 18th Northumberland Fusiliers, which was holding the Glory Hole, to attack La Boisselle. Captain Francis had just completed his arrangements for the attack, when it was counter-manded, as two Brigades of the 19th Division had been detailed for the job.

Communications with the party in the New Crater was established through the tunnel during the after-noon, and by nightfall Lieutenant Nixon had cleared it sufficiently to allow of the passage of a battalion of the 19th Division.

We must now turn to the 101st Brigade. Punc-tually to the moment, the leading waves of the 15th Royal Scots and the 10th Lincolns moved forward, followed by the rest of the Brigade. It was soon evident that the bombardment had by no means extinguished the Boche machine guns, which chattered with increasing virulence as the waves advanced, and our artillery barrage moved off the front lines of the German system. On the right, where No-Man's-Land was not quite so wide, the 15th and 16th Royal Scots got across, after suffering heavy but not crushing losses; but the 10th Lincolns and 11th Suffolks were almost wiped out, very few got over, though, as mentioned, a small party of Lincolns got into the New Crater, and we hear of small parties in other parts of the field, but, as effective units, those two battalions had ceased to exist by eight a.m.

Owing to the formation of the ground, General Gore could see nothing of what was happening after his troops had passed over the first two German lines, but several attempts were made to support the attack and subdue the machine gun fire. At ten a.m. three sections of 207th Field Company, R.E., were ordered to attempt the passage of No-Man's-Land, but the machine gun fire rendered it impossible. At one p.m. another attempt was made by thirty bombers of the Lincolns, and "A" Company, 18th Northumberland Fusiliers, met with no better success. Nearly all the Lincolns fell as they crossed our parapet, and the 18th Northumberlands suffered very heavily from artillery fire.

The first news received at 101st Brigade Headquarters was a message, timed ten a.m., from Major Stocks, commanding "C" Company, 15th Royal Scots, stating that had reached Peake trench, and had already beaten off two counter-attacks. So the battalion had reached its objective up to time.

The next report was not received by General Gore till midnight, 1st and 2nd July, but it is well to give its purport here.

Captain Brown, 11th Suffolks, and Lieutenant Robson, 15th Royal Scots, reported that they, with the remnants of the 101st Brigade were holding Wood Alley down to Round Wood, and were in touch with the 21st Division on their right. What had occurred was this :

Lieutenant Robson had been with Major Stocks, and "C" Company, 15th Royal Scots, about twelve men 16th Royal Scots, a few Suffolk lads, and one of the Lincolns, in Peake trench, but they were driven back by desperate counter-attacks, after an hour's close fighting. Every effort to extend to the left was met by heavy machine gun fire, and on that side the little party's flank was in the air. Major Stocks reformed the party with fragments of his own and other battalions of the Brigade, but was driven back, and was later reported wounded and missing. To Captain Brown and Lieutenant Robson the credit of maintaining our position in Wood Alley, which guarded the flank of the 21st Division, is awarded by their Brigadier, but they were soon joined by Captain Bibby's party of the 27th Northumberlands.

Lieutenant Robson was the only officer of his battalion, of those who took part in the assault, who came through untouched. Captain Brown also survived, and though wounded was able to remain at duty.

Another party of the Royal Scots and other units, under Captain Armit, of the 16th Battalion, had established itself in the Boche lines, not far from Captain Brown, but neither knew of the other's existence.

The 103rd Brigade early suffered the loss of its commander, who was wounded by a machine gun bullet in his observation post at seven-fifty a.m., and Lieutenant-Colonel Steward, D.S.O., commanding the 27th Northumberland Fusiliers, was sent for to take command. The battalions of this Brigade had followed the assaulting columns, and but little information regarding them could be obtained. Some men of 24th and 26th Battalions were reported to be with Acklom in the crater. Three officers and eighty other ranks, all that remained of the 25th, were said to be in our front line, about Keats Redan, having returned from the abortive attack up the Mash Valley. Later, some sixty men of 26th Battalion were reported to have got back, and to be in Tummel Street.

Second-Lieutenant T. W. Thompson, and a handful of the 25th Northumberlands, nearly reached Contalmaison, but were forced back. A small party of the 27th Battalion, of the same regiment, also made a great effort to reach its objective, but were forced back, and under Captain Bibby were holding Shelter Wood at ten a.m., and eventually joined the Royal Scots, and we shall hear of them later.

From information obtained later, and from evidence of those present at the taking of Contalmaison, it is amply proved that men of this Brigade did actually penetrate to that village on the 1st July, but none survived to tell the tale.

The situation at nightfall could not be described otherwise than unsatisfactory. The whole of the G.O.C.'s force had been launched in the attack, and though small parties were established at various points in the enemy's lines, it was doubtful whether they could hold out. There was considerable danger of a counter-attack on our main position from La Boisselle, and the officer commanding the Pioneers was ordered to organise the defence of the right brigade area, reinforcements of some Corps cavalry and cyclists being sent up. The left brigade area was taken over by the 19th Division during the afternoon.

On the right, in the 21st Division area, a trench had been opened across to the Boche front line, and the Staff Captain of the 101st Brigade, Captain Greig, 15th Royal Scots, attempted, with a small party, to carry food, water, and bombs to the remnants of the brigade in the front area. It was a painful experience wandering about the battle-field among the dead and dying, and in constant danger of running into the Boches. The party failed to find our men, but distributed their water to many wounded men, and handed over their bombs to a party of the 21st Division.

During the night of 1st/2nd, Lieutenant Ash, and twenty-seven other ranks of the 209th Field Company, volunteered to try to find the troops in the forward area, and succeeded in conveying to them a supply of bombs, etc., of which they were in sore need. The party only returned to its company at four a.m., and at nine-thirty a.m. Lieutenant Ash set out again with all four sections of the company, and worked on the consolidation of the positions till relieved by Engineers of 23rd Division on the night of 3rd/4th. The night of the 1st/2nd July passed without any great change in the position.

To the 19th Division, in Corps Reserve, had been entrusted the task of taking La Boisselle. Small parties of Cheshires of this Division reached Major Acklom's trenches through the tunnel during the night, and in the early morning of 2nd the rest of the battalion began arriving. The trenches became very congested, and there were heavy casualties from the enemy's artillery fire. Though supplies were being sent through the tunnel, but little reached Acklom's men, being made use of by intervening units. This was put straight on the evening of 2nd July, but the wounded, who could not be removed, suffered badly, though a doctor was sent up from the Field Ambulance.

The attack on La Boisselle was going on all day. During the afternoon Major Acklom received some reinforcements, among them three machine guns, and detachments, of 102nd Machine Gun Company, under Lieutenant Robson, and at eleven-five p.m. he was able to place on record : " Two Stoke's guns received, and placed in position. Plentiful supply of water and rations. Received men in good spirits. POSITION SECURE." His strength at midnight had decreased to five officers and one hundred and fifty-five N.C.O.'s and men.

We must now return to the parties of 101st and 103rd Brigades. The headquarters of the battalions of the 101st Brigade had not been allowed to go forward with the assaulting columns, but at nine p.m. an order was sent to them to go forward and try to straighten out the situation. This order did not reach the Lincolns or the 15th Royal Scots, but Sir George McCrae received it at nine-twenty, and started five minutes later to attempt to reach his men, but got held up for some hours by heavy artillery fire, and did not reach them till near daylight.

This Wood Alley party on the morning of 2nd was constituted thus :

	Officers	Other ranks	Total
15th Royal Scots	2	85	87
16th Royal Scots	7	137	144
10th Lincolns	0	4	4
11th Suffolks	1	14	15
27th Northumberland Fusiliers .	1	53	54
Total	11	293	304

With Captain Armit were about one hundred and forty officers and men, mostly of 16th Royal Scots, but there were also a few Lincolns and 24th and 27th Northumberland Fusiliers.

Sir George McCrae was placed in command of all troops of the Division in this part of the field, with Major Temple, 27th Northumberland Fusiliers, as his Staff Officer. A strong combination—the fearless "amateur," whose cheerful optimism soon spread through all his command, and the tried regular, who had then just made his twelfth trip "over the top."

The chief cause of anxiety was not what the Boche might do, but the exhaustion of the men, who had been without water since the previous morning, and had also consumed the food and used up most of the supply of bombs, etc., with which they had started on their perilous adventure.

Before noon on 2nd the arrival of carrying parties of the Pioneers, and others working with them, gave new life to the defence. Orders were received by Sir George McCrae to attack the German strong point, known as Scots Redoubt, and to attempt to join hands with the 19th Division on the left. The response was prompt. A party of the 15th Royal Scots, under Lieutenant Robson, captured the Redoubt after a sharp bombing fight, and took about fifty prisoners, among whom were three officers. A party of 16th

Royal Scots cleared about one hundred and fifty yards of the trench towards "Horse Shoe," but were stopped by a strong barricade, at which the Boche put up a good fight. The garrison's defence throughout the day was of a very active nature, producing constant bombing scraps.

A junction with Captain Armit's party was early established, and a considerable number of Huns, who were holding the intervening trenches, escaped along a communication trench towards La Boisselle.

The Boche was being reinforced, his communications being open to the rear, whereas ours, owing to the failure of our "moppers up," were menaced by the active enemy in Heligoland, The Kipper and Bloater, whose machine gun fire made it necessary for our parties to go round through the 21st Division area. This was a very slow business, not only on account of the length of the detour, but also because of the congestion—the trench across No-Man's-Land, and the approaches to it from both directions, being crowded with masses of men. Reinforcements, and carrying parties struggling forward, wounded painfully striving to crawl back, stretcher-bearers with their patient burdens stumbling along, all under periodic bursts of shell fire and constant streams of machine bullets passing overhead, made a veritable pandemonium.

All his available troops being engaged, our General obtained the loan of two companies of the 7th East Lancashire Regiment from the 19th Division and these did grand work. Crossing on the right through the 21st Division trench, they bombed along the Boche front line system to their left, and by five-thirty p.m. had cleared Heligoland, and taken fifty prisoners.

In the early hours of the night, reinforcements to the number of about four hundred rifles, composed of men from various units of the 101st and 103rd Brigades, were sent up to Sir George McCrae, and further supplies of food, water, and bombs. The 16th Royal

Scots' diary records with pleasure and pride that the
Quartermaster sent up full rations of fresh meat and
groceries, so that everyone had a much-needed square
meal.   Four sections of the 207th Field Company also
arrived, and strengthened the defences, so that all
danger of the Boche recovering the post was passed.

On the 3rd July the two companies of the East
Lancashire Regiment further cleared the Boche
trenches round Heligoland, and effected junctions with
the parties in Scots Redoubt and the New Crater.
The Boche made an attack on Scots Redoubt about
three p.m., but was driven back by the 16th Royal
Scots.

General Williams was not the man to stay at
home while his men were in a tight place.   During
the 3rd July he visited Scots Redoubt, and though few
had previously suspected him of being tender-hearted,
he was overcome, and with tears in his eyes he went
round the trenches, giving a cheery word to the men,
saying over and over again, " Well done, lads, well
done, you've done damned well."

Major Acklom's party, during the third, was not
inactive.   Guided by Lieutenant Rotherford and
Corporal Burns, Captain Longhurst, 23rd Northumberland Fusiliers, with one hundred men of various
battalions, pushed out to the right beyond the New
Crater, clearing that area without serious opposition.

During the third the 19th Division firmly
established itself in La Boisselle.   In this attack a
party of bombers did good work; they were led by
Captain D. H. James, our Trench Mortars Officer
and one of his officers, Second-Lieutenant Wylie.
Unfortunately, Captain James was severely wounded,
and we lost him, his place being taken by Captain
E. L. O. Baddeley.

Fighting went on all day, and, of course, there
was the usual shelling, but a lull set in towards
evening, and it was possible to walk about No-Man's-
Land with comparative safety and groups of men from

many battalions stood about discussing the wonders of
the deep dug-outs of La Boisselle. We all were
cheerful, in spite of the poor dead lying thickly around
us. The sun shone brightly. Were we not strolling
about at our ease within a few yards of what, three
days ago, was the Boche's front line? Things were
undoubtedly coming our way at last. The news from
the south was good : the French had made grand
progress, and our 15th Corps, on our immediate right,
had also made good. If our ambitious programme
had not been carried out, still we had established a
record of which we need not be ashamed. We had
broken into the Boche lines, and made good our
footing, thereby guarding the left flank of the 21st
Division, and greatly facilitating the capturing of La
Boisselle by the 19th. That our failure to achieve
complete success was not due to any lack of zeal on
our part was proved by the rows of dead lying in
regular ranks, as the machine guns had mown them
down, and the many wounded that had been carried
or painfully struggled back, or, alas, were still lying
out in areas where the stretcher-bearers could not
reach them, owing to the murderous fire with which the
Boche greeted every attempt to remove them.

During the night of the 3rd/4th the three
Infantry Brigades, and their attached Field
Companies, were relieved by Brigades of the 23rd
Division; under rather different circumstances to
those in which we had relieved them five months
earlier in peaceful Armentières.

The Pioneers were not relieved till early on the
6th, being employed for two days in the sad job of
burying the dead. They had been busy all the 3rd
carrying out supplies, and on the 4th a company went
once more to Scots Redoubt to take supplies to its
new garrison, while half of another company was
hailed from its gruesome task to aid in repelling an
expected counter-attack on La Boisselle, which, however, never developed.

D

The gunners through all these days had been working hard. After the " set piece " barrage of 1st July, they helped the infantry in every possible way, putting down barrages in front of points the Boche seemed inclined to attack, and bombarding places which our troops were about to attack. In some cases they had good sport, and enjoyed themselves, in witness whereof I quote from a Battery Commander's diary :

" 1st July. Light very bad at start, and impossible to see anything for some time. Discarded periscope, and observed from Kinfauns Street. When light got better, waves of our infantry could be seen crossing the support line, and disappearing over the crest into Sausage Valley. La Boisselle was to have been taken from the north, but this attack failed entirely with heavy loss, owing to the width of No-Man's-Land, and the wire not being properly cut. This fact did great damage to the attack of our Brigade (103rd), as they were enfiladed by machine gun fire from La Boisselle. Saw a machine gun detachment double down from La Boisselle and get into action at X.14.c. 5.05 against our people crossing X.20.a and b. Took the law into my own hands, stopped battery shooting per time-table, and turned one gun on to the machine gun. First round of shrapnel went right into them, knocking out some, and dispersing the remainder. One man presently returned for the gun which they had left on top of the parapet, and reached it just as my second round burst, and both man and gun disappeared. Silenced several other machine guns along south edge of La Boisselle. Later, saw several lines of our infantry retiring from X.20.a and b. They were being bombed by Boches, and first two lines went right back to our trenches. Got on to the Boches, and stopped the bombing, and the remainder of our men stayed in the Boche front line from X.20.a.4.7 to 8.3. They then started to bomb up towards La Boisselle, but began to get rather the worst of it from bombs and snipers. I turned odd guns on to various points where machine gun rifle fire and bombing came from, and eventually put them all out, and our people were left in peace, and started consolidating. It was nervous work strafing the bombers, as they were only fifty yards from our bombers. On one occasion a Boche was sitting right up on his parados in La Boisselle, and . . . bet me five to one that I would not get him first shot. The first round was one hundred yards over, and did not frighten him, and the second (H.E.) was an absolute direct hit, and blew him to bits.

"2nd July. A splendid day's shooting. . . . Our infantry (the 19th Division), crossing No-Man's-Land (to attack La Boisselle), began to take it in the neck from trench X.14.c.5.05 to X.20.a.9.9. Turned all guns on them with H.E. The trench was lined with riflemen, and there were at least three guns on the parapet. I started with three rounds of gun-fire, which burst perfectly, and absolutely flattened out the Boches. They only showed here once again, and six rounds of gun-fire finished them for good, and our infantry walked into the trench without losing another man. . . . We had several glorious targets, whole lines of trench absolutely full of Boches firing for all they were worth. The battery shot very well, got round after round of gun-fire H.E. right into them."

It is pleasant to read on 7th : "General Brydges (commanding 19th Division) was here to-day, and thanked me for our shooting, and for the information he had received from this observation post."

The gunners were not relieved with the rest of the Division, but remained in their positions, backing up the infantry of the 19th and 23rd Divisions with just as much zeal as they had shown in supporting us. Our diary writer records on 16th : "Got to the battery for tea, and slept in pyjamas for the first time for three weeks." When we return to the front again, in the next chapter, we shall find him and his gunners still there, busy and cheery as ever.

To give some idea of the work done by the guns during this period, it may be noted that in the first seven days of the attack two R.F.A. Brigades fired 43,496 rounds, and in eighteen days the guns of all calibres of 3rd Corps sent over 702,400 shells.

The Divisional Headquarters went back to Basieux, and the remnants of the infantry collected in Hennencourt Wood.

The casualties suffered in the three days' fighting, by the three Infantry Brigades, were :

101ST BRIGADE

	Kd.	OFFICERS Wd.	Msg.	Kd.	OTHER RANKS Wd.	Msg.	ALL RANKS
15th Royal Scots . .	7	5	5	44	244	233	538
16th Royal Scots . .	1	5	6	30	74	356	472
10th Lincolns . . .	4	10	1	66	259	162	502
11th Suffolks . . .	2	12	4	4	390	279	691
101st M.G. Co. . .	2	5	0	4	54	28	93
101st T.M.B. . . .	1	2	0	included in batts.			3
Total	17	39	16	148	1021	1058	2299

102ND BRIGADE

	Kd.	Wd.	Msg.	Kd.	Wd.	Msg.	All ranks
20th Northumberland F.	16	10	0	337	268	0	631
21st Northumberland F.	11	10	0	161	296	0	478
22nd Northumberland F.	7	14	1	198	319	0	539
23rd Northumberland F.	9	7	2	178	444	0	640
102nd M.G. Co. . .	1	5	0	6	24	0	36
Total	44	46	3	880	1351	0	2324

103RD BRIGADE

	Kd.	Wd.	Msg.	Kd.	Wd.	Msg.	All ranks
Brigade H.Q. . . .	0	1	0	0	1	0	2
24th Northumberland F.	4	12	2	13	307	282	630
25th Northumberland F.	4	13	1	5	0	468	491
26th Northumberland F.	8	12	0	51	11	165	247
27th Northumberland F.	3	16	1	4	180	335	539
103rd M.G. Co. . .	3	2	0	2	6	9	22
103rd T.M.B. . . .	1	4	0	0	3	29	37
Total	23	60	4	75	508	1288	1968

Total for three Brigades 6591.

These lists are copied from those in the war diaries compiled immediately after the brigades came out. It is evident that a different system of classification has been employed, as the 102nd show no men missing, apparently classing all who were absent as killed. Lieutenant-Colonel W. Lyle, of 23rd Northumberland Fusiliers, was last seen among his men, walking, stick in hand, about two hundred yards from the German trenches. Lieutenant-Colonel A. P. A. Elphinstone, commanding the 22nd Northumberland Fusiliers, was also killed. He had long retired from the Indian Army when the war broke out, but joined up joyously, and the fear that his age might preclude him leading his battalion into action was the only thing that worried him. When that was removed, he became the most cheerful member of the Mess. Major Heneker, who had been given command of the 21st Northumberland Fusiliers, shortly before the attack, was also killed. So that of the 102nd Brigade all the battalion commanders were killed. The 103rd fared but little better, Lieutenant-Colonel Howard being killed, and Lieutenant-Colonels M. E. Richardson and J. H. M. Arden, D.S.O., of the 26th and 25th Northumberlands, being wounded.

The clearing of the battle-field was a difficult task, as fighting went on over a large portion of it for some days, and many poor fellows lay out for a long time. This distressed General Williams greatly, and he was constantly on the move, hastening the work of the stretcher-bearers. On the 4th July he writes:

" . . . I am glad to say we got large numbers of our wounded in before the weather broke. . . . One poor man was so excited seeing me come, that he insisted, though I implored him not to do so, in undoing his pants and showing me his broken thigh. All very pathetic. A great many are wounds that may recover, I am glad to say, but of course many are gone for ever, and were killed outright."

On the 5th July the Corps Commander inspected the remnants of the brigades, and complimented them on their bravery and tenacity. He specially referred to valuable service that they had performed in guarding the left flank of the 21st Division, which, had our small isolated detachments not held firmly on to the positions they had seized, might have been seriously endangered, and in fact the whole attack would have been in jeopardy, and all our line down to the French might have been rolled up.

General Sir H. Rawlinson, K.C.B., C.V.O., commanding 4th Army, wired :

" Please convey to the 34th Division my heartiest congratulations on their successes. Whilst regretting their heavy casualties, I desire to express my gratitude and admiration of the gallantry with which they carried out their difficult task."

The casualties to the infantry rendered it impossible for the Division to remain in the line, unless it were speedily reconstituted, and therefore the 102nd and 103rd Brigades, whose effectiveness would take longer to restore, owing to the severe losses they had sustained in their higher ranks, were transferred to the 37th Division, their places being taken by the 111th and 112th Brigades of that Division. With the decimated brigades went the 18th Northumberland Fusiliers, though this battalion had only suffered slightly. Its inclusion in the troops to be relieved was apparently due to a loosely worded message describing the crushing losses suffered by the " Northumberland Battalions."

The exchange of troops took place without delay by buses and lorries on the 6th and 7th, the 9th North

Staffords replacing the 18th Northumberland Fusiliers.

The doings of our two brigades and Pioneers, while with the 37th Division, need not be detailed. They went into the line opposite Monchy au Bois, and then on the Vimy Ridge, where they had an exciting time in that area of mines. The two brigades were, for a time, amalgamated under command of General Ternan till reinforcements arrived, and their increased strength allowed of them acting separately. Brigadier-General H. E. Trevor, D.S.O., succeeded to the command of the 103rd Brigade.

CHAPTER IV

THE troops sent to replace the shattered brigades of the 34th Division were :

> 111th Infantry Brigade.—Brigadier-General R. Barnes.
> 10th Royal Fusiliers.—Lieutenant-Colonel H. White.
> 13th Royal Fusiliers.—Lieutenant-Colonel H. des Voeux.
> 13th Rifle Brigade.—Lieutenant-Colonel C. F. Pretor-Pinney.
> 13th K.R.R. Corps.—Lieutenant-Colonel R. Chester Master.
> 111th Brigade M.G. Company.—Captain H. S. Allfray.
> 112th Infantry Brigade.—Brigadier-General P. M. Robinson, C.M.G.
> 11th Royal Warwickshire Regiment.
> 6th Bedfordshire Regiment.—Lieutenant-Colonel F. F. Edwards.
> 8th East Lancashire Regiment.—Lieutenant-Colonel J. D. Mackay.
> 10th Loyal North Lancashire Regiment.—Lieutenant-Colonel R. Cobbold.
> 112th Brigade M.G. Company.—Major B. H. Puckle.

The 8th Division suffered so severely on the 1st July that it was withdrawn on the same evening, its place in the 3rd Corps being taken by the 12th Division. The 34th, although relieved in the front line by the 23rd Division, remained in the 3rd Corps, which was thus increased by one Division, and enabled to carry on the offensive. The 12th Division attacked Ovillers. The enemy fought well, but gradually was forced back. The fighting was very fierce, and the progress slow, each of the many lines of defence being stubbornly held. The 19th Division also captured La Boisselle, but not without severe fighting. The 23rd Division was able to push forward towards The Cutting and the northern edge of Contalmaison and Bailiff Wood. The fresh troops of the 34th Division were hurried up, some on the very day of their arrival, to assist in the operations by supplying, carrying, and working parties. The artillery of the 34th Division remained in action, covering the 19th and 23rd Divisions.

On 9th July the 112th Brigade took over a portion of the front from the 58th Brigade of 19th Division. The three Field Companies, having returned after refitting, started the construction of a road from the northern edge of Becourt Wood north-eastward down into the Sausage Valley, to join an old track running up that valley to meet the La Boisselle-Contalmaison road, and the Divisional dump was formed on this road in what had been the old Boche reserve line. This point was fortified by a company of the 9th North Staffords, and named Gordon Post. On the 10th the 111th Brigade took over the left sector of the Divisional front, in which 13th Rifle Brigade and 13th Royal Fusiliers were already. The front trenches were then about one thousand three hundred yards due east of La Boisselle, and the 25th Division had come in on our left. The relief was completed by three-thirty a.m., and at four a.m. General Ingouville-Williams took over command from G.O.C. 19th Division, and issued instructions to brigades to pursue a more active policy. Those who know the General will not infer from this that the policy of his predecessor had been unduly quiet.

The 69th Brigade, on our right, captured Contalmaison at four-thirty p.m. on the 10th—nine days and two hours after it was to have fallen to our 103rd Brigade, " according to plan."

In conjunction with this attack by the 23rd

Division, our two brigades were ordered to push forward strong patrols, and try to occupy a line of trench running from north-west corner of Contalmaison, westward to the fork formed by the junction of two tracks from Pozières and Ovillers, and prolonged northwards to the Pozières-Albert road, which it crossed about one thousand yards west of the former village.   This meant an advance of about five hundred or six hundred yards, and though the patrols pushed forward vigorously they did not make much progress. All the afternoon and evening the front line was heavily shelled, and the 13th Rifle Brigade, which was holding the 111th Brigade front lost two officers and several other ranks.   Later, an attack on the Boche line by both brigades was ordered, and had begun before the orders cancelling it reached the battalions concerned.   This sad contretemps caused severe losses.   The 13th Rifle Brigade advanced with " A " and " D " Companies in front, followed at a distance of about one hundred and thirty yards by " C " and " B "; when these latter had gone two hundred yards a runner of the 10th Royal Fusiliers rushed up, and handed the Commanding Officer a message that the attack was cancelled.   The order to retire was given, and the battalion retired to its original position.   The leading companies had penetrated to the third line of trenches and inflicted severe losses on the enemy, and captured two hundred prisoners before the order to retire was received.   The casualties in the battalion were twenty officers and about three hundred and eighty other ranks.   The Commanding Officer, Second-in-Command, Adjutant, and all four Company Commanders were in the casualty list.

The 112th Brigade also made a successful advance, but on retirement were followed by the Boche to within fifty yards of their trench, when the 6th Royal Warwicks put things straight by a bayonet charge.   It seems likely that the Boche was preparing an attack on our line when our advance forestalled him.

The 13th Rifle Brigade was relieved by the 10th Royal Fusiliers during the night, and on the 11th patrols from both brigades established themselves some two hundred yards in front of former line, and consolidated during the day. The 1st Division had come in on our right, and the 25th was still on the left. Further advances were made on the 12th, connection being made with the Divisions on our flanks. The 1st Division placed and maintained a post in Contalmaison Wood. Ovillers was still holding out, not more than half of it being in possession of the 25th Division, and machine guns from its north-east corner swept over our trenches.

The R.E. and Pioneers carried on the tramway from Chapes spur towards Gordon Post to relieve the mules, and a new communication trench was commenced, leading from the rear of La Boisselle to the forward line, which now it joined some three hundred yards west of Bailiff Wood. The Chalk Pit northeast of Contalmaison Wood was visited by a patrol of 10th Royal Fusiliers under Lieutenant W. F. Campbell, and found unoccupied. The shelling was steadily increasing, and life in these imperfect trenches was far from pleasant, very different to the orderly peaceful existence we used to lead before the push began. There was great uncertainty as to the whereabouts of the Boche, and we were in constant anxiety as to what he would do next, and even more exercised as to what we should be asked to do.

On the 13th we had to extend to our right, and take over a portion of the line from the 1st Division, up to the north-west corner of Contalmaison. On the 14th orders were received from the Corps that the 1st Division and the 15th Corps on our right would attack the Boche second line east of Pozières, and we were to co-operate by gaining ground towards that village. Considerable difficulty was found in drawing up the scheme for the operation, owing to the number of artillery units which were engaged in pounding Pozières—10th Corps from west, 19th Divisional Artillery, attached to 34th Division, from south, and the heavy guns of the 3rd Corps, supporting the attack of the 1st Division. However, eventually arrangements were made to lift the fire off the portion of the village to be attacked, and at six p.m. a lodgement was effected by a platoon of the 111th and two of 112th Brigade in a Boche trench about two hundred yards south of Pozières. About ten p.m. came news to the Divisional Headquarters that the Boche had ejected our men, re-occupied the trench, and placed machine guns in the gardens which projected to the south of the village, almost to the left flank of the trench. Orders were sent to the 112th Brigade to re-occupy the trench with two companies, and this job was entrusted to the 8th East Lancs. Of this we shall hear more later.

The position on this night was : 15th Corps hold Mametz Wood, 1st Division carry on the line westward along road to The Cutting, then along northern edge of Contalmaison, with posts in Pearl Wood. The 34th held from there to the 25th Division area, near Ovillers, all of which, except the extreme northeast corner, was in their hands. The 34th Division was, for most of the way along the trench known as the Brown line in the operation orders for the 1st July, but a chain of posts was held in front, including Bailiff's Wood.

The plan of the attack to take place on 15th in conjunction with the 1st Division, which was to advance from western edge of Bazentin le Petit Wood astride of the Boche second line east of Pozières, involved an attack on that village from the south by the 112th Brigade, supported by the 111th Brigade, which, after the 112th had occupied the village, was to pass through and attack the second line about the Windmill north-east of Pozières. The artillery bombardment commenced at eight-thirty a.m., and an hour later raked slowly back through the village.

The 25th Division, in the first orders, was to make a simultaneous attack from the west, but subsequently this was limited to patrol action. The 1st Division advance was to commence at nine a.m.; that of the 112th Brigade twenty minutes later. This brigade started from a trench which ran from the north-east corner of the Contalmaison enclosures westward for about one thousand two hundred yards, and it had between it and the Boche line about one thousand three hundred yards of rising ground, with very little cover after passing Contalmaison Wood, which was a little over one thousand yards from Pozières. The brigade advanced in artillery formation, battalion behind battalion. As each unit passed Contalmaison Wood it extended two companies in the front line, and two, fifty paces in rear, so that by the extension of the first three battalions was completed the brigade was in six waves. The 4th Battalion, the 10th Loyal North Lancs, followed, carrying S.A.A., bombs, etc., to form a dump at the Chalk Pit. Four guns of the Machine Gun Company were to support the attack from a point three hundred to four hundred yards west of the Chalk Pit, while two guns were to work up the depression to their right, and come into action from behind a small bank and a few shrubs. It was firmly believed at Brigade Headquarters when the operation orders were drawn up that a party of the 8th East Lancs was established in the German trench about two hundred and fifty to three hundred yards south of the gardens of Pozières, and it was only when late on the night of the 14th/15th the Commanding Officer was ordered to occupy this trench with two companies that it was found the trench was not in our possession. It was then too late to alter the plans of the attack.

The attack went well till the leading waves were within four hundred yards of the outskirts of the village, when the machine gun fire became so intense that no further progress could be made. The 10th Royal Fusiliers of the 111th Brigade was in support, the headquarters when the advance was stayed being about two hundred and fifty yards south of the Chalk Pit. The sorely tried battalions of the 112th began slowly to give ground, and there was a tendency to seek cover in the hollow road some two hundred yards from the entrance to the village, causing a dangerous block. The 10th Royal Fusiliers pushed on, " C " and " B " Companies being extended each on a two platoon front with their L.G. detachments in rear of the second line. " D " and " A " Companies followed in the same formation. The attack received new impetus, and the small orchard on the Albert-Pozières road, some two hundred yards from the entrance to the village, was occupied by " D " Company of the 10th Royal Fusiliers under Lieutenant Taylor, and a great effort was made to seize the boundaries of the village. A few men got in, but the machine guns took so heavy a toll of the assailants that the line fell back to the trench running through the orchard.

The headquarters of the 10th Royal Fusiliers, 6th Bedfords, 11th Royal Warwicks, and 8th East Lancs were all in the Chalk Pit, and there about two p.m. appeared General Ingouville-Williams, eager to see for himself how the day was going. Nothing daunted at the check under which the assault was suffering, he decided to renew the attack after a more severe bombardment.

Our Battery Commander, from his observation post in Kinfauns, records : " July 15th, Saturday. Heavy fighting in Pozières all day. This was the biggest bombardment of it, by all our heavies, I have ever seen. The whole place went up in brick dust, and when it was over no trace of a building could be seen anywhere. It was a wonderful sight, huge clouds of rose-coloured, brown, bluish black and white smoke rolling along together with flashes of bursts, the whole against a pale green blue sky and bright evening sunlight.''

Alas! the Boche machine guns and their plucky crews came through this hellish experience unscathed and undismayed, and when the 112th Brigade renewed the attack it was met by an even more destructive fire than in the morning, and, after making gallant attempts to establish itself in the village, was compelled to regain the cover of the trenches it had left.

The casualties this day were :

	Kd.	Wd.
11th Royal Warwicks	64	262
6th Bedfords	37	293
8th East Lancashire	53	268
10th Loyal North Lancashire . .	6	47
M.G. Company	1	2
T.M.B.	0	1
Total	161	873

Total for 112th Brigade, 1034.

The 10th Royal Fusiliers lost forty-two killed and one hundred and eighty-three wounded and twenty-four missing. It was relieved at once, but the last of the weary battalion did not reach the haven of the deep dug-outs in the Tara-Usna line till two a.m. the next morning.

The 112th Brigade was relieved during the 16th and night of 16th/17th by the 68th Brigade of 23rd Division, which had been lent to the 34th Division, as the 101st Brigade was not yet reorganised sufficiently to take its place in the line. Before being relieved, the 10th Loyal North Lancs had established itself firmly in the most westerly of the two orchards at the south-east end of Pozières, so that the sad losses of the 15th had not been quite in vain, for our line had been advanced about one thousand yards and a foothold obtained in the defences of Pozières.

The 68th Brigade made an effort to take Pozières on the 17th at eight p.m. after the usual artillery and trench mortar bombardment, but the Boche forestalled the assault by half an hour, putting down an intense barrage at seven-fifty, which, combined with the fire of about ten machine guns, defeated the attack, one company getting forward about one hundred yards, and another only twenty.

The Division was relieved on the 19th and 20th by the 1st Australian Division, which captured Pozières on 25th July after most severe fighting.

The old quarters were re-occupied : Divisional Headquarters returned to the château at Basieux, 111th Brigade went to Bresle, 112th to La Houssoye, 9th North Staffords to Bresle, into which elastic village the three Field Companies also squeezed themselves. The Field Ambulances were at Franvillers, Hennencourt, and Millencourt.

The 101st Brigade had remained in Hennencourt Wood busy refitting. The battalions were soon up to their full strength as regards numbers, but mere numbers do not make a battalion efficient or reliable. Esprit de corps, on which so much depends, cannot be obtained in a few days; bombers and other specialists take long to train, and the drafts that arrived, though of good stamp, were of many different units, and none had any experience in France. The 15th Royal Scots received two hundred and ninety-nine men from their 6th Battalion; these men had served in Egypt, but none of them had handled a Mills' bomb. The Suffolks drafts were from various battalions and regiments. The Lincolns was completed by parties of men from Northamptons, North Staffords, South Staffords, Middlesex, Oxford, Worcester, and Leicester Regiments, "and a few Lincolns." Many of these had only three months' service. Truly it was asking much of the few remaining officers and non-commissioned officers to expect them to weld such material into a first-class

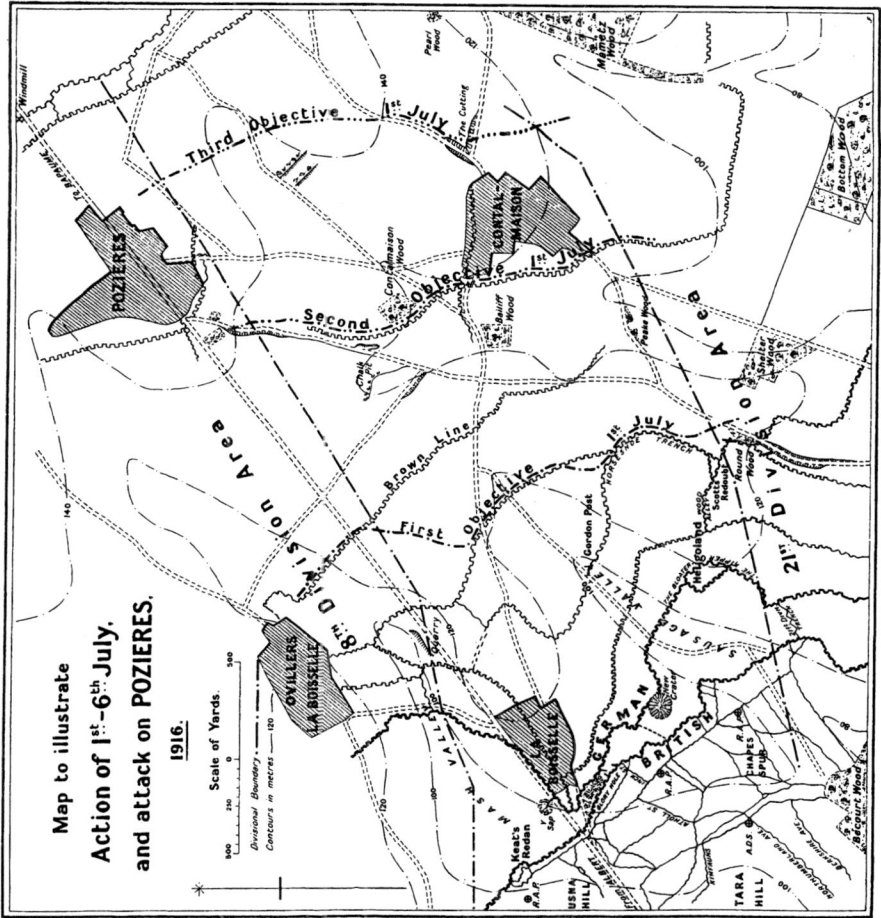

Map to illustrate
Action of 1st–6th July.
and attack on POZIERES.

1916.

Scale of Yards.

fighting instrument in a few days. Yet this is what
was demanded not once but many times during this
long-drawn-out war of every battalion staff, and the
certainty that this almost superhuman task would
have to be undertaken, after every push, emphasised
the wisdom of General Gore, in not allowing the Commanding Officers of the 101st Brigade to lead their
battalions on the 1st July.

It may not have been possible to avoid a man who
had been sent to England, either sick or wounded,
being seldom returned to his old battalion, but that
the army lost much in driving power thereby cannot
be disputed, and so great was this loss that next time,
if there is to be a next time, let us hope some means
will have been found to avoid it.

" On the 22nd the Divisional Commander, Major-
General Ingouville-Williams, C.B., D.S.O., was
killed whilst reconnoitring ground in the vicinity of
Mametz. He went out soon after lunch, accompanied
by the A.D.C., Lieutenant Grainger Stewart, 16th
Royal Scots, and about eight p.m. a telephone message
was received that the G.O.C. had been killed at seven
p.m. by a shell-fire, whilst walking back from Contalmaison, round the south end of Mametz, to meet his
car, which was at Montaubon. Exact spot was
Square X.30.a.3.7 on top of the bank."—Extract
from War Diary 34th Division.

So died the first commander and the maker of
the 34th Division—an absolutely fearless man ; a
stern disciplinarian, but with a tender heart : he
worked his men hard, but he loved them, and looked
after their well-being and comfort. Only two days
before his death he wrote : " Never shall I cease
singing the praises of my old 34th Division, and I
shall never have the same grand men to deal with."

All ranks felt they had lost a great leader and a
kind friend.

On the next day, at four p.m., he was buried in
Warloy cemetery. The funeral was attended by a

E

large number of the officers and other ranks of the Division, and by some of the 102nd and 103rd Brigades.   Of these more would have been present had they been able to overcome the difficulty of distance and transport.

On the 25th July Major-General C. L. Nicholson, C.M.G., arrived at Divisional Headquarters and took command of the Division.   He had succeeded our late G.O.C. in the command of the 16th Brigade, and was just completing his second year in the country.

On 31st, the Division went back into the line, this time rather farther east than before, and operating northwards instead of eastwards.   The 101st Brigades took over the front line east of Bazentin Wood to High Wood exclusive, 111th Brigade was in support in Mametz Wood, and the 112th in reserve in Becourt Wood.   The Field Companies were disposed : 207th with the 101st Brigade, 208th at Bellevue Farm, 209th in Mametz Wood.   Divisional Headquarters was in a camp about one thousand yards south of Albert.   The Divisional Artillery were still where they had been since they arrived in these parts early in May, viz., in their battle positions, though they had been having, for them, an easy time of late.

Our Battery Commander records : "July 21st, Friday.   Wagon lines moved to just west of Albert this morning.   Quiet day; we are supposed to be in rest, and can keep half our gunners off duty, but we have a subaltern at Battalion Headquarters in the Chalk Pit, and have a day and a night observation post, and may be called on to fire at any moment, so it is not much use as a rest."

The battery was moved about this time to the Sausage Valley, and on 28th we read : " I registered on the Windmill (north-east of Pozières) in the evening.   Our mess dug-outs have been well creosoted, but there are still a good many dead Boches to be

MAJOR-GENERAL SIR LOTHIAN NICHOLSON, K.C.B., C.M.G.
Commanding 34th Division, July, 1916—March, 1919

[To face p. 66]

removed from blocked-up entrances, etc.'' The next day he records that ten of these unwanted Boches were removed : '' Very smelly work; there are, we suspect, a good many left.''

Our artillery was not looking after us during this tour of the line, that duty being undertaken by the 19th Division gunners and two brigades of the 1st Divisional Artillery.

The 101st Brigade Headquarters was in an old German dressing-station on the north-west side of Bazentin le Petit Wood, and wasn't a salubrious place. It had been '' repaired with sand-bags, into which had been shovelled various parts of human anatomy, German I hope. As the weather was very hot, the smell was strong.'' . . . '' The Lincoln Headquarter staff slept for three nights in a deep dug-out a few yards from us, and then concluded that it was so stuffy it needed to be cleaned. They found they had been sleeping on three dead Germans. Ugh ! . . . The wood, a hundred yards to the south, was carpeted with corpses. . . . The smells, the noise, the unnatural shapes, and the bloody mess of shell torn bodies ! Life at Bazentin was unpleasant.''

Nor was life very pleasant farther back, the 112th Brigade in Mametz Wood being shelled on 1st August, and one battalion alone had forty casualties.

The position in the front trenches was somewhat peculiar, as we and the Boche shared what was known as the Intermediate trench. We had the eastern end, and the Boche the western. To mark the limits of our respective spheres of influence there were two barricades.

The 16th Royal Scots, who were in the front line, objected to the close proximity of the Boche, and spent the night of the 1st/2nd in unsuccessful attempts to oust him by bombing attacks, but the following night they were more successful, and after an all night battle they found themselves in possession of about one hundred yards of trench, and erected a new barricade. On the 3rd the 111th Brigade took over a portion of the line to the right of the 101st, extending nearly to High Wood, from 51st Division. This wood completely overlooked our front line.

On the night of the 3rd/4th an attack on a larger scale was made on the Boche portion of intermediate. Originally this was to have been part of an operation in which the Anzacs and 2nd Division were to join, but early on the 3rd the Corps notified that these Divisions would not attack, but desired the 34th to carry out its share as previously arranged. The plan of attack was that after a heavy bombardment of the Boche line by the artillery and Stoke's guns for about two minutes the barrage was to rake back some two hundred yards, and remain there for ten minutes, and then gradually decrease in violence, and cease altogether after one hour unless the Brigadier asked for its continuance. As soon as barrage lifted off the Boche trench the assaulting columns were to break in. A machine gun was to be established in the line as soon as it had been captured, and a party from 207th Field Company was to aid in the consolidation, while a company of the 9th North Staffords was to dig a communication from our old to our new line.

The assault was to be carried out by two companies of the 16th Royal Scots and two companies of the 11th Suffolks. The bombardment was duly carried out, and at one a.m. Brigade Headquarters waited anxiously for news, but none came. The Boche barrage made communication very difficult, and it was three a.m. before anything reliable was known, and then the news was bad. It appeared that owing to the two companies of Royal Scots and the right company of the Suffolks losing their way, they had not reached their assembly points in time to participate in the attack, which had been carried out by "B" Company of the latter battalion, lead by Captain Brown of Scots Redoubt fame. This company took the left of trench, and started bombing to its right. It blocked the communication running back to Switch trench, and was doing well, but heavy pressure was brought to bear on its right, and in spite of reinforcements, which were sent across, it was forced slowly to the left, the trench becoming very congested.

An attempt was made to renew the attack, but by the time the columns could be reorganised it was getting light, and the effort failed. Unfortunately, Captain Armit, who had done so well in the early July fighting, was reported as " missing, believed killed." Lieutenant Mackenzie was the only one in this second attempt to enter the Boche trench, and he fell dead as he did so.

The Pioneers were not able to start work till three-thirty a.m., and the communication trench was only eighteen inches deep when daylight forced them to stop work. It being, therefore, impossible to support " B " Company, it was ordered to retire, which it did, with its tail well up, bringing with it nearly all its wounded and two Boche machine guns. Altogether a very fine performance, which shows that but for the failure of the other companies, the operation would have been completely successful. The company lost Second-Lieutenant M. Tallon and four other ranks killed, and Second-Lieutenants A. C. Mason and Maxwell and seventy-one other ranks wounded, and nineteen men were missing.

Later we paid still more dearly for this failure.

There was constant fighting in this trench. On the next night the 15th Royal Scots, who had relieved the 16th, made another bombing attack, but a crushing barrage made the attack a failure, and prevented the Lincolns, who had relieved the Suffolks, from co-operating. On the following night, just as the 15th Royal Scots were about to attack the barricade again, the Boche hopped over and took two bays of our trench, but by daylight the Scots had driven him out and taken fifty yards of his trench and erected another barricade.

The 112th Brigade relieved the 101st on 6th, the relief being concluded by seven-fifteen p.m. Two battalions were in the front line, one in support supplying working parties, and one in reserve occupied in carrying up water from Mametz Wood to the front troops, a distance of about three thousand yards.

At two a.m. on 8th the East Lancs, who were next the barrier, made an attempt to push the Boche farther down the trench, but the wily Hun had dug a deep pit on his side of the obstacle, and this foiled the Lancashire lads.

During the night of 8th/9th the 6th Bedfords made a plucky attempt to take this wretched Intermediate trench, which had now become a very sore subject with us all. After the heavies had treated the obnoxious trench to two hours of their best, the Field Artillery were to barrage the rear of the trench so as to prevent any reinforcements reaching it. The attack was not to take place till nine-thirty p.m., two hours after the heavies had stopped, and when it was thought that the Boche, judging from our previous behaviour, would think that all danger was over for the night. The Bedfords were to push out five patrols each of an officer and twenty-five other ranks, which were to steal across the intervening space, which varied from eighty to two hundred yards, and suddenly attack the trench. As soon as they were in they were to signal for the remainder of the two companies and a company of the 9th North Staffords, who were to come over and help hold and consolidate the line. The 8th East Lancs were to bomb down from their barrier as soon as the Bedford boys were in, and the 46th Brigade, 15th Division, was to co-operate with machine gun fire.

Alas! the Boche was too wide awake. A quarter of an hour before the attack was started he put down a smashing barrage with his heavy guns from the

direction of High Wood; under this the patrols left
our trench and attempted to get across to the Boche
line, but they were caught by a terrific hail of machine
gun bullets and though they stuck bravely to the job
it was evident that success could not be achieved, and
at twelve-fifty a.m. on the 9th they were ordered to
retire. Their casualties were three officers and eighty
other ranks, and alas! some wounded were left
behind.

On the 11th the turn of the 10th Loyal North
Lancs came. At two a.m., immediately on the tail
of a heavy bombardment, " C " Company, under
Lieutenant J. A. Garratt, sprang out of our trench on
the right of the barrier, and dashed along the top of
the Boche trench, hurling down bombs on its
occupants. " A " Company, under Lieutenant W.
H. Proctor, followed, and passing " C " pushed on,
sprang down into the trench, and bayoneted the
defenders, clearing the trench up to the Martinpuich
road. Lieutenant Duggan, with a building party,
then put up a barricade fifty yards from the road,
which was completed by two-fifty a.m. Both the
Company Commanders and their Seconds-in-Com-
mand, Second-Lieutenants Wadeson and A. F.
Gordon, having been wounded (the latter died later),
Duggan took command and beat off three determined
counter attacks, with heavy loss to his assailants. At
seven a.m. " B " Company took over the three
hundred yards of trench won by " C " and " A,"
and later a company of the 9th North Staffords came
up and consolidated the gain. The casualties were:
killed, one officer, twenty other ranks; wounded, three
officers, seventy-seven other ranks.

On the night of 12th/13th the 11th Royal
Warwicks made an attack on the remaining portion
of this hateful trench, after an intense bombardment
and co-operation of neighbouring troops. When they
had got in the Tunnelling Company was to blow up a
communication trench to the newly taken line. The

Boche, however, put up such a terrific artillery barrage and machine gun fire that the attack failed after getting within twenty yards of its objective. The attempt to blow up the communication trench failed owing to some defect in appliances. The battalion lost : killed, one officer and eleven other ranks; wounded, two officers, one hundred and nine other ranks; missing, two officers and thirty-seven other ranks. It is unusual and pleasant to have to record that the Boche appeared friendly and allowed the stretcher-bearers to work unmolested.

Our time in the hell pot of the Somme was over, and by six p.m. on 15th August the 1st Division took over our line without incident, and we went back to our old quarters, Basieux, Franvillers, Bresle, etc., whence a few days later the move to our first love, Armentières, took place. Here on 22nd we parted with the two brigades and the Pioneers of the 37th Division, who had done such good work with us, and got back our own brigades and men of the pick and rifle.

Note by General Nicholson regarding Intermediate Trench

The Intermediate trench which gave us so much trouble was eventually taken by the 1st Division, which relieved the 34th. The method adopted was to dig a line of trench from a point in our trench east of the barricade, in such a way that it eventually ran in rear of the portion of Intermediate trench which was held by the enemy. The result was that all reinforcements and supplies for the enemy in Intermediate trench were cut off, and the garrison eventually surrendered.

The failure of the attacks made by the 34th Division was due to various causes : (a) not only the Intermediate trench, but our own front line, were under

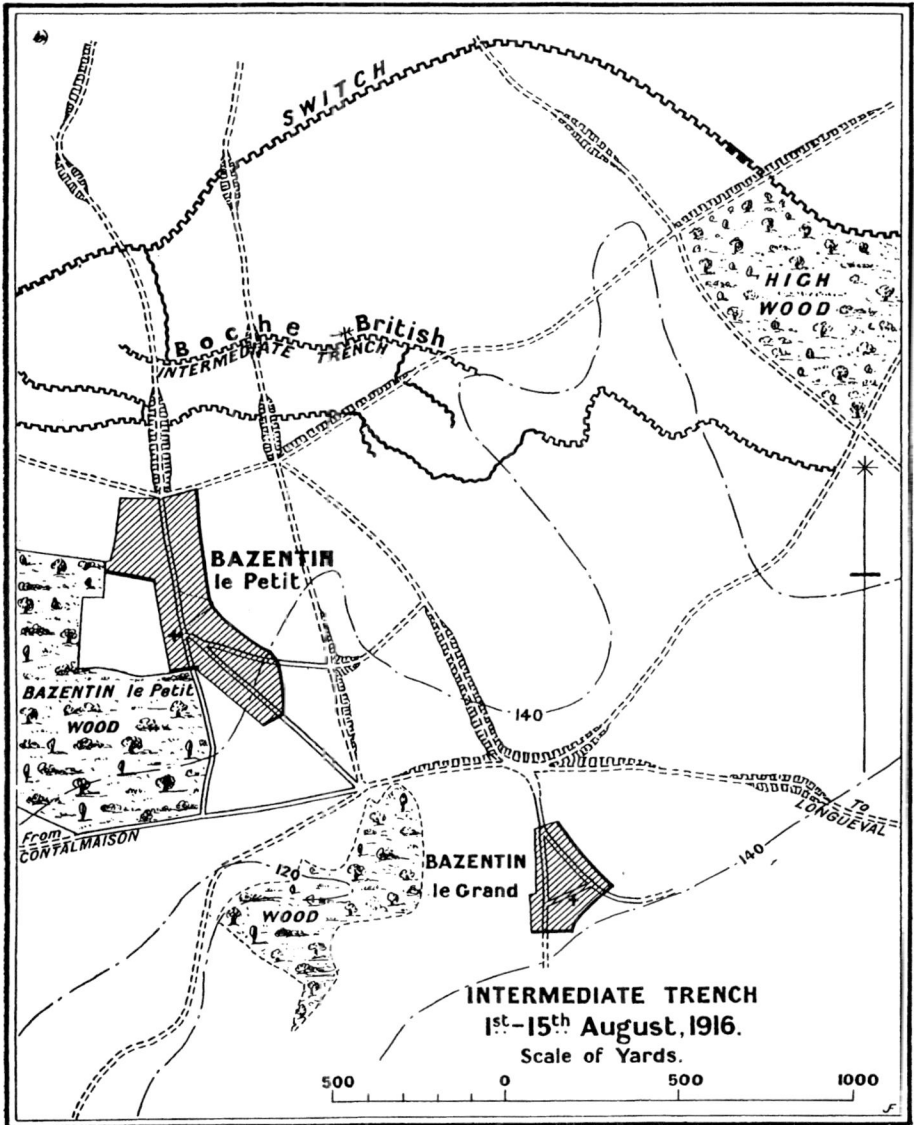

SWITCH

HIGH WOOD

Boche British
INTERMEDIATE TRENCH

BAZENTIN
le Petit

BAZENTIN le Petit
WOOD

From
CONTALMAISON

140

120

BAZENTIN
le Grand

WOOD

TO LONGUEVAL

140

INTERMEDIATE TRENCH
1st–15th August, 1916.
Scale of Yards.

500   0   500   1000

enfilade observation from High Wood; (*b*) the enemy's artillery could bring enfilade fire on both trenches; (*c*) last, but not least, the attacks, after that of the 3rd/4th August (owing to circumstances beyond divisional control), were carried out as isolated operations, and never as part of an attack on a wide front.

CHAPTER V.

THE happy reunion of the old Division with which the last chapter terminated was only to endure for a few days, for on the 25th August the 103rd Brigade and 18th Northumberland Fusiliers departed for the Somme region, where they were attached to the 15th Division, which was about to take part in the big offensive of the 15th September, prior to which it was necessary to give the troops a rest, so the 103rd Brigade was called on to hold their divisional front for about twelve days. As the brigade was very short of trained men, the 18th Northumberlands was sent along with it.

It is unecessary to go into details of the doings of this party. They spent an uncomfortable fortnight holding the line just in front of Martinpuich, in very unsavoury trenches, and under a considerable amount of shell fire. The 15th Division, refreshed by their rest, took over the line again on the 12th September, and triumphantly carried all its objectives on the 15th, on which date our brigade and Pioneers went forward again to aid in the consolidation.

By the 22nd September they were back with us, and filled us up with stories of the wonderful new war chariots which they had just seen make their debut. It is to be feared that some of them let their imagination run riot, for the writer was solemnly asked whether it was true that the armour of the tanks was twelve inches thick.

In the meantime the rest of us had settled down

74

to "peace time" war, and, save for the sad gaps in our ranks, it was like old times. The 101st Brigade took over the right section of the divisional front, and the 102nd again took the left. The left of our line included the Lille road, which, during our last visit, had been in our neighbour's area. It was not a change for the better, as it brought Chard's farm and Leith walk, both very unhealthy regions, within our line. From Chard's farm inclusive, the line extended southwards to the Bridoux salient inclusive, the dividing line between the right and left sections being a short distance south of the Rue du Bois.

The Divisional Staff went back to their old quarters in Croix du Bac. The 101st Brigade Headquarters returned to Rolanderie, but General Trevor Ternan secured a very fine billet known as Crown Prince House, which was a great improvement on the old house in Rue Marle.

The Divisional School, which had been closed for the holidays, i.e., the Somme episode, was reopened on 1st September, by the G.O.C., Major Warden, 16th Royal Scots, being appointed Commandant. Schools of all sorts sprang up all round us, and the demand for victims was so great that Commanding Officers complained that the fact that there was a war on had apparently been overlooked.

Diversions of other sorts also favoured this idea. In one diary we read : " Started at eleven-forty-five a.m. with . . . and . . . and motored to Wisques. Lunched at St Omer, to see a trench mortar and mine consolidation exhibition. Got there rather late, and did not see it well, but the crater consolidation was indifferent. A large crowd of officers there, rather like the Grand Military at Sandown, without the fairies. Met many people I knew." And again, " Rode over to training ground near Bailleul to see 51st Division horse show. Saw some very good jumping and some indifferent riding—and this is war ? "

Armentières was much as we left it. The

pâtisserie with its pretty waitresses still flourished. The fair Lucienne still welcomed her guests with smiles, and danced while they dined, and played draughts with the favoured ones when they had finished.

We resumed our old friendships, as the following extracts from a letter show :

" We are comfortably settled down among old friends again, and have considerable hopes of being left in (comparative) peace to admire the brown and yellow colourings of the trees, and the autumn sunsets and the MUD.

" We were greeted with broad smiles when we arrived—from the yellow haired urchins playing on the road, and the magnificent *garde champêtre*, who whacks them when they are naughty; from former landladies and expectant shopkeepers. The widest smile of all was from my old civilian foreman, Gustave. The industrious she-farmers, with extraordinary little available labour, have been getting in the harvest to within a mile of Mr Boche, and are now preparing to plough up again as close as the authorities will allow."

The pluck of the Frenchwomen is a constant source of wonder and remark in all diaries of which I have kindly been allowed the use.

" There is a house close by here where a mother and her daughter are still living. The mother refuses to budge, although two shells have burst in the farm : one in the yard outside their living-rooms, and one actually in their bedroom. They keep chickens, and sell coffee to the soldiers, but appear to have no other means of livelihood. The son has run away; he was frightened. . . ."

The Division now belonged to the 2nd Anzac Corps, the headquarters of which were in Bailleul, in which quaint, old-fashioned town an officer's club was opened under the auspices of the Corps Commander, Sir Arthur Godley, who also thoughtfully arranged for buses to bring officers from 'Armentières and other distant parts of his command to Bailleul on certain days of the week. General Headquarters this winter organised lectures on general subjects, and I find the following entry regarding one given in Bailleul : " I have seldom enjoyed an hour more than to get out of the dog fight and hear a civilised lecture by a pundit again."

Profiting by experience gained during our last sojourn, we devoted much labour to draining our area, improving our accommodation, and in general to making ourselves comfortable. My friend " Red Tab " records : " I had to have huts shifted or built, baths arranged for, rest-houses, boot drying rooms, and heaven knows what besides. I forget how many huts I built. I stole a good few before the Division tumbled to it. I had big gangs on to some of them, knocked them down, carted them away, and had them erected in our lines. At last the Division smelt a rat, and ordered a minute census of huts, but it was too late, mine were up and as innocent looking as if they had always been there.

" We were settling down for the winter, so I had to make sure that every man went into the line in dry gum boots, and came out to dry service boots and putties. As to socks, I had to see that every man in the line got a dry clean pair every morning. That was easy, as we had the big laundry at Armentières in those days. The gum boot stunt was more difficult, as the changes had to be made near the front line in the dark. However, we fitted up one or two ruined looking steadings with racks and braziers, organised a system by which men going in left boots and putties at one end and went out in gum boots at the other, and vice versa for out-going companies. . . . We had also rest-houses in the support line, one to each battalion front. These were in cellars of ruined houses, and necessarily very close to the front line. In the rest-house a man who had collapsed from cold after being some hours in a listening post, where no movement was possible, or one who had fallen into a shell hole and got wet through, or a man simply knocked out by fatigue, could be brought. He was stripped, put into dry blankets before a fire, given soup and cocoa while his clothes dried, and sent on his way generally fit again after a few hours. . . . Finally we had an 'up and down canteen,' also near the front line. In this canteen all through the night a man or officer could get hot soup, tea, or cocoa on his way up from or down to the trenches. It was a great boon to men coming out of the line after their spell, and starting on a four or five mile trek to billets at two a.m. on a bitter winter night.''

The writer, speaking of the old light duty men who got the much-sought-after jobs of taking care of these places : '' They could live in a fug which is absolutely indescribable, and that is what everyone wants at the front.''

The big laundry which made the Red Tab's job as regards clean socks so easy was a big show well run by '' Q.'' There every man in the Division got a weekly bath and an entire change of underclothing. It gave employment to a large number of women and girls, many of them fugitives from the Boche ridden parts of France and Flanders, to whom the regular pay was a godsend.

When the 103rd Brigade returned from the Somme, it did not remain with us, but became the infantry of '' Frank's Force,'' a temporary Division, under command of Major-General Franks, R.A., which was formed to take over the sector on our left, in which it relieved a Brigade of the 51st Division. The artillery for the Force were our 175th Brigade Field Artillery and '' A '' Battery, 152nd Brigade Field Artillery. With them went 209th Field Company and '' C '' Company of the Pioneers.

Thus we had all our brigades in the line, and the pleasant periods of comparative quiet, whilst in

Divisional Reserve, were no longer known to our infantry. The gunners had returned with us, and went back to their old jobs and carried on with their usual zeal and efficiency. The Pioneers were most of them at " Half-way House," a farm opposite which they named " Pig Farm " from their Christmas dinner, which, in the form of five fine porkers, was fattened up there on the kitchen refuse. They had detachments in the Bois Grenier line, and their headquarters were in a palatial residence just across the railway.

The Boche, during this period, was less troublesome in the back area, and few shells fell round La Vesée, l'Armée, Grispot, and Bois Grenier, but was far more active with his Minnies. He was very troublesome with these missiles, especially about Chard's Farm and the head of Leith walk, which was constantly being blown in.

Our trench mortars, Batteries X, Y, and Z Mediums, and V Heavy, together with the three Light Batteries belonging to the Infantry Brigades, were busy replying. The Mediums and Light were in action almost every day till we were relieved, cutting wire and blowing in the enemy's parapet. During the preparation for, and the execution of, the various raids they were very active, and reading the record of their daily activities one realises that it is probable the Boche records of this period would contain as many allusions to trench mortars as ours do to Minnies. " V " Battery does not appear to have been very successful with its new weapon, which had hardly reached the state of perfection which it did later. I find a record of one round descending in our own front line, and my memory takes me back to a wet day in the trenches when a very doleful individual told me a sad tale of one of his shots having dropped into a battalion cook-house, which was fortunately empty at the time, and of his subsequent interview with the Commanding Officer.

Early in September a period of activity commenced. Our gunners and trench mortar men treated the Boche to quite heavy bombardments for five days, and then the infantry raided his trenches. These spasms of violence were the main feature of our second sojourn in Armentières.

The even tenor of trench warfare was disturbed by constant small attacks on the Boche, with the object of obtaining prisoners, inflicting damage on his trenches, causing him as many casualties as possible, and generally keeping him on the jump. As to whether we attained our object, or whether whatever results we did obtain were worth the cost, opinions differed considerably. Some maintaining that as we were at war it behoved us to fight as much as possible, others saying that between offensives it was sound to sit as still as possible, others again . . . but it is useless to attempt to reproduce all that was said, and we will content ourselves with chronicling our doings.

Between the 15th September and the 12th February we carried out twenty-two of these minor operations, of which thirteen may be classed as successes; that is, we got into the Boche line and did more or less damage. In the remaining nine cases the party failed to get into the Boche front line, either on account of the thickness of uncut wire, the depth of the water in the borrow pit, or on account of the strength of the Boche resistance either by artillery barrage or with rifle, bomb, and bayonet. Even in these unsuccessful ventures the Boche must have suffered considerably from the attentions of our gunners and trench mortar men, who co-operated vigorously on most occasions, though a few silent raids were tried, i.e., attempts to make surprise entries into the Boche trenches without any artillery or trench mortar bombardment.

It is impossible to give details of all these little episodes, but we will attempt to give a general description of a raid and all the preparations, etc., that it involved.

Firstly, the spot to be attacked had to be selected. This was generally done by the Brigadier and the officer commanding the battalion which was to carry out the raid. Then a rough programme had to be drawn up by the Battalion Commander, and this had to be thrashed out with the Brigadier, the Commander of the Field Artillery group covering the front concerned, and the trench mortar and machine gun men. When a definite result had been arrived at, the Divisional Commander's views had to be taken. This all accomplished, the personnel of the party were struck off all other duty, and billeted together and treated just like a team in training for an important sporting event. Every effort was made to get them as fit as possible, and much trouble was taken to ensure that every man knew exactly what he was expected to do. The raid was practised repeatedly over a flagged course, representing the trenches to be attacked.

The Boche was a great believer in wire, and expended much trouble and material in this form of defence. The chief difficulty before the raiders was, as a rule, the Boche wire. Efforts were made to cut this by a previous bombardment, extending over some days, and not confined to the special points to be attacked. Occasionally Bangalore torpedoes were used. These were explosive contraptions manufactured by the Royal Engineers, which were inserted into the Boche's wire and then fired, just before the party rushed the trench.

Besides the real raids we also troubled the Boche with dummy raids, generally in another part of his line just before we made the real attack. A dummy raid might consist only of a bombardment, or of the firing of Bangalore torpedoes coupled with the exhibition of dummy figures in No-Man's-Land.

Raids varied considerably in importance; many

F

were made by no more than thirty men, others were
larger; one of the largest, if not the largest, was led
by Lieutenant-Colonel C. P. Porch in person, the
party numbering thirteen officers and two hundred and
thirty-seven other ranks of the 23rd Northumberland
Fusiliers, and twelve sappers of the 209th Field
Company. It was eminently successful, but the
casualties were heavy.

During the training of the party, No-Man's-
Land, between the jumping off place and the point of
entry into the Boche line, would be patrolled constantly
by selected leaders, so that, however dark or stormy
the night, they might be able to guide the party safely
to its objective.

When all was ready the party would be brought
as near as possible in lorries, and make its way up the
communication trenches to the front line, and wait
patiently till the minute fixed for it to emerge. The
guns and trench mortars would get busy, and the
machine guns would chatter. The Boche would
perhaps reply, but he was rather inclined to treat
us with contemptuous silence. The party would
creep out, make its way stealthily across the maze of
shell holes, ditches, and drains, and assemble as near
to the Boche wire as the protecting barrage would
allow. At the appointed hour the guns, with uncanny
accuracy, would lift from the front line and enclose
the area in which the party intended to operate in a
wall of shells. The raiders would push through the
gaps in the wire, wade the chilly borrow pit, often
nearly breast deep, scramble over the parapet, and
drop into the trench and get busy according to plan.
Sometimes two parties would push ahead down a
communication trench some distance, then turn out-
wards and swing round so as to take the front line in
rear; sometimes a party would push to right and left
down the front trench, a third blocking the communication trench a short distance down. Occasionally the
Boche withdrew entirely from his front line, and, as

soon as he knew where we had entered it, put down a heavy barrage on that portion. This was very rough on the raiders, who had come to kill or capture Boches and find "identifications," i.e., souvenirs, from a study of which something could be learnt of our enemy's movements, for if the trenches were empty, all their troubles and the losses they were sure to suffer from the Boche barrage would have been incurred in vain. It was better when the Boche stood and fought, a wild scrimmage in the dark, bombs and bayonets, and if concrete emplacements withstood the efforts of the bombers, a shout for the sapper with his explosives, and a determined rush to clear the trench and hold back the Boche till the explosion told that his work was done. With Boches who would not surrender, or refused to come out of their dug-outs, there was no time to parley—a bomb or a bayonet was their portion—for time was short; prisoners were quickly passed back to the collecting party waiting at the point of entry, and when the O.C. gave the agreed on signal all hurried back, and the journey back across No-Man's-Land was commenced, but it was often necessary to wait in shell holes till the Boche barrage had died down. A warm welcome and good fare awaited the party on its return to our line, and congratulations and immediate rewards were theirs.

Many very gallant deeds were done in these little affairs; in fact a raid that was well pressed home, and brought back prisoners and identifications, was a triumph of care in organisation and great gallantry in execution.

Every Brigadier and Battalion Commander pays generous tribute to the extreme accuracy and effectiveness of the artillery support and preparation, and the small amount of retaliation to which the Boche treated us, is, in more than one account, attributed to the excellence of our gunners' counter-battery work. Our losses in these stirring little fights varied greatly, but totalled up to a considerable number.

The Boche only raided us once, and then he was successful in carrying off a machine gun and its crew.

By the end of November the 3rd Australian Division relieved Frank's Force, and we got back our 103rd Brigade and the other details which had been on loan with it.

Several changes had taken place in the organisation of our gunners. In May the Howitzer Batteries were distributed among the other brigades, so that we had four brigades, each of three-eighteen pounder batteries, and one of Howitzer. In August the 176th Brigade was broken up, and the number of guns in the other brigades raised to six-eighteen pounders per battery, with one battery of four Howitzers. In January the 175th Brigade was taken from the Division, and became an Army Brigade.

Our Battery Commander's diary contains allusions to the amount of paper flying about at such times : " *Re* new establishment, handing over surplus, and indenting for deficiencies, I foresee lots of worries."

He had other troubles about this time :

" 28th August, Monday. Light bad in the morning. Went to front line in the afternoon to register, but found wire broken. Considerable delay in finding and mending the break, and then when only one gun was registered a terrific thunderstorm came on. Seldom seen such rain. Got soaked, and the whole place flooded in a short time, and to finish matters I stepped on a floating trenchboard and shot full length into about two feet of muddy water."

" August 31st, Thursday. Group scheme in the afternoon. D Battery, just behind us, shot a lot in that morning, and a 5·9 battery turned on to them, and later shortened and put about seventy rounds all round us, including three into the houses. One was a direct hit on the roof of No. 2, but beyond smashing the burster roof and knocking down the partition

THE CHEQUERS
Aladdin, Christmas, 1916

[To face p. 85]

wall of the house did no damage. Got all the men cleared to a flank directly they started, and nobody got hit. They shortened on to us just after I had left for the observation post to carry out the scheme. Shot the left section which is in the old orchard, until the wires went."

In the absence of bigger game our sporting friend turned to ratting, and about this time most days end up with some such entry as, " Got six rats in the evening," or " The doctor came round in the afternoon for ratting, and stayed to dinner. Only got two rats, but rooked the doctor badly at poker."

Our divisional artillery horse show came off on the 30th September, and our Battery Commander notes against that day. " Spent the morning, up to one-thirty p.m., in the observation post, while Chris went to the show. Brewitt came up here for the afternoon, and Milligan relieved me. Biked to the show, and got there just in time for the jumping. ' Good Hope ' refused first jump twice and second once, and then did the course faultlessly. He and one other were the only ones to clear the gate, without touching. However, they threw him out over the refusals. Headquarters won the mess cart, ' A ' won the officers' charger and non-commissioned officers jumping, and we got two seconds in the section driving."

Our theatrical company, " The Chequers," provided a most excellent pantomime about Christmas-time, the ancient tale of Aladdin forming the basis of the story. One of the attractions were two real French actresses, whose looks were a good deal better than their acting. We were all very grateful to Lieutenant Thomas and his troupe, and they played to full houses during the whole time they performed.

Tradition says that the presence of these ladies, owing to some irregularities in their passports, caused some heated correspondence between various important personages, and troubled Divisional Headquarters more than did the Boche.

On 22nd December the Commander-in-Chief, Sir Douglas Haig, inspected such details of the Division as could be spared from the trenches and gun positions. The force was drawn up along the Armentières-Estaires road. This road was, in many places, visible from the ridge behind the Boche lines, but as the Huns had hitherto shown themselves complacent as regards traffic passing to and fro, this fact had been overlooked when the road was selected for the inspection. The morning before the review was, fortunately, uncommonly fine, and General Nicholson, motoring in to Armentières, noticed how much it was under observation. Not wishing to put too great a temptation in the Boche's way, he called on the Pioneers to get the whole length screened before the next morning, which they managed to do, but even with the protection thus afforded it was surely rather impertinent to hold a review along a road well within range of the enemy's guns. However, all went off well. The troops formed up in line on south side of the road between Erquinghem and Fort Rompu. Order from right to left : H.Q.R.A., the 152nd, 160th, 175th F.A. Brigades and D.A.C., 208th Field Company R.E., Headquarters and one company 18th Northumberland Fusiliers, Headquarters 101st Infantry Brigade and 10th Lincolns, Headquarters 102nd Infantry Brigade and 20th, 21st, 22nd, 23rd Northumberland Fusiliers, Headquarters 103rd Infantry Brigade and 24th Northumberland Fusiliers, A.D.M.S. and details of 102nd, 103rd, 104th Field Ambulances and Divisional Train. The Commander-in-Chief arrived at Erquinghem Bridge at twelve-ten p.m. and rode along the line with the Corps Commander, our G.O.C. and staff. (What a chance for the Boche gunners over against us on Aubers Ridge, and the sun came out too, which made our screens

seem a very poor protection.) Arrived at the end
of the line Sir Douglas halted, and the whole force
marched past in column of route, played past by the
band of the New Zealand Rifle Brigade. The verdict
was : " Turn out very good, troops very steady in the
ranks, and marching excellent, especially the R.A."
The Commander-in-Chief expressed himself very
pleased, and subsequently sent a complimentary
telegram to the Corps.

So ended the first year of our stay in France—in
the trenches in front of Armentières, where our experience of war had begun.

The following statement of our losses represents
in cold figures an immense amount of suffering and
misery—a heavy item on the debit side of our account
with the Boche.

34th Division Statement of Wastage for the year 1916.

KILLED		WOUNDED		MISSING		SICK		TOTAL	
Off.	O. R.	Off.	O. R.	Off.	O. R.	Off.	O. R.	Off.	O. R.
158	1364	439	9501	125	3015	111	1467	733	15,235

During our stay in Armentières several members
of the committee which raised the Tyneside Brigades
paid a visit to the Division, not by any means their
first or last. Among them were Sir Charles Parsons,
Sir Thomas Oliver, Sir Johnston Wallace, and
Colonels Reed and Cowan. They visited the line and
saw a " strafe," which General Ternan inflicted on
the Boche for their special benefit. They also had
a peep through the loophole of an observation post
on Kemmel Hill, and were present at a distribution of
" immediate rewards " for the Somme fighting by
Sir H. Plumer.

We were pursuing the even tenor of our way,
when suddenly, at eleven-ten a.m. on 26th of January,
a telephone message was received at Divisional Headquarters directing the immediate relief of the Division
by the 3rd Australian Division, to be completed by

ten a.m. the next morning. The reason for this
sudden move was that since the 19th there had been
very hard frost, the thermometer registering twenty
degrees of frost almost every night, and in consequence
the marshes and inundations north of Boesinghe,
which formed the defence of the Belgian front, were
frozen so solidly that a Boche attack across them
became practicable, and it was necessary to have troops
ready to meet such an attack should it come off.   This
cold spell lasted till 11th February, and caused much
suffering to the troops in the line, which, however,
was trifling compared with what some had to undergo
on the night of the relief, for many men, owing to the
suddenness of the move, were houseless and blanket-
less that night.

The Divisional Headquarters was in cottages in
Fletre; the troops were scattered about Meteren,
Cæstre, Goderswalde, Berthen.

Lieutenant-General Sir A. J. Godley, K.C.B.,
K.C.M.G., our Corps Commander, paid a visit to
many units, and thanked us for the good work that
we had done in the trenches during our stay in his
corps area.

Our gunners, strange to say, had come out with
us, and they and the infantry now enjoyed a spell
of "rest," which meant strenuous training.   This
was interrupted temporarily by three batteries from
each brigade having to go back into the line to support
a couple of raids, which had been in preparation before
we were withdrawn from the line.   These have already
been alluded to.

On the 29th January, 207th and 209th Field
Companies and the Pioneers started off to make the
ways straight for us in the Arras region, which was
to be the scene of our next adventure.   They had one
day in buses, and four on their feet in very cold
weather, with snow underfoot and bright blue skies
and sunshine overhead.

The rest of us trained hard.   The 103rd Brigade

moved to the Tinques area, but the remainder stayed round Fletre till 18th February, when we started on our march to our new quarters, in the 3rd Army area. On the 19th the Division lost its G.S.O.1, Lieutenant-Colonel R. H. Mangles, D.S.O., Royal West Surrey Regiment, who was transferred to the War Office for training purposes. This was a severe loss to the Division, for he had been with it from its first days in France, and knew every unit thoroughly and was known and trusted by all. One who had every opportunity of knowing describes him as " One of the best men and ablest Staff Officers I have ever met." His place was taken by H. E. R. R. Braine, D.S.O., Royal Munster Fusiliers.

At this time there were also other changes in the staff. Brigadier-General A. D. Kirby, who had been with the Division as C.R.A. from Sutton Veny days, went to 2nd Corps, and everyone missed his cheery presence, but none but the G.O.C. and his own corps knew the full extent of our loss. His place was taken by Brigadier-General Rettie. Our C.R.E., Colonel A. C. MacDonnell, also left us for an appointment in England, and we had no more cause to wonder at his energy as we met him in all weathers and at all times of day and night in unexpected parts of the trenches, bent on seeing for himself how the work was progressing. Lieutenant-Colonel A. C. Dobson, R.E., was our next C.R.E. Major W. Neilson, Argyll and Sutherland Highlanders, who had been with the Division as G.S.O.2 since August, 1916, was also transferred to the 15th Corps Staff, and was relieved by Major C. R. Congreve, D.L.I.

The march was uneventful, and the weather fine. It was pleasant moving through the country which had not been touched by the Boche, and it was pleasure to see the columns swinging along, the picture of health and training. Our journey came to an end on 24th February, when the 102nd Brigade took over the centre sector of the 17th Corps front and lost three killed, one wounded, and one missing. Our holiday was over.

The 102nd Brigade Headquarters were in the Malterie in St Catherine, a huge building of several stories above ground and two below, which also housed a very large number of all ranks and of many units. There were two battalions in the front line, and two in support.

During this period Divisional Headquarters was at Hermaville, the Reserve Brigade was at X hutments, Ecoivres, and the third brigade in the back area round about Chelers training.

The portion of the line which the 34th had to take over extended from a point about two hundred yards north of the St Nicholas-Bailleul road, some one thousand five hundred yards almost due north. It was known as the "K section," from the fact that the names of the various mine craters, which formed such prominent features in it, all began with K.

The British had taken over this portion of the line from the French in the winter of 1915-16, and had not altered the French system of communications, which was based on Arras; therefore, when our advance troops arrived, they found all the communication trenches running north-east from St Nicholas, a suburb of Arras, which under the new arrangements would not be in the divisional area. It therefore became necessary to reconstruct the whole system, so as to admit of it being worked from St Catherine. This entailed an immense amount of work, which fully occupied our advance party of Royal Engineers and Pioneers until our arrival. Every advantage was taken of existing trenches, but much new work had to be done, and the hard frost, which lasted till 11th February, made all digging very difficult, and the thaw which followed impeded the work almost more, by causing the sides of the trenches to fall in.

However, on our arrival we found the system remodelled, and access to the front line obtainable by communication trenches which started from various points on the Lille road and led across the Roclincourt Valley and over the Chalk Farm plateau.

The weary work of preparation for the " push " began. Long lines of patient, weary men plodded slowly through the narrow muddy trenches laden with all the requirements of modern war; big working parties toiled through the night at clearing old trenches for assembly purposes and other preparatory works. Time was short, and there was much to be done.

Labour battalions had not yet been brought to the aid of the fighting units, and in spite of every effort to spare the troops unnecessary labour, a very severe strain was placed on them, the effects of which were felt later.

On the C.R.E., Lieutenant-Colonel A. C. Dobson, was thrown the responsibility of the execution of the mutifarious works required, and a special organisation was called into existence for their completion. Major Glendenning, 207th Field Company, was placed in charge of all these works on the whole divisional front. Under him worked, in each brigade area, an officer and a section of each Field Company, and two officers and one hundred men of the Sapping Company of each brigade, and in addition three companies of the Pioneers and one thousand one hundred men from the brigade in the line were employed wherever they were needed, and if these were not sufficient more help was given by the brigade in X hutments at Ecoivres.

The " Q " preparations were on even a more complete scale than those for the 1st July, 1916, and it was fortunate that though deprived of his C.R.A., G.S.O.1, G.S.O.2, and C.R.E. on the eve of preparing for the push, the powers that be had left our G.O.C. his A.A. and Q.M.G., Lieutenant-Colonel O. K. Chance, who, in spite of bad health, stuck to his job till the fight was over, and the wisdom and completeness of his arrangements had been proved.

On the 24th February news arrived from the 5th Army that the Boche on its front had suddenly disappeared. Patrols hastily pushed out by the 102nd Brigade, which was holding the line, showed that on our front the enemy was still present and on the alert.

Later, the probability of the wily Boche trying to anticipate our assault by sneaking off appears to have impressed itself on General Headquarters, as on the 23rd March the Division received orders to be ready to attack on twenty-four hours' notice. No easy job, when located on a narrow front and considerable depth. Nothing came of it, however. The Boche, on the contrary, was very active, and raided us three times, but was beaten off on every occasion without obtaining the coveted identification.

We carried out two raids, obtaining an identification on one occasion, and bombing some dug-outs on the other. For his conduct in the first raid Second-Lieutenant R. E. Baty, 21st Northumberland Fusiliers, who was wounded, was awarded the Military Cross.

The Boche got into a very nervous state, bombing his own wire of a night, and generally behaving in a jumpy manner. He also treated us to several heavy bombardments by artillery and trench mortars, but these were nothing to what our gunners gave him. Guns of all sizes jostled each other behind our lines, and were very active. Many of these long range monsters, though living among us, did not belong even to our army, and were in no way concerned with our particular Boches, but were dealing very faithfully with those in front of the Canadians, far away to the north. Our trench mortars, supplemented by five batteries from 2nd and 17th Division, were arranged in three groups and cut wire continuously.

Our bombardment began at six-twenty a.m. on

4th April, just five minutes after a successful discharge of gas bombs from Levin projectors, then a new contrivance, the effectiveness of which must have made the Boche wonder whether he did well when he introduced gas as a weapon of offence. The gas cloud was seen from an aeroplane to move low over the Boche trenches and back for some distance. Unfortunately a carrying party of the 24th Northumberland Fusiliers, which did very well, suffered a good many casualties, so fewer bombs were available than had been intended.

The bombardment lasted practically continuously till the assault was delivered on the morning of the 9th, but its intensity waxed and waned. Each day, at a different hour, it rose to its maximum, making the Boche think that zero hour must have arrived. We hoped that when day after day nothing happened after these bursts of frightfulness, he would be put off his guard. The enemy retaliated on our front line and battery positions, but not very heavily, though on the first day we had between fifty and sixty casualties in the line.

On the 7th, to get identifications and frighten the Boche, raids on an extensive scale were carried out. By this time each brigade had one battalion in the front line, and from each battalion front three officers and one hundred men broke into the Boche line. The parties were found by the 16th Royal Scots, 20th and 25th Northumberland Fusiliers. The raids were successful. Three prisoners were obtained, and many casualties inflicted. The Royal Scots lost Captain Cowan and Second-Lieutenant J. Watson, seven other ranks missing, and three other ranks killed. Second-Lieutenants L. W. Pollett, J. Thompson, and J. F. Ridley of the 20th were wounded, and the first named was also missing. Two other ranks were missing, and eight wounded. The 25th lost two other ranks killed, ten wounded, and Second-Lieutenant Howard was missing. There was much fierce hand to hand fighting in these raids.

Captain Cowan and Second-Lieutenant Pollett were found severely wounded, but alive, in German dressing-stations when we captured the position on 9th April.

CHAPTER VI

THE BATTLE OF ARRAS—I

BEFORE describing the attack of 9th April, it is necessary to give some idea of the position to be assaulted, and the plan which was to be followed. The task of the 17th Corps was to capture the southern extremity of the Vimy Ridge, and the low land along the left bank of the Scarpe River. To the 9th Division fell the duty of dealing with the low country and the adjoining slopes. Included in their area were the strongly fortified villages of St Laurent Blangy, Athies, and, farther back, Fampoux; in consideration of the strength of this portion of the hostile line the 4th Division was detailed to support the 9th.

On the left of the 9th was the 34th, the front of which lay roughly between the Bailleul-St Nicholas and Bailleul-Roclincourt roads. To the left of the 34th was the 51st Division, beyond which came the Canadian Corps, which had the tough task of capturing the Vimy Ridge as far south as Thelus, a strongly fortified village standing well above the southern end of the ridge and completely enfilading the troops of the 17th Corps during their advance. On the success of the Canadians depended that of the 17th Corps, and in the same way the success of the 9th Division depended largely on the 34th taking the high ridge terminating in the farm, Le Point du Jour, whence the low ground to the south was commanded.

The German defences consisted of three main trench systems, known to us as the Black, Blue, and

95

Brown lines.   The Black line was the rearmost of the Boche's four front system trenches, the first of which was from eighty to one hundred and fifty yards from our line, and the last about five hundred to six hundred.   The total length of this line was about one thousand seven hundred and fifty yards.   The Blue line was mostly a single trench.   The southern seven hundred and fifty yards of the system consisted of a sunken road, a shallow valley filled with wire, and a railway cutting, roughly parallel to one another, and covering a depth of two hundred and fifty yards at the northern end and about four hundred at the southern.   The length of the Blue line along the trench was about two thousand four hundred yards, and there was a deep re-entrant, the flanks being only some seven hundred to eight hundred yards, and the centre about one thousand three hundred from the Black line.   The Brown line was roughly one thousand three hundred yards in rear of the Blue, and consisted of a double line of trench, partly wired.

All these three lines had to be taken, and a new line, called the Green (east of Brown line), had to be dug by the evening of Z day.   The Green line was to be sufficiently in advance of the Brown to give good observation over the forward slope of the ridge towards the next German line.

From all the information available before the attack, it appeared as if the most difficult part of our task was the capture of the southern portion of the Blue line, above described, and generally spoken of as Wire Valley.

The Division was to attack with its three brigades in line.   Each brigade was to have two battalions in the front line (" A " and " B " Battalions), and two in support and reserve (" C " and " D " Battalions).   " A " and " B " Battalions were to be drawn up as near the German front line wire as possible an hour before zero on the day of assault.   At zero hour (actually five-thirty a.m.) the barrage was to fall on the German front line for four minutes, during which time the leading waves of the assaulting columns were to creep up as near as possible. At zero, plus four minutes, the barrage was to lift direct to the second trench, and after resting there three minutes, to the third, and, after another three minutes, to the last trench, or Black line, as a creeping barrage at twenty-five yards a minute. At zero, plus thirty-five minutes, the barrage was to move forward again from Black line for twenty minutes, and then remain stationary till zero, plus two hours and six minutes. The "A" and "B" Battalions were to follow the barrage as closely as possible up to the Black line, and then occupy themselves in mopping up that system consolidating and reorganising during the one and a half hours that would elapse before the barrage moved forward from its protective position towards the Blue line.

In order to make quite sure of capturing the Black line, either "C" or "D" Battalion of each brigade was to be brought up near enough to render help if required, but every effort was to be made to prevent it becoming involved in the fight for the Black line, unless absolutely necessary, as its real rôle was, in company with the other reserve battalion, to capture the Brown line later on.

At two hours after zero, "A" and "B" Battalions were to be formed up as close to the protective barrage as possible, and six minutes later were to advance again behind its kindly curtain to the attack of the Blue line, which they were timed to reach in about forty-five minutes, but as the Blue line bent away from them in the centre, those on the flanks would reach it first, and must needs wait till the barrage and the following infantry in the centre should reach their goal.

Four hours were allowed for the mopping up and consolidation of the Blue line, during which time the gunners would protect the infantry by keeping a pro-

G

tective barrage some distance in front of them. During this pause the " C " and " D " Battalions of each brigade were to be brought up, and, if necessary, reorganised, so as to be ready to take their places as near as possible behind the barrage by zero, plus six hours and forty minutes, and follow it forward to the Brown line six minutes later. The Brown line was to be reached in forty-six minutes, and during the mopping up and consolidation the ever reliable artillery was to keep its protective curtain of fire some three hundred yards in front, thoughtfully leaving gaps through which patrols might safely advance to explore the country beyond, with a view to the occupation of the Green line overlooking Bailleul and Gavrelle.

The Machine Gun Companies of each brigade were temporarily, with the exception of one section (four guns), taken from the control of the Brigadiers and employed under the command of Major Hellaby, 103rd Machine Gun Company. On Z day they were mainly employed in barrage work, keeping a hail of bullets just in front of the infantry.

In some parts of the line, where the width of No-Man's-Land was not enough to allow of our artillery safely putting a barrage on the German front line, the trench mortar batteries took their place and maintained an efficient barrage.

The right group of the artillery, under command of Lieutenant-Colonel Warburton, consisted of three eighteen pounder batteries of 160th Brigade, and an equal force of the 17th Division. This group covered the front of the right Infantry Brigade. Covering the front of the centre Infantry Brigade, were six eighteen pounder batteries of 86th and 311th Army Field Artillery Brigades. The left Infantry Brigade was covered by the three eighteen pounder batteries of the 152nd Brigade, and an equal force of 17th Divisional Artillery. This group was commanded by Lieutenant-Colonel W. G. Thomson, 152 Brigade.

After capture of Blue line two Artillery Brigades

were to advance to positions in the Roclincourt Valley, and on the capture of the Brown line two were to move forward into No-Man's-Land.

The three Field Companies and the Pioneers were to be employed in opening up communications as the assault progressed, and elaborate arrangements were made for getting supplies and material forward by pack animals and on wheels. Till needed, the Field Companies and Pioneers were to remain in dug-outs in Roclincourt Valley.

So much for the plan, now for its execution. The morning of the 9th April was dull and misty, with signs of rain. By four-thirty a.m. Divisional Headquarters had received the word "Complete" from all three brigades, meaning that the assaulting battalions were in their final positions. At five-thirty the guns roared and the barrage fell all along the Boche line.

All went well for some time, and for over two hours the anxious staff at Divisional Headquarters, in Chausée Brunehaut, received nothing but cheering messages, of trenches occupied up to scheduled time, and batches of prisoners arriving. At nine a.m. the Contact Aeroplane reported that flares were seen from the Blue line on the fronts of the 101st and 102nd Infantry Brigades, showing that on that portion of the field the programme had been carried out, but news from the 103rd Brigade gradually got worse, and it was soon evident that there was a hitch somewhere on that front.

The leading battalions of this brigade were the 24th and 25th Northumberland Fusiliers. They got into the enemy's front line without much trouble, and at six-twenty a.m. the brigade ordered the Battalion Headquarters to cross No-Man's-Land. In doing so Lieutenant-Colonel E. W. Hermon,[1] commanding the

---

[1] Lieut.-Colonel Hermon, formerly of 7th Hussars, went to France in King Edward's Horse, but finding service in that Corps not exciting enough, asked to be given an infantry command.

24th, was killed. This was a serious loss, especially occurring at such a moment. Lieutenant-Colonel Moulton Barrett, commanding the 25th, got over safely, but found things in a far from satisfactory state.

The trench mortar barrage covering the attack was most efficient, and under it " A " and " B " Companies of 25th Northumberland Fusiliers took the support line without much trouble, and " C " and " D " passing through them while they were reforming, followed the barrage, according to plan, to the Black line. The captured trenches were mopped up; many prisoners, two Maxims, and eight Minenwerfers were captured.

In due course the companies were formed up behind the barrage for the advance on the Blue line. By this time all the officers of " C " and " D " were either killed or wounded. When the barrage lifted, " A " and " B " Companies advanced. " A " on the right, with " C " following in support, were favoured by the conformation of the ground, which gave them some cover from the machine guns higher up the slope on their left, and about eighty men, under Second-Lieutenants J. G. Kirkup and J. Snee, the only two company officers left standing, reached the Blue line, and pushed along it to the left, having been pushed rather to the right by the troops of the 152nd Brigade. Captain Beattie Brown and Lieutenant McLachlan, M.C., were both killed in the Black line, and at the end of the day in these two companies only two officers and five sergeants remained unhurt.

" B " Company, on the left, came under very heavy machine gun fire from its left. The troops on its left of the 152nd Infantry Brigade, 51st Division, had been delayed, and on their arrival they also were held up by these machine guns, and eased off to their right into the 34th Division area. The 26th Northumberland Fusiliers also came up from behind, and increased the confusion, as all advance in this part was stayed by the machine guns on the 152nd Brigade front, men of many units with but few officers being crowded in the Mittel Weg. Lieutenant-Colonel Moulton Barrett sent parties up the Zehner Weg and Gaul Weg to attempt to deal with these machine gun pests and reach the Blue line, and also reported matters to his brigade.[1] The 27th Northumberlands, the remaining battalion of the brigade, was ordered up, and the 152nd Infantry Brigade, having reorganised, another advance was made, and eventually the Blue line was captured throughout its length, but not till too late to make a further advance at the appointed time. One was attempted by the 26th and 27th Northumberlands, but the heavy machine gun fire from their left flank held them up. It was then decided that without complete reorganisation no further advance was possible, and the two battalions dug in beyond the Blue line, connecting with the 102nd Brigade on the right in the Gavrelle Weg, and the 152nd Infantry Brigade on the left.

Having told the worst, we can now turn to the brighter side of the picture. In the right and centre

[1] Thanks to the kindness of Major T. Reay, I am able to give some interesting particulars of one of the parties. "Captain Huntley and Bryan had gone forward up a communication trench to see what they could do. Huntley was killed on the way up, while spying through his glasses. (I saw his body there afterwards.) Bryan went on alone and killed the two gunners, so that the Blue line was made safe for the other people who were to push on later in the day. The two witnesses said they saw Bryan stab the two gunners—they saw his bayonet flashing. I saw the ground afterwards, and examined the machine gun position. It had a wonderful field of fire, and had held up the brigades on our right and left. It had caught our people as they came over the ridge, about three hundred yards in front of the machine gun position. Our men and the men of the Scottish Division (on our left) were lying dead almost in a line, just on the ridge. But for Bryan, the Division would never have reached its objective that day."

"No. 22040, Lance-Corpl. Thomas Bryan, Northumberland Fusiliers. For most conspicuous gallantry during an attack. Although wounded, this non-commissioned officer went forward alone, with a view to silencing a machine gun which was inflicting much damage. He worked up, most skilfully, a long communication trench, approached the gun from behind, disabled it, and killed two of the team as they were abandoning the gun. As this machine gun had been a serious obstacle in the advance to the second objective, the results obtained by Lance-Corpl. Bryan's gallant action were far-reaching."—*Supplement to "London Gazette," 8th June,* 1917.

areas the 101st and 102nd Infantry Brigades took all their objectives strictly according to plan, and the Brown line was occupied by two-thirty p.m. The leading battalions of the 101st were the 16th Royal Scots and 11th Suffolks. The enemy's artillery fire was weak, and his rifle and machine gun fire feeble, most of his men being caught in their dug-outs. His trenches were badly shattered, and the Black line was occupied and consolidated without severe loss. In fact "A" Company of the Suffolks reported the Black line captured without loss. The 15th Royal Scots, in support to the 16th, was ordered to follow closely, so as to escape the barrage, which it did successfully, but became involved in the fight, so that the three battalions entered the Blue line practically together, at about seven-fifty a.m. The wire in the valley and other obstacles were found less formidable than had been expected.

In the Blue line the 16th Royal Scots established connection with the 11th Battalion of their regiment, which was the left battalion of the 9th Division. The line was carried on by the 11th Suffolks, on whose left flank the 21st Northumberlands arrived a little later, having suffered severe casualties among its officers. The left battalion of the 102nd also reached the Blue line without any particular difficulty, and on both brigade fronts the attack on the Brown line was launched almost up to time, but the 15th Royal Scots, through having been involved in the attacks on the Black and Blue lines, could only muster about one hundred men, with Captain Harrison, Second-Lieutenants Dakers, Fisher, and Satchel, the last being wounded. This battalion therefore could not cover its front, and while keeping in touch with the 5th King's Own Scottish Borderers on its right left a gap of about a hundred yards between it and the Lincolns on the left. The Lincolns had picked their way through the German barrage, which was heavy but spotty, and arrived just in time to take part in the final advance. The wire in front of the Brown line was found uncut, and in places some delay occurred, during which the Royal Scots and Lincolns came under direct fire of some 77 m.m. guns, and suffered some casualties. In front of the former the Boche infantry made no fight, some forty putting up a white flag and surrendering.

The Lincolns lay down while a few men cut lanes through the wire, and then pushed on, and the Brown line was taken without much resistance. On the right, the Royal Scots found that what our airmen had taken for a track, was, in reality, a trench covered with corrugated iron, so that consolidation was easy. No. 1. Section 101st Machine Gun Company, under Second-Lieutenant Beveridge, arrived opportunely, and punished the Boches returning towards Oppy. The 20th Northumberlands on the right of the 102nd Brigade reached the Brown line, but with considerable loss.[1]

The 23rd Northumberlands encountered considerable resistance in and about the Brown line. Captain Herm, M.C., did good work cutting through the wire under heavy fire. Both of the trenches, which in this part composed the Brown line, were taken by a bayonet charge, in which Captain Herm was wounded.[2]

With the 20th and 23rd Northumberlands the 22nd also arrived at the Brown line, and occupied the western of the two trenches. The other two battalions, after leaving a garrison in the eastern trench, pushed on and formed outposts on the Green line. The left flank of this brigade was unprotected, owing to the 103rd Brigade being held up near to the

[1] Its casualties in the day amounted to: killed, one officer, thirty-one other ranks; wounded, ten officers (three died subsequently), two hundred and eight other ranks (six died); missing, thirty-nine other ranks. Its strength in the morning having been twenty officers and five hundred and fifty other ranks.
[2] This battalion's casualties that day amounted to about one hundred and sixty-five. Only one officer, Second-Lieut. Ashworth, lost his life. Lieut.-Colonel C. P. Porch, D.S.O., handled his battalion with great skill, and displayed his usual cool bravery.

Blue line, and posts were thrown out on this flank, and later the 22nd [1] was ordered to occupy the Graveller Weg from the Brown line to the Railway, which operation was carried out during the night, and connection established with the 26th Northumberlands on the right of the 103rd Brigade.

To strengthen his front line General Gore ordered up the 16th Royal Scots from the Blue to the Brown line, where it took up its position on the left of the Lincolns about six-thirty p.m., its headquarters moving into the western Brown line at eleven-thirty p.m. [2]

Lieutenant Simms brought up No. 4 Section 101st Machine Gun Company about seven-forty p.m., and covered all gaps in the Blue line. The artillery covered itself with glory. Every report comments on the accuracy and volume of the barrage, and General Ternan only voiced the feelings of all ranks when on the 10th he thanked the artillery for making the progress of his brigade through the German lines so easy during yesterday's engagement.

At twelve-thirty p.m. the 86th and 311th Army Field Artillery Brigades moved forward to their advanced positions in the Roclincourt Valley, and at five-twenty-five p.m. the three eighteen pounder batteries of 160th Brigade moved off to take up new positions in what was recently No-Man's-Land. At one-fifteen p.m. the 17th Divisional Artillery, which had been lent to our General, left us to join its Division, which was held in readiness to exploit any success gained.

The situation of the different infantry units at nightfall on 9th are shown on Map. It will be

[1] The 22nd Northumberland Fusiliers lost during the day and night, Second-Lieuts. J. E. Calkin, W. P. H. Brounger, A. D. Gibson, and thirty-six other ranks killed; seven officers and one hundred and sixty-seven other ranks wounded, and sixty missing.

[2] Its casualties were estimated at three hundred and nineteen other ranks killed, wounded, and missing. Second-Lieuts. E. J. P. Thompson and A. D. Flett were killed, and six officers wounded. Every officer of "A" Company became a casualty.

noticed that all objectives had been gained on about half the divisional front, and that the failure of the 103rd Brigade, and the brigade on its left, to reach the Brown line had necessitated the 102nd Brigade throwing back its left flank along the Graveller Weg to connect with the Blue line.

On the whole there was a reason for the General and all concerned to feel fairly satisfied, and confident of the morrow, and orders were issued for the seizure of the remainder of Brown and Green lines at dawn.

Major Congreve, G.S.O.2, was deputed to settle the details of the attack with Brigadier-General Trevor, at whose disposal were placed the 1/5th Gordon Highlanders of 152nd Infantry Brigade, and 21st Northumberland Fusiliers of 102nd Brigade. Three companies of the 18th Northumberland Fusiliers were also sent up to hold the Blue line, and set free the 27th Northumberland Fusiliers. At one a.m., 10th April, the Commanding Officers of the 1/5th Gordon Highlanders and 21st, 26th, 27th Northumberlands, met Major Congreve at the headquarters of the 27th in a German dug-out in the Blue line, and all details were arranged. The share of the artillery was to shell the communication trenches leading from the Brown to the Blue line, and put down a barrage east of the former. The assault started at five a.m., and was a complete success. The 26th and 27th Northumberlands met with some organised opposition, coming under heavy machine gun and rifle fire from Maison de la Cote, which, with its covered approaches, was evidently the key to the local situation. Stoke's mortars were sent up, but " Captain Neeves had organised the whole battalion, and worked round the left flank with Lewis guns along the Gaul Weg, and also on the right along the sunken road. They assaulted, but the enemy ran away. Our men were exhausted, owing to heavy going and bad weather during night of 9th/10th, and could not catch them. The men entered the eastern Brown line, and, standing up, fired at the enemy running down the slope, and cheered lustily. Lewis guns did execution at long range." [1]

Patrols were pushed out to the Green line, and after some time the battalion got in touch with the 51st Division troops on its left, and the 26th Northumberlands on its right, and by nine-thirty a.m. the cheering news reached General Nicholson that the whole of the Brown line was securely held.

The night of the 9th/10th had been a very severe trial of the endurance of the troops in the front area, where there was very little cover. Heavy rain began towards evening, and the wind rose to a gale. The rain changed to snow, and daybreak brought no relief to the sorely tried men, who, exhausted by the hard work before and during the assault, were not in the best condition to bear such a strain. This awful weather lasted till the 13th, which made the sufferings of the poor front line troops terrible, and those of the unfortunate wounded had best not be dwelt on, although the arrangements for clearing the battlefield were good, and Colonel Bliss and the R.A.M.C. of all ranks worked their hardest.

Although sympathising with his weary troops in all their troubles, General Nicholson felt bound to call on them to make a special effort to dig in the Green line, push forward patrols towards Bailleul and Gavrelle to capture guns, and try to locate the enemy. On our right the 4th Division, which had passed through the 9th capturing Fampoux and the Hyderabad redoubt, and on our left the 51st were similarly employed. The day passed in readjusting the boundaries between brigades, and generally straightening out matters.

The arrangements made by Lieutenant-Colonel Chance for supplying the needs of the troops in the

---

[1] War diary, 27th Northumberland Fusiliers.

new positions had worked splendidly, and, in spite of the awful weather, Captain Wilson, 18th Northumberlands, had by eleven p.m. on 9th, stocked a dump with S.A.A. bombs, food, and water close behind the Blue line, by means of the pack mules.

The patrols found no enemy anywhere near our front, except a small party in Towy trench, and the 16th Royal Scots captured six prisoners in a gun-pit, in which also was a seige gun. Many guns were found abandoned, and claimed by the lucky finders, and will no doubt in time find their way to various towns and villages in the old country.

Although the enemy could not be found by our patrols, reports from airmen and artillery F.O.O.s gave warning of a concentration of troops, which portended an attempt to recover the Maison de la Cote by a counter-attack from Bailleul. General Trevor made all necessary arrangements, and when the attack developed, about seven-fifteen p.m., the 152nd Art Brigade caught the columns in such an accurate and overwhelming barrage that they melted away.

During the night the 51st Division took over a portion of the line held by the 103rd Brigade, which was withdrawn to the Black line as divisional reserve, and the 101st and 102nd Brigades held the whole divisional front, each with three battalions in the front line and one in the Blue line as brigade reserve. The three companies of the 18th Northumberlands, which had been in Blue line since the previous night. rejoined their battalion.

On the 11th General Nicholson spent about seven hours going all over the newly acquired territory, looking into all matters affecting the comfort of the troops and the defence of the line, and also the preparation for a further move, should such be ordered. Towy trench, which ran forward from our Brown line towards Gavrelle, was occupied by the 16th Royal Scots as far as the Bailleul-Fampoux and St Laurent

Blangy-Gavrelle cross-roads, near which we got in touch with the 4th Division.

The weather continued awful, but the consolidation of the Green line was pushed on with, though the rain and snow made digging almost impossible. The Hun did not worry very much, though he indulged in fits of hate at intervals, but the weather made life absolutely miserable.

Our total bag up to now was eighteen officers, seven hundred and eighty-six other ranks, fourteen twelve pounder guns, two howitzers, fifteen trench mortars, and about thirty machine guns.

Early on the 12th the 2nd Division relieved the 51st on our left. On our right the 9th Division relieved the 4th and attacked Greenland Hill unsuccessfully, which led to our 101st Brigade getting a heavy dose of shells.

The state of the men in the front lines was getting very bad, and companies of the 18th Northumberlands were sent up to relieve those who were most exhausted, so that it was without much regret that General Nicholson received a visit on the 12th from General Laurie, commanding the 63rd Royal Naval Division, who came to arrange for taking over our line.

On the 13th the weather began to improve. The 2nd Division passed through Bailleul unopposed. Our patrols on 11th and 12th had been in and through the southern edge of the village without finding the enemy, and they now pushed out farther towards Gavrelle, keeping in touch with those of the Divisions on our flanks.

On the 14th the weather improved still further, which made the relief and the long treks it involved a little easier for the tired men. By midnight 14th/15th we were out of the line, some in billets, some in camps, some in bivies, and some in lorries or buses *en route* for the back area. Our Artillery, Field Companies, and Pioneers, although badly in

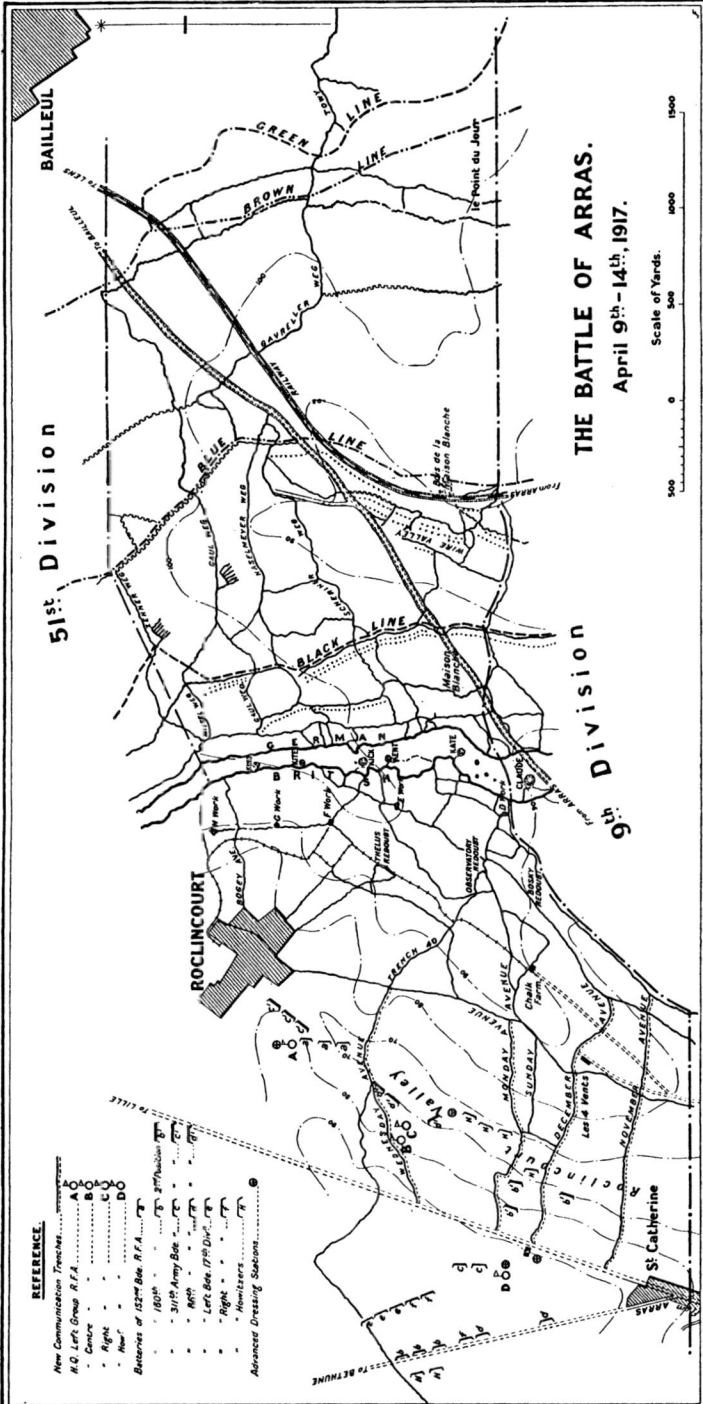

THE BATTLE OF ARRAS.
April 9th–14th, 1917.

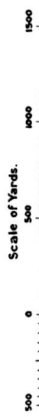

Scale of Yards.
500   0   500   1000   1500

BAILLEUL

51st Division

9th Division

ROCLINCOURT

St Catherine

GREEN LINE

BROWN LINE

BLUE LINE

BLACK LINE

GERMAN

BRIT

REFERENCE.

New Communication Trenches.
H.Q. Left Group R.F.A.
  A
  B
  C
  D
Batteries of 152nd Bde. R.F.A.
  180th
  31/1st Army Bde.
  104th
  Left Bde. 17th Div.
  Right
Advanced Dressing Stations.

need of rest, could not be spared, and had to remain behind to work with other formations.

Our casualties during the six days of the offensive were :

	Officers	Other ranks	Total
Killed	37	304	341
Wounded	94	1980	2074
Missing	1	314	315
Sick	5	32	37
Totals	137	2630	2767

Rather different to the appalling totals of the first few days of the previous July, but still heavy enough to make one think furiously, when one remembers that in all reports the barrage is described as feeble, and the machine gun fire as weak.

The effects of the cruel weather are shown in the reports of the next six days, during which four officers and three hundred and sixty-eight other ranks were evacuated on account of sickness.

The Divisional Headquarters went to Chelers, 101st Brigade in and round Maizieres, 102nd about Orlencourt, and 103rd in and about Bailleux aux Corneilles. The Field Ambulances were with their brigades.

NOTE.—During the action of the 9th/10th April, another V.C. was won by a Northumberland Fusilier, the record of which, in the *London Gazette* of the 8th June, 1917, is as follows: " No. 40989, Pte. Ernest Sykes, Northumberland Fusiliers. For most conspicuous bravery and devotion to duty when his Battalion (27th), in attack, was held up about three hundred and fifty yards in advance of our lines by intense fire from front and flank, and suffered heavy casualties. Pte. Sykes, despite the heavy fire, went forward and brought back four wounded, he made a fifth journey and remained out, under conditions which appeared to be certain death, until he had bandaged all those who were too badly wounded to be moved. These gallant actions, performed under incessant machine gun and rifle fire, showed utter contempt for danger."

Pte. Sykes was an Irishman of Mossley, near Manchester, who joined the West Riding Regiment on 24th August, 1914, but was transferred to the Northumberland Fusiliers, after being wounded in the foot at the Dardanelles.

CHAPTER VII

ONCE again the weary task of refitting, filling up the vacancies, training specialists, and trying to make a mob of recruits into fighting force had to be gone through, and time was very short. In fact we were back in the front line, and over the top again, within a fortnight.

Besides the severe casualties among battalion officers, General Nicholson was at this critical time deprived of the Commanders of the 102nd and 103rd Brigades; the latter was gripped by the sciatica fiend, and the former, to quote his own words, "had come to the end of my tether, and reluctantly had to acknowledge that there comes a time when one must step aside for a younger man." General Ternan was the last of the three Brigadiers that came out with us. He had held command of the 102nd Brigade from the very beginning of its existence, and had thoroughly identified himself with it, and knew all his battalions. When the war began, after service in many parts of the Empire, General Ternan was, as he describes himself, "a dug-out, having retired as a Brigadier-General in 1907," but, as with many of us, the war put back the clock ten years for him, and he tramped his trenches with the best of his brigade.

The command of the 102nd Brigade fell to Major N. H. T. Thomson, Seaforth Highlanders, who joined on 22nd April, and that of the 103rd to Brigadier-

General C. J. Griffin, of Lancashire Fusiliers, who did not arrive till the 25th, and found his brigade back in the line again, holding the front line, after the unsuccessful operations of the 23rd April, during which the 103rd Brigade had acted as reserve to the 51st Division.

The brigade left Arras early on the 23rd, St George's day, and moved through Blangy Park, on the bank of the Scarpe, in all the glory of a spring morning. The attack on the whole 3rd Army front was then in progress, and it was hoped that the brigade would be able to move forward after dark and form a line of outposts east of Roeux, but the result of the fight did not allow of this, and the 26th Northumberlands, during the night of 23rd/24th, dug a line west of Roeux almost from the railway to the Scarpe. A very gallant effort was made by a platoon of this battalion, under Lieutenant Shackleton, to capture the château and chemical works, but these were full of machine guns, and the platoon suffered severely, its leader being killed.

The 103rd Brigade had only been out for seven days, and our Field Companies and Pioneers had not been out at all. Our gunners were still covering our old front, now occupied by the 37th Division, our present front being covered by the guns of the 51st Division. During the late operations our infantry had lost thirty-one per cent of its trench strength, and the reinforcements since received, mostly new indifferently trained men, many of whom had not yet been under fire, only brought our battalions up to an average trench strength of five hundred and twenty all ranks, therefore as a fighting force the Division compared badly with that which broke into the enemy's lines on the 9th April.

General Nicholson took over from General Harper, 51st Division, at ten a.m. on 25th, with his headquarters in old German dug-outs in the railway cutting east of St Laurent-Blangy, which had formed part of the German second system before the 9th Division expelled them on 9th. The front line ran from the bank of the River Scarpe, about seven hundred yards west of Roeux, north-north-east to the railway along the Cusp, Care, Cap, and Ceylon trenches, skirting the château and the buildings north of it. To the north of the railway the line curved forward close to the buildings round the station, and then crossed the Roeux-Gavrelle road, just north of the cross-roads, and continued along the Clover trench, northwards, parallel to the road some five hundred yards till it was joined by the Clyde communication trench, which formed the boundary between the 34th and 37th Divisions. When the 103rd Brigade took over this portion of the line on 23rd/24th April the connection between the right of Clover and the left of Ceylon trench, south of the railway, was very incomplete, and the only communication by which access to the front line could be obtained was Cam, which was very shallow. Snipers and machine gunners, well concealed in the buildings near the railway, made all movement difficult and dangerous, while the enemy's artillery were particularly active. The enemy held the Chemical works and the buildings north and south of the railway, including the château. It would have been a nasty bit of line to take over at the best of times, even with seasoned troops, and to have to do so with a troop of which a considerable proportion had never been under fire, two days before delivering an attack, was particularly unpleasant.

However, General Nicholson made the best of it. On the night of the 26th/27th, Cam communication trench was dug down to a safe depth by the 24th and 25th Northumberlands and two companys of the 18th, which battalion had rejoined us on our again coming into the line.

The consolidation of the centre of the line near the railway proved most difficult, as the Boche was

very vigilant, and by night kept up such a constant
discharge of Very lights that his snipers and machine
gunners took heavy toll of our working parties.
While reconnoitring this portion of the line on the
night of the 25th/26th, Major Reay, temporarily in
command of the 26th Northumberlands, was so
severely wounded that he never rejoined. On the
previous day, 24th April, he had had a very nice
little bit of shooting, for after taking over from the
1/4th Seaforths, he was troubled by some snipers in
a house and wood in his rear. A few rounds of Stoke's
set the game moving, and for a few minutes there was
some rapid shooting at the " Running Man " by a
Lewis gun and the Battalion Headquarter's personnel.
At four-thirty on the 25th April the Corps Commander held a conference with the headquarters of
the 34th and 37th Divisions at General Nicholson's
dug-out, and broke the news that the two divisions
were expected to take Greenland Hill and Roeux on
the 28th. Truly, not much notice. Especially as the
operations of the 23rd had put the Boche very much
on the alert. The 6th Corps on our right, south of
the Scarpe, and the 13th on our left, were also attacking. Operations on so large a scale naturally
demanded considerable interchange of views between
the many staffs concerned, so that it was not till
twelve-fifteen a.m. on 27th that the final orders were
received from the Corps. In the afternoon the Corps
Commander visited Divisional Headquarters, and
came in for one of the heavy doses of 5·9's that Fritz
delighted in sending over.

The scheme of attack, as far as the 34th was concerned, was simple. The two brigades in the line,
101st and 103rd, were to advance straight through
to their objective, which was a line to be dug one
hundred yards east of Roeux on the right, and Cupid
trench on the left. The 102nd Brigade lent one
battalion, the 20th Northumberlands, to the 101st,
and the remainder was in divisional reserve. The

II

101st Brigade had in front of its right Roeux village, a straggling collection of houses with gardens, with a front of some seven hundred yards, extending from the River Scarpe to the cemetery, which was opposite the 101st Centre. The village stretched back about eight hundred yards. Between it and the British lines were various copses and lines of trees. About six hundred yards from the cemetery was the château, whence to the railway was a line of irregular buildings with gardens, with the extensive and solidly built chemical works slightly in rear. The railway ran almost at right angles to the objective, and was the dividing line between the two brigades. Just north of the railway were some more buildings, which extended about three hundred yards, beyond which the ground was open. The Boche had undoubtedly a very strong position, and one admirably suited for the use of his favourite arm, the machine gun.

The 101st Brigade was disposed with the 15th Royal Scots on the right next to the Scarpe, the 10th Lincolns in the centre, and the 11th Suffolks on the left. The 16th Royal Scots were utilised as moppers up, two companies behind the 15th and one behind each of the other battalions. The 20th Northumberlands were to occupy the front line as soon as it became vacant. The 103rd Brigade had the 24th Northumberlands on the right and 25th on the left, the 27th in support and 26th in reserve. Two guns of the 103rd Machine Gun Company went with each of the two leading battalions.

The day is classed as a thoroughly bad one by General Nicholson. It began badly, continued badly, and ended worse. The only bright spot was the defeat of a counter-attack on the 101st front. The assault was delivered at four-twenty-five a.m. The barrage was not as accurate as on the 9th, owing to lack of opportunity for reconnaissance, the nearness of the lines in places, and other causes. On the left it fell behind the enemy's front line, and in the centre it was ragged, missed the houses south of the railway, and was not heavy enough to extinguish the machine guns in the wood. The result was that along the whole line the attack was met by such terrific machine gun fire that it was doomed to failure from the start, though on the two flanks the 25th Northumberlands and 15th Royal Scots got far into the Boche line. The 24th, being opposite the buildings north of the railway, which were full of machine guns, made practically no progress, and the portion of the 27th which was supporting it was also held up, both battalions suffering severely. The 25th, on the extreme left, farther from the nest of machine guns, though met by heavy rifle and machine gun fire from an unregistered trench two hundred yards east of our line, and from the chemical works, did better; indeed some of the battalion got within bombing distance of Cupid trench and dug in. Some of the 27th came up on the left, and reached the top of Cash trench, and were in connection with the troops of the 112th Brigade, which had reached Cuthbert trench. But the position was unsatisfactory, the men of these two battalions being scattered in shell holes between the Roeux-Gavrelle road and Cupid trench under heavy rifle and machine gun fire from their front and right, and from a pocket of Boche in their rear. They could not get forward, but they held on till dark, awaiting orders. The Machine Gun Companies lost all their officers and thirty-five other ranks.

The Suffolks met with much the same fate as the 24th Northumberlands, being met by machine gun fire from a trench untouched by the barrage and from the buildings. They made no progress, and at five-thirty a.m. Major Tuck, Second-in-Command, being sent up to reorganise the battalion, found only five officers and about three hundred other ranks in our front line, including about sixty men of the 16th Royal Scots moppers up. Some of the Suffolks got as far as the houses near the chemical works, and stayed till dark, when they returned with some prisoners.

On the right of the Suffolks, the Lincolns made a good start in the face of terrific machine gun fire, but by five-fifteen a.m. they were held up all along their front. Captain Newton with some twelve men were in the south end of Corona trench, about twenty yards from Clip trench. The enemy had a blocking post in Corona, and a machine gun in a house just behind, which made progress impossible. From Captain Newton's post the line bent back to a point about two hundred yards from our old front line, the men being in shell holes here and there. Captain Worthington at the right, having some twenty men with him, started consolidating in a shallow trench. The enemy made a slight counter-attack on the right of Corona, capturing about thirty men, most of whom were wounded. Seeing that things were in a bad way, Major Vignoles, who was in command, went forward, and about six a.m. collected all the men he could find, and sent them to join Second-Lieutenant Dawson, who was holding the junction of Ceylon and Corona trenches with a few men. Major Vignoles also sent up some Lewis guns and Stoke's mortars, and got them into action. Captain Newton also received a reinforcement of Lewis guns, with which he did considerable execution on the enemy in the houses north of the cemetery, till the guns and their crews were destroyed by heavy artillery shelling. He then retired to Ceylon trench, leaving a bombing post in Corona. The Lincolns had now some forty men collected in Ceylon, and were in touch with the Suffolks on their left, but had not established connection with the 20th Northumberlands, who were farther to the right, in Cusp trench. Captain Worthington's party had been reduced to only ten men, and about eight a.m. he was forced to retire to Care trench, and a little later was killed by a shell.

Some of our men were now seen retiring from

east of Mount Pleasant Wood, closely followed by the enemy, who came on in six waves, covered by heavy machine gun fire from the château and artillery fire on Mount Pleasant Wood. Lance-Corporal Riggall, with a Lewis gun detachment of the Lincolns, held on in the centre of the line till his gun was put out of action and all his men became casualties, and then managed to escape.

The counter-attack was pushed with vigour, though the flanks were broken up by the rifle and Lewis gun fire of the Lincolns from Ceylon and 20th Northumberlands from Cusp. Some two hundred or more of the enemy penetrated into Care and Colne trenches and Mount Pleasant Wood, and thirty or more got through the wood into Ceylon. The situation was extremely critical, but it was effectively dealt with by Major Vignoles, who handled his small reserve with the utmost gallantry and skill, and by Lieutenant-Colonel N. A. Farquhar, commanding the 20th Northumberlands, who sent his " A " Company to bomb the Boche out of the trenches they had occupied, and turned his Lewis guns on them as they quitted, causing them heavy losses. Sergeant MacCrae, with a party of the moppers up of 16th Royal Scots, held on to a bombing post at the north of the wood throughout the attack, effectively checking the Boche. Finally some twenty or thirty Boche in and round the wood surrendered, and by twelve-thirty p.m. the danger was over and the Northumberlands and Lincolns set to work to repair damage and strengthen the line. The counter-attack was made by the 65th I.R., which had come straight up from Biaches. The forces opposite to us this day were : north of the railway the 185th I.R., from the railway to the cemetery cross-roads, the 65th R.I.R., and thence to the Scarpe the 6th I.R. It was the last named which met the attack of the Royal Scots. The machine gun fire here was delayed, and the first waves had got across, but it then came with terrific violence, and cut off the rear wave. Second-Lieutenant Walker, of " C " Company, 16th Royal Scots, was in charge of the last mopping up platoon, following the last wave of the 15th, and was the only officer that got back from the assault. His party was held up by the machine gun fire, and eventually regained our lines. Of the remainder but little information could be obtained at the time. A few wounded struggled back, and a little information was gathered from German prisoners.

I am able now to give a full account of this very gallant attack from an account supplied me by Lieutenant Leonard Robson, who took part in it. The 15th Royal Scots had " D " Company on the right next the river. This company was commanded by Captain Pagan, a very gallant member of the Church Militant. " A " Company was on the left, under Lieutenant Dixon. These were followed by the moppers up of the 16th Royal Scots, and then came " C " and " B " Companies of the 15th, under Lieutenants Wilson and Robson.

The line was formed in No-Man's-Land about midnight, and at zero they advanced and entered the wood. This was found strongly wired and full of machine guns, which must have taken heavy toll of the attackers, but as it was very dark Robson can give no particulars. Another informant speaks of losses from snipers posted in the trees. They stumbled through the wood, and beyond it the going was better. In the ruined village little opposition was met with. They found themselves under the fire of our own guns, evidently having outpaced the barrage. Lieutenant Robson now found himself with some of the moppers up, and as they stayed to attend to the village he went on alone along the road towards the river. It gradually got lighter, and he came on Captain Pagan and two or three other officers and some one hundred and fifty to two hundred men. Being a little early they reorganised the line along the road already mentioned, and when the barrage had moved on they followed it to their objective. Captain Pagan took the right of the first line, and Lieutenant Robson the left; the centre was traversed by a ditch five feet wide. From each half a Lewis gun and bombing squad was sent forward about one hundred and fifty yards, and Lieutenant Robson's left flank being in the air he placed a Lewis gun and bombing post on that side.

The party was at this time entirely isolated, but it held on patiently, trusting that other troops would soon appear on its flanks and from the rear. "We felt rather pleased to be living up to our reputation." Alas! no help came. Digging was almost impossible on account of the marshy nature of the ground, and the shell holes were full of mud. In this parlous state the little party was attacked by parties of the enemy, who crept round the left flank, and fire was opened from machine guns and rifles in the gardens and house on its left rear. Lieutenant Robson did not dare attempt to crush these pests by rapid rifle fire, as his supply of S.A.A. was getting low. About seven-thirty a.m. one of our planes came over, and the party lit flares. At perhaps eight-thirty a.m. a counter-attack was made against the right of the line, and Lieutenant Robson, handing over charge of his section to Lieutenant Fisher, crawled in that direction, under a heavy fire. He found that the men on the right were out of ammunition, and that Captain Pagan was severely wounded. The casualties in the little line of Scots had been very serious, and it was evident that a withdrawal was imperative. An effort to hold the road was frustrated by the enfilade fire from the village, and when refuge was sought in the wood it was found to be held by the enemy, who saluted them with machine gun and trench mortar fire. "So far as I could judge, we were by this time reduced to about thirty men, many of whom were wounded. I myself had a bullet through my right thigh and a hit in my back, though this latter must luckily have been stopped by something in my haver-sack.'' Lieutenant Robson then tried to save the remnant by swimming up-stream under cover of the bank, but this proved impossible, and the end soon came. ''Presently I found myself being helped to my feet—minus equipment—by two of my men under enemy supervision.'' On his way to the rear of the German lines he passed lines of machine guns in shell holes, each with a couple of men, and farther back six battalions at intervals. '' So evidently they were taking no chances of a break through.''

Thus disastrously, but surely very gloriously, ended the attack of the Royal Scots. The casualties of the 15th alone were eighteen officers and three hundred and ninety-nine other ranks.

The moppers up of the 16th Royal Scots had, as Lieutenant Robson puts it, been mopped up, and he had as a companion in misfortune Captain the Honourable M. B. Lyon, who had commanded one of these companies.

Divisional and Brigade Headquarters could obtain but little information of what was happening in front, and even battalion commanders knew little, for the enemy's machine gunners took heavy toll of the runners, and the artillery fire on the area between Battalion and Brigade Headquarters was heavy, cutting the cables and making communication very difficult. It was at first hoped that the 103rd Brigade attack had succeeded sufficiently to make it possible to use the positions gained as a jumping off place for an attack on the chemical works from the north, but later information showed that this was quite impracticable, and after much discussion with Corps Headquarters it was decided to attempt a surprise attack early the next morning, and in the meantime the remnants of the shattered battalions were, as far as possible, with-drawn to their positions of the morning. By the evening the 101st Brigade, plus the 20th Northum-berlands, only totalled about twenty-five officers and seven hundred and ninety other ranks, and the three battalions of the 103rd which had been engaged were in no better condition. In the evening Captain Harris, R.A.M.C., medical officer of the Lincolns, took a party out to search for wounded. Many were brought in, including two or three of the 51st Division, who had been lying out since the attack of the 23rd April.

To prepare the way for the surprise attack the heavies treated the chemical works, between ten p.m. and midnight, to a bombardment, their guns and howitzers firing over five thousand rounds.

The attack on the Chemical works was delivered by the 22nd and 23rd Northumberlands. The former battalion was to take over Cawdor trench, as far as Cam, from the 103rd Brigade, and the latter Ceylon from its junction with the Corona to the railway from the 11th Suffolks. At three a.m., without any artillery bombardment, they were to attempt to surprise the Boche opposite them and capture the buildings north and south of the railway, including the château and Chemical works, and press on to the Corona trench beyond. The right flank was to rest on Ceylon, and the left on Cam trench. Unfortunately, both battalions had a long way to come, and it was not possible for them to receive their orders till late. The 22nd received the orders from General Thomson himself, who visited Battalion Headquarters at eight-fifty p.m. The battalion moved off at ten p.m., and reached its assembly position at one-fifteen. It experienced great difficulty in getting along in the trenches, crowded with men of the 103rd Brigade. No one in the battalion had been in these trenches before, nor had any reconnaissance of the ground ahead been possible. Information as to the exact whereabouts of the enemy was lacking; it was even uncertain whether he was in the portion of Calabar immediately in front of the battalion, or in the next trench east.

The prospect was far from pleasing, and yet the 22nd was better off than the 23rd, which was much farther back and received its orders so late that, though no time was wasted, the companies could not reach their destinations till four a.m., just one hour after the time fixed for the assault. As soon as General Thomson heard this disagreeable news he sent orders to the 22nd to delay its attack, but, unfortunately, these did not reach the battalion in time, and at three a.m. the advance began. " D " Company was on the right, and " B " on the left, each with three platoons in the front line and one following to " mop up."   " C " Company was in support, and " D " in reserve. The enemy was found in Calabar, and quickly ejected. The buildings east of the trench were occupied, but further progress was impossible, owing to intense grazing machine gun fire from north, east, and south. The intensity of the last showed that the 23rd had not yet reached its objective, so " B " consolidated the northern part of Calabar, which was the only cover obtainable, while " D " withdrew to Cawdor via Cam, but a small party of eight, including Lieutenant Robson and Second-Lieutenant Simson, held on in a short section of trench about eighty yards east of Calabar, in spite of the enemy's efforts to dislodge them, only withdrawing when ordered to do so, as the position was quite isolated.

Lance-Corporal Reay, with a patrol, broke through a hostile bombing post on the right, crossed the railway, and got in touch with the left of the 23rd Northumberlands. This battalion arrived at its jumping off trench, Ceylon, from its junction with Corona to the railway, in a very exhausted condition, after a long trek in the dark over an unknown route. At four a.m. " A " Company advanced up Corona, with " B " and " C " on its left moving over the open, while " D " remained in reserve. " A " drove the enemy with bombs down Corona as far as the road east of the château, and then emerged from the trench, only to be cut down by terrific machine gun fire, but held on till ordered to retire down Corona as far as the junction of that trench and Clip, which was the limit to which " B " and " C " had been able to reach. " C," on the extreme left, next the railway, got almost up to the station, but no further progress was possible. The machine guns were numerous, at least five being located in the château, and four or five more in the buildings south of railway, and they were used most skilfully. The positions gained were held by both battalions throughout the day, in spite of a local counter-attack in the evening, which was beaten off with loss to the enemy.

There was now only one unengaged battalion in the Division, and those which had been in action had all suffered severely, so that it was necessary to relieve us, and this was done by the 4th Division between nine p.m. on 30th April and two-thirty a.m. on 1st of May.

Our casualties during the ten days that our last spell in the line had lasted were :

	Killed		Wounded		Missing		Total
Officers ...	21	...	46	...	39	...	106
Other ranks	213	...	1123	...	1202	...	2538
	234		1169		1241		2644

Our losses among the infantry were equivalent to forty per cent, and at the time of our relief the average strength of a battalion, including reinforcements received and details left behind when going into action, was forty-eight per cent under establishment.

Lieutenant-Colonel O. K. Chance, A.A. and Q.M.G., who had been in bad health for some time, but had stuck to his post while the Division was in action, was obliged to go to hospital, and, after an operation, was sent home, and never rejoined us. This was a severe loss, for Colonel Chance had been with us practically all the time we had been in France, and had seen us through the Somme and Arras battles in a manner that inspired confidence in all ranks. Those in the line felt that, whatever might happen, they would never be let down by "Q" as long as O.K. was there. His place was taken by Lieutenant-Colonel R. M. Tyler, D.S.O., Durham Light Infantry, who had previously been Brigade-Major 101st Infantry Brigade.

The relief of the Division was completed by a quarter past four on the morning of the first of May, and General Nicholson handed over command of the line to General Lambton, commanding the 4th Division, at ten o'clock, and after seeing his Brigadiers and the em-bussing of the 101st Brigade, and paying a visit to General Fergusson at Corps Headquarters, drove to his new headquarters at Le Cauroy. It is probable that, like all the rest of us, he never wished to see Roeux and its Chemical works again.

Our artillery, as usual, was left behind, and 102nd Machine Gun Company also remained in the line for a few days.

After a few days in the back area of the 17th Corps, we were transferred to the 19th Corps, but our gunners stayed in action. The rest of us by the 9th May were in billets far away in peaceful country much enjoying the change. The Divisional Headquarters were at Bernaville; those of the three brigades at Pernois, Fienvillers, and Fieffes, with their battalions round them. The three Field Companies were at Gorges, Vacquerie, and Canaples. The Pioneers settled comfortably at Candas, and could hardly believe that they were to be "out" for a spell. It was their first real "rest" since they came out to France. From the 10th to the 26th we trained hard. The changes requisite to meet the more or less open fighting which the partial breaking of the German trench system had brought about were carefully worked out, and a course of instruction devised to fit the troops to meet them.

Attack on RŒUX, 28ᵗʰ April, 1917.

Scale of Yards.

500   0   500   1000

CLYDE

CADIZ

CAM

CAWDOR

From FAMPOUX

From ARRAS

25th Nthd Fus.

CLOVER

From GAVRELLE

CASH

CUTHBERT

CUPID

GREENLAND
HILL

To DOUAI

To FLOUVAIN

24th Nthd Fus.

CALABAR

Suffolks

RAILWAY

Station

Chemical Works

Chateau

CEYLON

CLIP

CORONA

Objective

Camy

Mt PLEASANT
WOOD

SCARBART

COLNE

15th R.S.

20th D.F.

Ditch

Rœux

la Scarpe River

From MONCHY

During this training every effort was made to break down the cult of the bomb and to re-establish the rifle as the infantry soldier's chief weapon. These efforts bore fruit on Greenland Hill, where the counter-attacks were defeated by rifle fire, and the confidence in the rifle thus gained was again evident in the repulse of the many counter-attacks on the Cologne Farm position in August and September, 1917, and still more in all the defensive fighting in April and March, 1918.

Much time and care was devoted to night operations, outposts, wood fighting, village fighting, and shell holes; how to make better 'oles out of any in which you might find yourself, if your attack were held up. Everything possible was done to get the Division up to a high standard of efficiency. To prevent men getting stale, and to keep them fit, games of all sorts were encouraged, and most units indulged in sports. Altogether this was a pleasant as well as a useful interlude. Colonel Porch sums it up in the war diary of the 23rd Northumberlands : " Autheux. Pretty village, good billets, fine weather, good training area, and rifle ranges." What more could the quality want?

The only fly in the ointment was the scarcity of reinforcements. The total wastage from all causes during May was five hundred and forty-two non-commissioned officers and men, and we received reinforcements numbering one thousand four hundred and sixty-one, so that the increase was only nine hundred and nineteen, which did not go far towards filling the deficiency of forty-eight per cent in establishment which existed at the commencement of the month. So great was the shortage of men that battalions were temporarily reorganised as three companies, and the 15th Royal Scots could only find men for three platoons of three sections in each of their three companies.

On 12th May Brigadier-General E. C. W. D.

Walthall, D.S.O., joined the Division as C.R.A., General Rettie receiving another appointment. During the time we were out training, our gunners got only a few days out of action and did not get farther back than Roclincourt Valley. The strain on the personnel was very great, and yet when called on the guns never failed us. Day or night their barrage came down within a few moments of a S.O.S. going up.

All things must have an end, even rest and training, and on the last day of the month, by ten a.m., General Nicholson was again in command of the left section of the 17th Corps front line, relieving General Robertson commanding 17th Division. His headquarters were in a camp near St Nicholas, and our front a little to the north and to the east of that we had held last, but Roeux, with its chemical works and other buildings, which we had good cause to remember, had fallen on the 10th May before a gallant assault of the 4th Division. This was the 9th attack made on the position by British troops, and three days later the Boche made a desperate attempt to recover the lost positions, but the 51st Division, which had relieved the 4th, beat him off.

The 101st Brigade held the right of the line, and the 103rd the left. The former had bad luck, for a thunderstorm broke over the area just before it went into the tenches, and torrents of rain fell, which made the communication trenches almost impassable.

What was known as a minor operation was to be carried out by the left brigade of the 9th Division and the right brigade of the 34th. A small affair, just a little straightening out of the line, with the object of improving our position and forcing the Boche either to dig a new line on the crest of Greenland Hill, or to abandon the crest and dig on the reverse slope. The execution of this was entrusted to the 102nd Brigade of the 34th, and the 27th or Lowland Brigade of the 9th Division. The 102nd took over from the 101st on the night of 4th/5th June. Our front line trenches were Cuba and Conrad. The 102nd held Cuba from the left of the 27th Brigade at its junction with Cinema and Cambrian, and Conrad as far as Curse, beyond which the 103rd carried on the line to the divisional boundary at Civil. The objectives of the 102nd were : (1) Curly and Charlie trenches, (2) Cod and Cuthbert trenches, from the junction of the latter with Charlie to the left of the 27th Brigade objective in Cod, where a line parallel to the railway from Crook cut that trench.

There was to be no doubt about the weight of the barrage, for besides our own two R.F.A. Brigades, which now came back to us, our C.R.A. had under his orders the 50th, 255th, and 293rd R.F.A. Brigades, two brigades of 13th Corps Field Artillery, and two sixty pounder batteries, which gave him one hundred and twenty-six eighteen pounders, thirty-eight 4·5 howitzers, and twelve sixty pounders, and in addition the Corps heavy artillery were going to lend their aid. Twelve guns from the three Machine Gun Companies were also to be employed on barrage work. All Stoke's mortars of the three Brigade Batteries were to assist in searching No-Man's-Land, etc. The 102nd Brigade had the 20th, 21st, and 22nd Northumberlands in the front line, and the 23rd in support. The three assaulting battalions had their three companies in line, each in four waves; the leading two waves were to capture and mop up the first objective, while the third and fourth were to pass through and take and hold the second. The 103rd Brigade was to assist and put the finishing touch to the job by joining up the left of the second objective with our existing front line at Curse trench. Six platoons of the Lincolns were to carry, etc., for the 102nd Battalions.

Zero was at eight p.m., and the barrage fell with a crash on the Boche in Curly and Charlie trenches. After four minutes, which to those under it must have seemed an hour, it lifted one hundred yards, and the stormers were in all along those trenches save in the centre of the right battalion, where the barrage had not exterminated the Emma Gees and their wonderfully brave and efficient crews. At this point the attack was held up short of the first objective. On the left the assaulting waves came under heavy machine gun fire from Wit trench on the left, and of the platoon especially detailed for the capture of the junction of Charlie and Cuthbert trenches only the commander and two men reached their goal. There was stubborn fighting in Charlie and Curly. The Boche held on bravely here and there, and fierce struggles with bayonets and bombs took place, but our men showed their superiority with these weapons and with their rifle grenades, so that the enemy was cleared out of the whole of the first objective, save in a small portion in the 20th Northumberland area, where they held on till the following afternoon. The fighting in the first objective was not allowed to interfere with the capture of the second. The third and fourth waves of the attackers, disengaging themselves from that scrap in a manner that reflected great credit on their training, passed on close behind the barrage and established themselves in Cuthbert and Cod, and by midnight on both brigade fronts the objectives had been seized, save for the pocket of Boche in the 20th Northumberlands part of Curly. Even two hours earlier, matters had advanced enough for General Thomson to order up two platoons of "D" Company, 18th Northumberlands, to dig a new communication trench, to be called Costa, from Cuba to Charlie, and two sections of 208th Field Company, under Lieutenants Nesham and Morris, with their attached infantry to make strong points. The 26th Northumberlands, 103rd Brigade, started on the new trench, which was to join up their front line from Curse trench with the recently acquired line, but were unable to complete it, owing to some defect in the tracing and the heavy fire brought to bear on them. Captain G. Stewart and Second-Lieutenant O. H. Sprenge were killed, and there were about sixty other casualties.

The enemy did not acquiesce in our appropriation of his trench. He kept up a heavy barrage on our communications all night, rendering the work of the Lincolns carrying parties difficult, but the careful leading of Second-Lieutenants Bousfield, Finnertz, Steemson, and Bannister enabled their platoons to dodge the barrage with the loss of only three killed and seven wounded. On the left, between midnight and two a.m. on 6th, the enemy made several bombing attacks under trench mortar barrage, but was beaten off with rifle grenades. Not discouraged, he attacked more than once from Whip trench, but the rifle fire of the garrison of Cuthbert was so effective that finally the Boche had to resign himself temporarily to its loss. On the right he made two strong counter-attacks, the first of which was smashed by the fire of our gunners and the infantry in Cod trench, but the second achieved partial success, for a short time driving in our posts in Cod, but was driven off Curly, and eventually out of Cod, by rifle and machine gun fire.

At four a.m. the Pioneers had connected Cuba with Charlie by a serviceable trench called Costa, and the Royal Engineers had constructed a strong point round its head. Cod and Cuthbert were held by posts which were well wired, but some Boche still hung on to a portion of Curly, where they remained till arrangements were completed to oust them, which was about two p.m., by which time Stoke's mortars had been got into position and opened fire on the Huns, and the 20th Northumberlands attacked them on the left from Charlie. This was too much for the enemy, who bolted over the open, but on being fired at by Lewis guns from the posts in Cod, two officers and seventy-two other ranks returned to Curly and sur-

I

rendered. Four heavy and two light machine guns and a " pineapple thrower " were captured at the same time. This completed the task set the 102nd Brigade, but the tired troops had still to fight to maintain their hold, and to suffer heavy spells of shelling. At ten-four p.m. the S.O.S. went up from the extreme right of the 20th Northumberlands, and two minutes later our artillery barrage dropped exactly in the right place, and the attack fizzled out.

However, at twelve-thirty a.m. on 7th the Boche had another try, this time on the 22nd Northumberlands, on the left of the line. The attack was pushed with great vigour, and under cover of an intense trench mortar bombardment a lodgment at the junction of Charlie and Cuthbert, and our lads, fighting hard, were driven back some ninety yards down the former, and a Stoke's mortar had to be blown up to prevent it becoming a prize. The left post in Cuthbert was also driven southwards down that trench. The survivors of the small post at the junction of the trenches held on for some time, considerably delaying the attack, and by the energy of the officers and non-commissioned officers, within twenty minutes the ejected troops were re-formed, and, the supply of rifle grenades running short, they counter-attacked with such vigour over the open that the Huns made a clean bolt of it, and the garrison of the centre post in Cuthbert put matters to right in that trench. Second-Lieutenant A. W. D. Mark, M.C., did excellent service on the extreme left, where his platoon beat off several attacks. Indeed, Colonel Acklom had good reason to be proud of all his lads that day. Daylight showed many dead Boche in front of our line, and a machine gun was left in our hands.

The 23rd Northumberland Fusiliers had been in reserve, but its machine guns had assisted in the defeat of the counter-attacks. Its casualties numbered twenty-two, Lieutenant-Colonel Porch being included in the number of wounded.

During the 7th June the enemy attempted several attacks, but all were stopped by our ever-watchful gunners and machine gun men before they had time to develop. Several more posts were established in Cuthbert and Cod trenches during the 7th and 8th, and during these nights the 18th Northumberlands dug Coke and Cry trenches, thus connecting the new front line with that held by the 103rd, and making everything shipshape and secure.

At three-twenty-five a.m. on the 8th the 102nd Brigade, which had by then been constantly engaged for fifty-five hours, was relieved by the 101st, and went into divisional reserve. The 101st strengthened the line, putting out some more posts in Cuthbert and Cod every night. The Boche made no more efforts to regain the lost ground, but showed his wrath by shelling the whole of our area, fore and aft, pretty severely for several days. Then his behaviour improved, and before our relief it left nothing to be desired.

General Nicholson handed back the command of the line to G.O.C. 17th Division, and returned to his old quarters in Hermaville Château.

This was our last appearance in the Battle of Arras. It was a pleasant ending, which helped us to forget the misfortune of our second visit, sandwiched between the successes of our first and our last.

The 102nd, which had borne the brunt of the last battle, came well out of the test, and the Divisional and Brigade Staffs might well feel satisfied with the results of the special training. The high value the enemy placed on the positions captured was shown by the strenuous efforts which he made to recover them, and the troops that, after storming them, held them in spite of those efforts, surely deserved the highest praise.

The 21st Northumberlands lost the following officers : Captain C. M. Joicey, Second-Lieutenants G. Bailie, A. V. Knox, S. G. H. Purnell, H. J. Elias, R. Armitage, T. V. Scattergood, killed, and five wounded, including Captain Rev. J. McHardy. The 22nd had Captain T. H. Waugh and Second-Lieutenant W. K. Simson killed, and Lieutenant H. McDonald was missing. Our total losses were : Killed, sixteen officers and one hundred and seventy-six other ranks; wounded, thirty-two officers and nine hundred and nine other ranks; missing, one officer and one hundred and fifty-seven other ranks. From accounts of prisoners and other sources we learnt that our opponents, the 1st and 3rd Battalions of the 463rd Regiment, were nearly wiped out. Our bag of captures for the month was six officers, one hundred and seventy other ranks, twelve machine guns, and one Granatenwerfer.

So, with our tail well up, and smiling faces, we turned our backs on Roeux and its chemical works, and departed *quo fata vocant*.

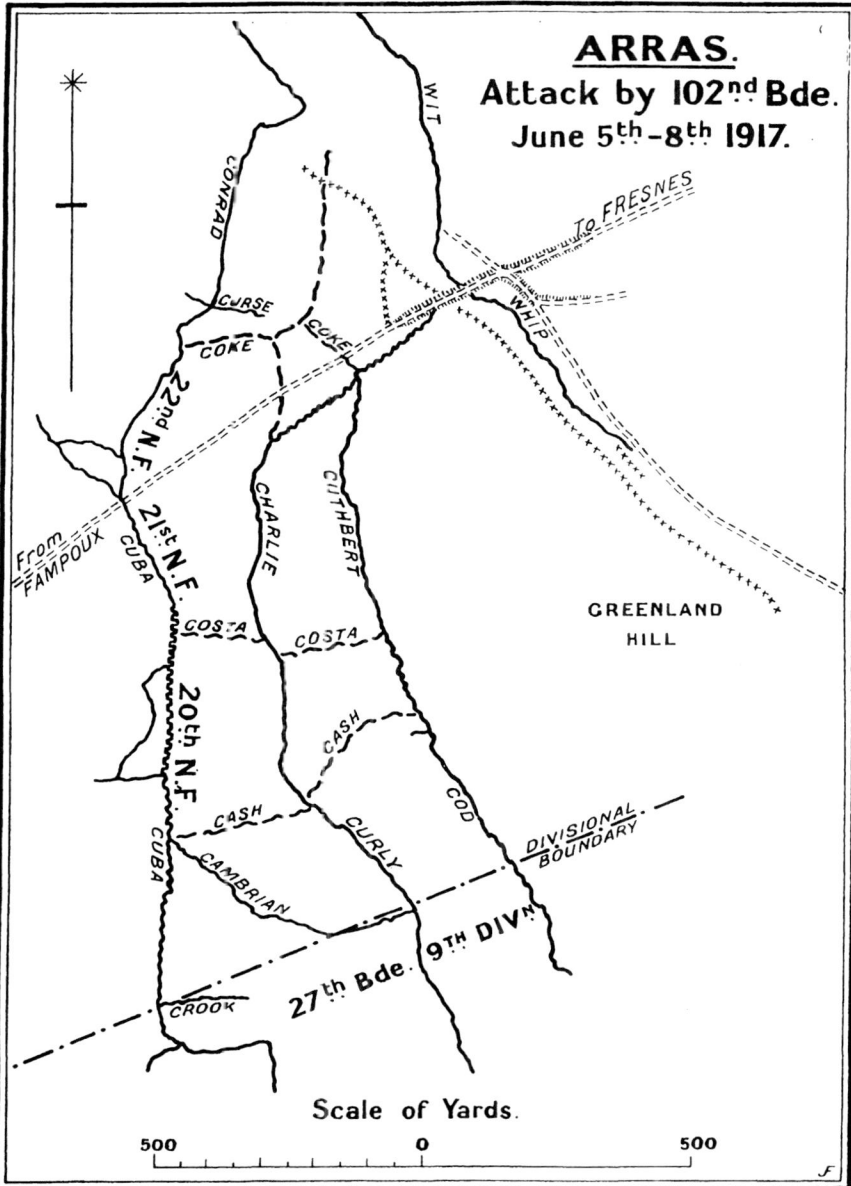

ARRAS.
Attack by 102nd Bde.
June 5th–8th 1917.

CHAPTER VIII

HARGICOURT

THE Division spent the rest of June, and the first few days of July, cleaning up, refitting, replenishing its depleted ranks, and training in the back area of the 17th Corps, which had become quite like home by now. The replenishing of the ranks was not satisfactory; in fact, the return for June shows that the reinforcements received fell short by over four hundred of the wastage which had occurred.

The 103rd Brigade underwent reconstruction. The 24th and 27th Northumberland Fusiliers were amalgamated into one battalion, known as 24th/27th Northumberland Fusiliers, and the 9th Battalion of the same regiment was brought into the brigade.

The 18th Northumberland Fusiliers were detached from the Division, and left on the 30th June by train for the far famed " salient," where they were employed, with other Pioneers, on special railway work. We met them there later on, when our fate took us into that abominable area. The rest of us moved away from the Arras neighbourhood early in July, and by the 6th we were in the Cavalry Corps area; Divisional Headquarters in Peronne. We only halted there a few days, during which time we supplied working parties for clearing away the debris in the town, and had opportunities of studying the results of the awful destruction deliberately carried out by the Boche before he retreated.

During the 8th, 9th, and 10th the 101st and

102nd Infantry Brigades took over the Hargicourt-l'Omignon River section of the 3rd Corps front, relieving the 4th and 5th Cavalry Divisions, and at nine a.m. on 10th General Nicholson took over command with his headquarters in Nobescourt Farm.

The country here, and the lines held by the opposing forces, were quite different to any we had been in before. The country had been wilfully laid waste when the disciples of Kultur retired earlier in the year. I cannot improve on the following extracts from letters, which have been kindly lent me : " All the villages round here have suffered the same fate. Practically every house ruined . . . certainly every one has had a charge fired in it, and many of them have been burned. . . . A village wrecked by continual shell fire is a melancholy sort of sight, but it is a very different one from one destroyed after careful preparation, and with a certain fiendish sense of humour. It forces you to the conclusion that a live Boche is a mistake. . . ." " Wrecking farmhouses, cutting down ornamental shrubs, smashing farm implements (all laid out in a row for the purpose), sawing through spokes of farm carts, fouling ponds and water supplies, were all items of the official programme, but I think that breaking *one* wheel of each perambulator must have been a spontaneous burst of humour on the part of individuals. . . ." Again the Boche has shown himself a bad judge of character. The peevish destruction of purely civilian property has had a great effect in stiffening up the French, and has saved us from paying fancy prices for brick rubble, timber, strawberries, currant tart, and gooseberry fool. You can't think how thankful we are to find close to a hole in the road, the material necessary to repair it. Fancy if *we* had blown that house down. . . . I wonder if Fritz knows what a good turn he has done us in the provision of R.E. material, and if he remembers that he forgot to destroy fruit *bushes* as well as fruit *trees*."

To quote again, "The country is open and undulating like Salisbury Plain, and we hold some high ridges with low ground in front. In most places, however, we are some little way from the Boche, and the lines are not dug in or organised in the way that we have been used to. Everything is more opened and scattered, and we walk about in the open in what seems to be an extraordinary reckless fashion, after our experiences in other parts of the line. . . . We can ride up the Battalion Headquarters in the line, and so are able to take along plenty of kit and make ourselves comfortable."

While we held this part of the line the Infantry Brigade Headquarters were, for right and left brigades in the line, Vraignes and Hervilly respectively, and for brigade in reserve, Bernes.

Accommodation was hard to find, owing to the ruined state of the countryside, and "Q" had a difficult task to provide shelter for all, but with tents and huts it was accomplished, and in a short time baths were in full swing at Montigny Farm, Bernes, and Hamelet, and Expeditionary Force Canteens were opened at Roisel, Montigny, Hancourt, and La Chapellette.

Our front line consisted chiefly of posts. Commencing from the right, where we were in touch with the 22nd Division of the French Army (in whose area south of the Omignon River we had a machine gun post), our first post was known as Lone Tree post; it stood at the southern end of Ascension Spur, not far north of the Pontru-Bellenglise road, and had good command over all the country to south and east. The line was carried northwards along the forward slope of the spur by a series of posts, the first named Dragoon, and the others numbered from one to nine, which was the last in the right brigade area. About three hundred yards in rear of this line was a second line, on the reverse slope of the spur, from Cressy trench (which, though farther back, was a front line trench), on the south, close to Pontru to Molly on the north, between Ascension and Le Grand Priel Farms. A little to the north of Cressy trench was a tumulus, which stood some fifty feet above the general level, from the top of which an excellent view could be obtained, wherefore the Hun shelled it frequently. Farther back was the intermediate line, a line of trenches known as Mareval, Cooker, Dean, and Orchard. They stretched along the top and eastern slopes of the spur, which lay between Mareval copse on the south and the village of Le Vergier on the north.

The left brigade front line consisted of a line of posts extending northwards across the top of Buisson Ridge, across the valley and up the other side round the eastern edge of Villeret and east of Hargicourt villages, and across another depression and up the far side till it met the line held by the 35th Division. From the Quarry, east of Hargicourt, northwards, the line was a nearly continuous trench. East of Hargicourt were two farms, or what had been farms, known as Unnamed Farm, which we held, and Cologne Farm, held by the Boche. Here the lines were close together, but at the northern end, and opposite Villeret, the distance between them increased to about eight hundred yards.

In the rear of the left brigade front the intermediate line was called Priel Wood trench, Fervacque trench, Cote trench, and Hargicourt trench. The Boche, as usual, had the best position, especially on the left. He held a ridge more or less parallel to our main line of defence, which denied us observation over his Hindenburg line, and allowed him to see a good deal more than was pleasant for us, of what went on between our outpost line and our main line. It was therefore decided that he was to be pushed off the highest part of the ridge, which was opposite our left, and General Nicholson was told to do this. Thus vanished the dreams of a peaceful rest cure which some of us had been indulging in.

Our gunners had come out of the Arras battle on the 1st July, having been continuously in action since February, and for the greater part of that time hotly engaged in the great offensive, so that they might well think they were entitled to a spell of rest, but by nine p.m. on 10th July they were in action again on our new front. The right group, commanded by Lieutenant-Colonel W. G. Thomson, consisted of the 152nd Brigade, and two batteries of R.H.A., and three howitzers of 298th Brigade, R.F.A. The left group was composed of Lieutenant-Colonel W. M. Warburton's 160th Brigade and one battery of 295th Brigade R.F.A. We had therefore twelve thirteen pounders, eighteen eighteen pounders, and nine 4·5 howitzers covering the right brigade, and twenty-four eighteen pounders and six 4·5 howitzers covering the left brigade.

Owing to the width of No-Man's-Land on the right all the trench mortar batteries were in the left group. They did not get into action till near the end of July. They made use of some German 77 m.m. guns, which we had brought from Arras battle-fields, and a new heavy mortar was received which gave satisfaction.

July passed without any incident of great importance. The monotony of trench warfare, to which we had been accustomed, did not trouble us here. The distance between the lines, and the change in the systems of defence, required different tactics, the chief of which was a great increase in the number and range of our patrols. Every night several small parties issued from our posts, and searched the country in front; as the enemy carried out the same policy, encounters were not infrequent. Even if no Boche were met, the work was highly exciting, and calculated to develop the initiative and resourcefulness of the patrol leaders. There were two small attacks by the enemy, both of which were beaten off. The first was on 14th July, when, after a few minutes' intense bombardment, the enemy attacked our positions in Indian trench and Unnamed Farm, held by the 23rd Northumberlands. Most of the Boche were stopped by artillery, Stoke's, and machine gun, but some got into the latter post, whence they were quickly ejected by a bombing attack up the former trench. The extremity of Indian trench was blown in by a big shell, and a Lewis gun and its crew were missing. Our other losses were : Two killed and ten wounded. The Stoke's mortars got off one hundred and seventy rounds, and contributed greatly to the success of the garrison. The other little affair was at the right of the line, where the enemy attacked Lone Tree post on the night of the 21st, and was driven off with the loss of six, left dead on our hands.

At the end of July, the 101st Brigade, which had been relieved by the 103rd earlier in the month, relieved the 102nd in the left sector, and to facilitate the coming operations the divisional front was extended northwards to include Rifleman's post. During the 101st Brigade's second tour of front line duty, the Lincolns dug almost every night, and connected up the posts along the brigade front. It was a somewhat ticklish task, as it was not quite certain which of the buildings in front were occupied by the Boche, as he changed his dispositions from time to time. However, the battalion worked hard and silently, and the job was safely accomplished before the brigade went out into divisional reserve and trained for its next undertaking. The value of careful training, and rehearsals over spitlocked models of the trenches to be attacked, was fully appreciated, and no detail, however small, was overlooked or neglected. In addition to his own brigade, General Gore was given the use of the 20th and 23rd Northumberlands, 207th Field Company, R.E., the 101st

L.T. Mortar Battery, and two mortars of the 102nd Battery. The 102nd Brigade also assisted by the loan of four companys for carrying up material, etc.

The position to be carried comprised a system of trenches constructed on the Cologne Ridge, about two thousand yards west of the Hindenburg line, and overlooking our position in the Villeret-Hargicourt Valley. It extended from the northern end of Malakoff support to the southern end of railway trench, at the railway cutting. Two objectives were named in the operation orders, the Black and the Red lines. The former ran from the north corner of Malakoff trench, along Sugar-New-Pond and Railway trenches; the latter from junction of Malakoff and Malakoff support, southwards along the latter, then to the east of the Sugar factory and along Bait trench thence a line through shell holes east of Railway trench to the railway. South of Bait trench this was to be a line of posts.

The 101st Brigade put all its four battalions in the first line, in the following order, from right to left : 15th and 16th Royal Scots, 10th Lincolns, and 11th Suffolks. The 20th Northumberlands was in reserve behind the railway embankment, south of Slag quarry. A company of the 23rd Northumberlands was to make a bombing attack up Rifle Pit trench, and join hands with the Suffolks on the left of the Black line, the remainder holding the old line. The 26th Northumberlands, on the right of the 15th Royal Scots, were to be ready to co-operate under the orders of their own Brigadier. The 21st and 22nd Northumberlands of 102nd Brigade supplied a company to carry up stores, etc., for each of the assaulting battalions of the 101st Brigade.

The artillery treated the enemy to the usual preliminary bombardment, and on 25th to a special "Chinese" barrage, with a view to ascertaining where he was likely to put down his barrage when the assault was delivered.

Along the greater part of the front concerned, the width between the opposing lines was considerable, and in these portions it was necessary that the assaulting troops should be drawn up before zero hour, some distance in front of our line. To ensure this being properly done, a tape was put down during the night by a specially chosen officer, and a small party of each battalion. This job required skill and care. In fact, a Boche patrol did come in contact with the covering party of the Lincolns, but was disposed of without any alarm being raised.

The forming up was carried out in absolute silence, and at four a.m. on the 26th August all the four battalions of the 101st Brigade were in position, and the Boche over the way had no suspicion of the imminence of the attack.

At four-thirty a.m. the barrage came down. The eighteen pounders opened on a line approximately two hundred yards east of Cologne Farm road; all other guns and howitzers concentrated on points of importance in rear of the enemy's front line. A heavy machine gun barrage swept the lines, by which reinforcements could reach the positions attacked. The assaulting waves closed up to the barrage. After four minutes the barrage lifted fifty yards, and began to creep to the enemy's front line, and the leading waves of the attackers followed till they were close to his wire. The barrage rested on the front line for three minutes, and then lifted one hundred yards east, and the first waves of each battalion rushed through gaps in the wire and dropped into the German front line trench, where they took necessary action with the garrisons thereof, while the second wave passed on and formed up behind the barrage, which crept forward at fifty yards a minute. At four-forty-five the fiery curtain and its following line of infantry reached the enemy's second line, paused there two minutes, then jumped forward two hundred yards to give the infantry room to deal with the Red line, and then crept forward for another two hundred yards and stayed there.

Such is a brief account of the action, but some details must be given. We will begin on the left. The company of the 23rd Northumberlands experienced no difficulty in clearing Riflepit trench, capturing six prisoners in process. The trench was consolidated, and connection made with the 11th Suffolks, in Malakoff support. This battalion had some hand-to-hand fighting at the junction of Sugar and Malakoff trenches, and suffered from a machine gun's fire till its crew was killed. The centre company, "B," lost ground a bit getting through Malakoff Farm, but this had been foreseen, and the troops on right and left bombed inwards down the support trench, so that the Red line was occupied up to time. The officer commanding "D" Company materially facilitated the consolidation of this part of the objective by seizing the adjacent portion of Triangle trench, in which he took thirty prisoners.[1]

To the right of the Suffolks the Lincolns found that our artillery and heavy trench mortars had dealt so faithfully with Sugar and Pond trenches that they were almost obliterated. What remained of the garrison was either killed or captured in the dug-outs. 'A' machine gun and Granatenwerfer were found in Sugar trench, and in the factory the whole garrison of twenty was either killed or captured. The

[1] " No. 15092 Corporal Sidney James Day, Suffolk Regiment (Norwich). For conspicuous bravery. Corporal Day was in command of a bombing section detailed to clear a maze of trenches still held by the enemy. This he did, killing two machine gunners, and taking four prisoners. On reaching a point where the trench had been levelled, he went alone, and bombed his way through to the left, in order to gain touch with the neighbouring troops. Immediately on his return to his section a stick-bomb fell into the trench occupied by two officers (one badly wounded) and three other ranks. Corporal Day seized the bomb, and threw it over the trench, where it immediately exploded. This prompt action saved the lives of those in the trench. He afterwards completed the clearing of the trench, and established himself in an advanced position, remaining for sixty-six hours at his post, which came under intense hostile shell, grenade and rifle fire. Throughout the whole operations his conduct was an inspiration to all."—*Supplement to the " London Gazette,"* *17th October, 1917.*

Lincolns reached Bait trench, their final objective, a few minutes before the 16th Royal Scots, and a small pocket of Boche, which held on in that trench between the two battalions, was promptly dealt with by bombing attacks from north and south. Some over-zealous Lincoln lads pushed on into Ruby Wood, which was beyond the limits laid down for the advance, and found it empty. All returned safely, though some waited till dark before returning.

The following is from an account by a Lincoln officer : " The enemy was apparently surprised at the rapidity with which our attack was pushed home, and put up a very poor fight. Many of them came rushing out to our men, screaming, with their hands up, and some tried to throw their arms round K———, calling him Kamerad ! A few fought till our men were on them, and *then* threw up their hands, but our men finished *them* off. The ones that did not fight were taken prisoners, and were so anxious to get to our lines that in many cases they started running in twos and threes across No-Man's-Land towards our trenches, without waiting for an escort. We had posted police to take over prisoners who were brought down, but when they saw these men coming over, they just whistled and beckoned them, and they came to heel like well-trained dogs ! It must have been amusing to see the invincible German soldier whistled to heel like a poacher's lurcher ! "

The 16th Royal Scots found Pond trench almost wiped out, and experienced but little opposition in reaching Bait, but on the extreme right about one hundred Boches put up a good fight, and then retired across the open, giving the rifles and Lewis guns of the Scots good targets. Thirty-five prisoners were taken.

The final objective of the 15th Royal Scots was a line of dug-outs and posts. This had not been as faithfully dealt with by the artillery as the remainder of the enemy's line, and it was found strongly

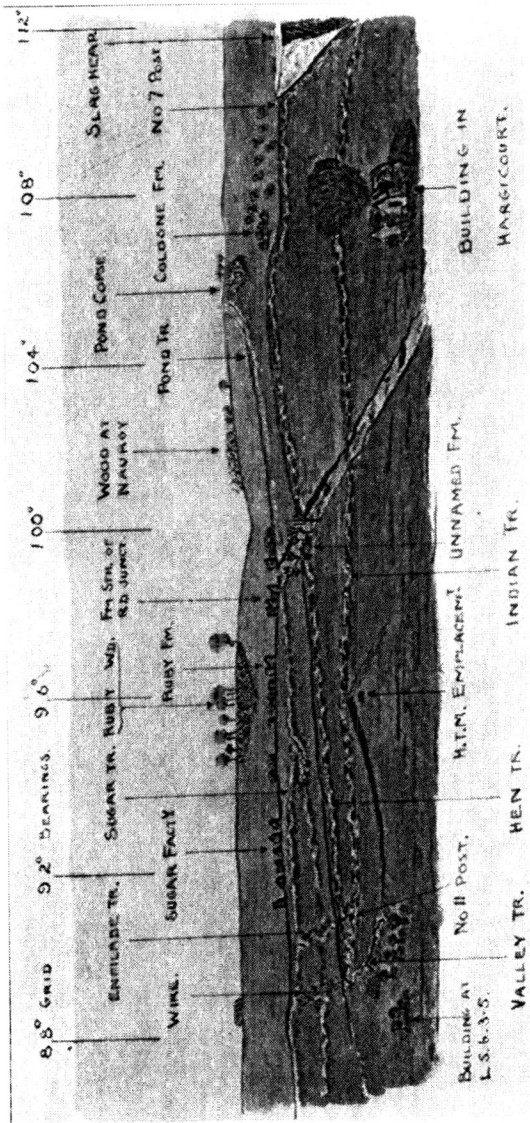

88° GRID 92° BEARINGS. 96° 100° 104° 108° 112°

WIRE. EMPLADE TR. SUGAR TR. RUBY WD. Fm. Smr or WOOD AT POND COPSE. SLAG HEAP.
R.D. JUNCT. NAUROY.
SUGAR FACTY. RUBY Fm. POND TR. COLOGNE FM. No 7 POST.

BUILDING AT No II POST. M.T.M. EMPLACEMT. UNNAMED FM. BUILDING IN
L.S.6.3.5. HARGICOURT.
VALLEY TR. HEN TR. INDIAN TR.

COLOGNE FARM POSITION

From a sketch made August 19th, 1917. W. A. Vignoles, Major.

[To face p. 112]

manned, but the 15th, in spite of heavy casualties, ousted the defenders, but were themselves immediately counter-attacked from Farm trench, and forced back down Railway to its junction with Pond trench, where a block was established. The brigade diary records at noon : "16th Royal Scots, 10th Lincolns, 11th Suffolks, and left of 15th Royal Scots all right. Right of 15th Royal Scots been fighting all the morning to maintain its position against counter-attacks and bombing attacks. Difficult to keep up supplies, owing to heavy barrage in Villeret Valley and to machine gun and sniper fire from north end of Farm trench and shell holes west of it.''

All the battalions report that in the actual assault they suffered little, but after being driven out the Boche made us pay dearly for our success by bombarding his late trenches very severely. He made several unsuccessful counter-attacks during the remainder of the day, which were defeated with severe loss.

The Flying Corps had its share in our victory; planes of 59th Squadron and 3rd Brigade, R.F.C., flew low over the enemy while he was assembling to counter-attack, and did much execution with their machine guns.

Prisoners taken during the day spoke with terror of the execution done among the counter-attack columns by our machine gun barrages.

Our Battery Commander had stopped keeping his diary before this, which is a great loss, but fortunately I have the following from another source. While fighting his guns, from his observation post he spotted a Boche counter-attack forming up, and the battery got off three hundred rounds in five minutes into the thick of the column. My informant adds that counter-attack did not progress.

Altogether, the 26th August may be put down as a most successful day, and it was only the situation on the right flank which dimmed its glory. The enemy still held part of Railway trench, his advance posts being in continual conflict with the 15th Royal Scots, the battle swaying backwards and forwards, and causing considerable anxiety. During the night and the next day the consolidation of our gains was pushed on energetically, in spite of hostile counter-attacks and barrages and heavy rain, which began on evening of 26th, and from midday on 27th continued without stopping for a moment for twenty-four hours, making the existence of the troops in the trenches very wretched, and almost completely stopping all digging.

It had been recognised from the beginning of the preparation for this operation that we had neither troops nor guns enough to extend the objective sufficiently to the south to take, at one operation, Farm trench and the high ground south of Railway trench, on the Villaret Col, whence the enemy looked along the back of Cologne Farm Ridge and down the Hargicourt Valley. Therefore two battalions of 103rd Infantry Brigade (9th and 24th/27th Northumberlands) had been previously detailed to take this high ground by a night attack of the night of 26th/27th August. To prepare for the attack the artillery, during the afternoon of 26th, did much unostentatious wire cutting, and after dark the objective was well dosed with thermite shell.

Owing to the weather, which had by then made all movements very difficult, the 24th/27th Northumberlands were late in arriving at the jumping off place, and the officer commanding the 9th did not feel justified in pushing on alone, and withdrew his battalion. The 24th/27th, though late, advanced, and Lieutenant Burne and some thirty men of his platoon reached Farm trench, which at that spot was not occupied, and were found there at daylight by Colonel Guard, 15th Royal Scots. The rest of the battalion was withdrawn. Fighting continued on this flank all the 27th. A bombing attack, made by the Royal Scots up Farm trench, failed, owing to the rain making the Mills' bombs so slippery that they could not be thrown, while the Boche could use his stick bombs with effect.

The weather was so bad that General Nicholson decided to postpone further operations against Farm trench, and in order to make the right flank of the newly won trenches safe, the two left posts of Villaret system were pushed forward, and on the night of the 28th/29th the 12th Yorks, who were temporarily replacing our Pioneers, cannected these posts with the right of the 101st Brigade position by a trench and wire fence.

Early on the 29th the 101st was relieved by the 103rd Brigade. The exhausted battalions were withdrawn from the waterlogged trenches, which they had captured and held so well in spite of many counterattacks, and, with infinite labour in the worst of weathers, had deepened and made strong with wire throughout their length.[1]

The more graphic pen of a correspondent sums up the impression made on him by these strenuous days : " Certain square miles have been turned into a hell from which men have come back (some of them) looking twenty years older, with staring eyes that see nothing. Add to intense shelling by both sides, a pouring rain that hardly stopped for days, and imagine what sort of time the infantry had living in a crater field where the light clay had been turned over and over and rapidly turned into a bottomless clay. . . ."

General Gore published a special order, which ended thus : " On previous occasions I have had reason to be proud of commanding the 101st Brigade, but never more than on this occasion."

[1] The following officers were killed: Lieutenant J. R. Devene, 15th Royal Scots; Second-Lieutenant Smith, 16th Royal Scots; Lieutenant R. C. Lodge, Second-Lieutenant J. S. McHoul, 10th Lincolns; Second-Lieutenants Branfoot, Simons, and Thomas, 11th Suffolks; Second-Lieutenants E. E. G. Alderwick and R. W. F. Danvers, and Second-Lieutenant R. C. Waitt missing. The other causalties among the battalions engaged were: officers, 30 wounded; other ranks, killed, wounded, and missing, 733.

General Byng, commanding the 3rd Army, called at General Nicholson's headquarters on the 29th, and complimented him on the success attained.

Information obtained from Boche prisoners showed that our attack came as a surprise; even when the barrage dropped on them they only thought it meant a raid on rather a bigger scale than usual.

About this period the divisional front was sub-divided afresh. The 4th Cavalry Dismounted Brigade, which was temporarily placed under General Nicholson's orders, took over the right sector, from the Omignon River to north of Grand Priel Farm; the centre sector extended thence to Post Slag and the junction of Bait and Pond trenches; thence to the north was the left sector.

The Cavalry Brigade, composed of British and Indian Cavalry from the Indian contingent, was energetic in patrolling, capturing several prisoners, and keeping the right flank secure.

Although the operations at the end of August had driven back the Boche, and given us a good view over parts of the Hindenburg line, while denying him observation over much of our own, his continued possession of the high ground we had tried to take on the night of 26th/27th August, made the situation in the Hargicourt Valley and the rear of Cologne Farm Ridge unhealthy for reliefs, ration parties, etc. It was therefore decided that the Hun must be driven off this ground.

On 31st August a reconnaissance was made by General Nicholson, with a view to settling exactly how much of these Boche trenches we must take. On the next day he discussed the matter with the Corps Commander, and it was determined that the 102nd Brigade, holding the centre sector, should take what we required on the 8th September. To give the Brigade the necessary opportunity of training, it was relieved on the following night by the 101st, which only came out of the left sector on the morning of the

29th August. This brigade at this time was so weak that it required three battalions to hold the front line, which was usually done by two. The Lincolns could only muster a trench strength of two hundred and seventy, and the other battalions only averaged four hundred and fifty rifles. The casualties during September, during which month the brigade took part in no offensive, were one hundred and forty-two. During the last week of the month large drafts were received just in time to be trained during the next spell of " rest."

The 26th Northumberlands had a disagreeable affair on the night of the 2nd/3rd September, when they lost Second-Lieutenant N. A. Hunter, killed, P. N. Dixon, missing, and ten men killed and wounded, in an attempt to take a trench junction on top of a knoll in Triangle trench, which commanded two Hun trenches, and whence the Hun troubled us with machine gun and sniper fire. The Boche was very tender at this point, resenting all attempts to oust him. On the night of the 8th/9th September, while the 102nd Brigade was attacking farther south, an officer and thirty men of the 24th/27th Northumberlands, under the thermite bombardment, actually captured the point, killing many of garrison, and bringing back thirty Boches and one 'dog, with a loss of only one killed and seven wounded, but on the following night the Huns re-took the junction under a terrific trench mortar bombardment, rushing the trench on top of a returning wiring party. This was a nuisance, and we were anxious to have another shot at it, but higher authority said No'!

The 102nd Brigade having trained and rehearsed the forthcoming attack, returned to the line on the seventh. The eighth was spent in preparations, making up loads of wiring material, issuing the many requisites of a soldier who is about to " offend," etc. The Hun interfered greatly with this by bombarding our front and our dumps with heavy stuff. He also shelled the whole area concerned very heavily, while the assaulting battalions were forming, but in spite of this, at the time named in operation orders, eleven-forty-five p.m., the 21st and 23rd Northumberlands were duly formed up along the tape, in front of our line and three hundred and fifty yards from the Boche's trenches. Each battalion had two companies in the front line, each in four waves, of which the first was to cross the enemy's trench and form a screen on the far side, the second was to mop up the trench, and the third and fourth were to consolidate it. The other two companies were to carry up stores, wire, etc., cross the trench, without interfering with scrap, and proceed at once to run a line of wire along the whole front. At twelve-fifteen a.m. on 9th the guns started, a creeping barrage on the right, the main point of attack, a thermite bombardment of the left sector front, and the attack of the 24th/27th Northumberlands, already described, meant to deceive the Huns; also a heavy bombardment on Quenet Copse on our extreme right.

The creeping barrage moved forward perfectly, and the assaulting waves, following it, occupied the Boche line without trouble, save on the extreme right, where the right company of the 21st Northumberlands found the wire still in position, and in the morning mist lost direction, inclining to the left, so that the full length of Farm trench was not occupied, and sniping from this portion down the valley showed General Nicholson that the whole objective had not been captured. Elsewhere, however, our success was complete. In many places the enemy were seen to bolt as our men neared the trench, and in the trench itself were found many rifles and sets of equipment left by the fugitives. At one-thirty a.m., having heard of the success of the frontal attack, General Thomson ordered the 20th Northumberlands, holding the northern portion of Railway, to clear the remainder of that trench. Four bombing parties, of ten men

each, very soon cleared the trench, capturing four
Boche, and killing about twenty, and joined up with
the 23rd Battalion, without themselves suffering any
casualties.

To make his hold on the new trench secure,
General Thomson set two companies of the 22nd
Northumberlands, and two platoons of the Pioneers,
to work on a communication trench, to be called
Turnip Lane, which was to connect Martin post with
the right of the new line, but the Boche shelled the
area so hard that only some two hundred yards were
dug to a depth of two feet. In the meanwhile the
consolidation and wiring of the new line was pressed
on vigorously, and by daylight all was ready for the
reception of visitors. The first to arrive was a party
which counter-attacked on the right, and receiving a
warm reception, retired, but bombing was kept up
on this flank till noon, and a second attack was made
at eight a.m., but met with no better success than the
first.

The enemy on the right was very active with
his light trench mortars, and his snipers made all
movement in rear of the captured position most
difficult. It was one of these gentry who wounded
Colonel Porch while he was superintending the
consolidation work of the 23rd Northumberlands.
This was the third time that this good soldier and
much-loved commanding officer was wounded, and, to
our loss, he never rejoined us.

From dawn till eleven a.m. the Boche gunners
gave us a little respite, but from that hour onwards
they troubled us sore.

An effort was made by the 21st Northumberlands
at four-fifty p.m. to complete the task they had been
set by bombing southwards down the trench as far as
the top of the hill, but the Boche had chosen that
particular moment for attempting to turn them
out of the portion they held. The result was a heavy
bombardment by the guns of both sides, much bomb-

ing activity around the block in the trench, and no progress on either side. The night and the whole of the 10th passed without any incident of importance, except heavy hostile shelling, and at three a.m. on 11th we captured the remainder of our objective— a neat bit of work, carried out by a frontal attack from Villaret posts by two companies of the 22nd Northumberlands, preceded by a creeping barrage, and a flank bombing attack along Farm trench by " C " Company of 21st Northumberlands. This latter attack met with much resistance, and came under such heavy shell fire that the three bombing parties, one in and one on each side of the trench, had to call on the carriers following them for assistance, which was readily given, and the trench was cleared as far as the left flank of the 22nd Northumberlands, but the help of the 23rd farther up the trench on the left had to be requisitioned to aid in the consolidation. By four-forty-five a.m. General Thomson had the pleasure of reporting that the whole trench was in his hands, and wired along its whole front. Once again all arrangements for the reception of visitors were completed in good time. The first counter-attack, at six-thirty a.m., was easily defeated, but the enemy again advanced in close order at nine-thirty a.m. against the 22nd Northumberlands, whose rifles and Lewis guns wrought so faithfully with the dense mass that he did not repeat the performance.

The following morning, at two o'clock, General Thomson handed over the line to General Gore, and the 102nd Brigade marched off merrily to divisional reserve.

The bag of these three days amounted to some seventy prisoners, eight machine guns, two Granaten-werfer, a great many rifles, etc. The enemy's casualties were heavy, but the chief gain was the improved tactical position, which made a surprise impossible.

HARGICOURT
26th – 29th Aug. & 9th – 11th Sept. 1917.

Front Line 26th Aug. — — —
Black " " " —·—·—·
Red " " " —+—+—+
Forming " 9th Sept —+—+—+

A – Point on which right flank rested at daybreak 9th

B-C Objective of 2 Coys. 22nd North.ld Fus. on 11th Sept.

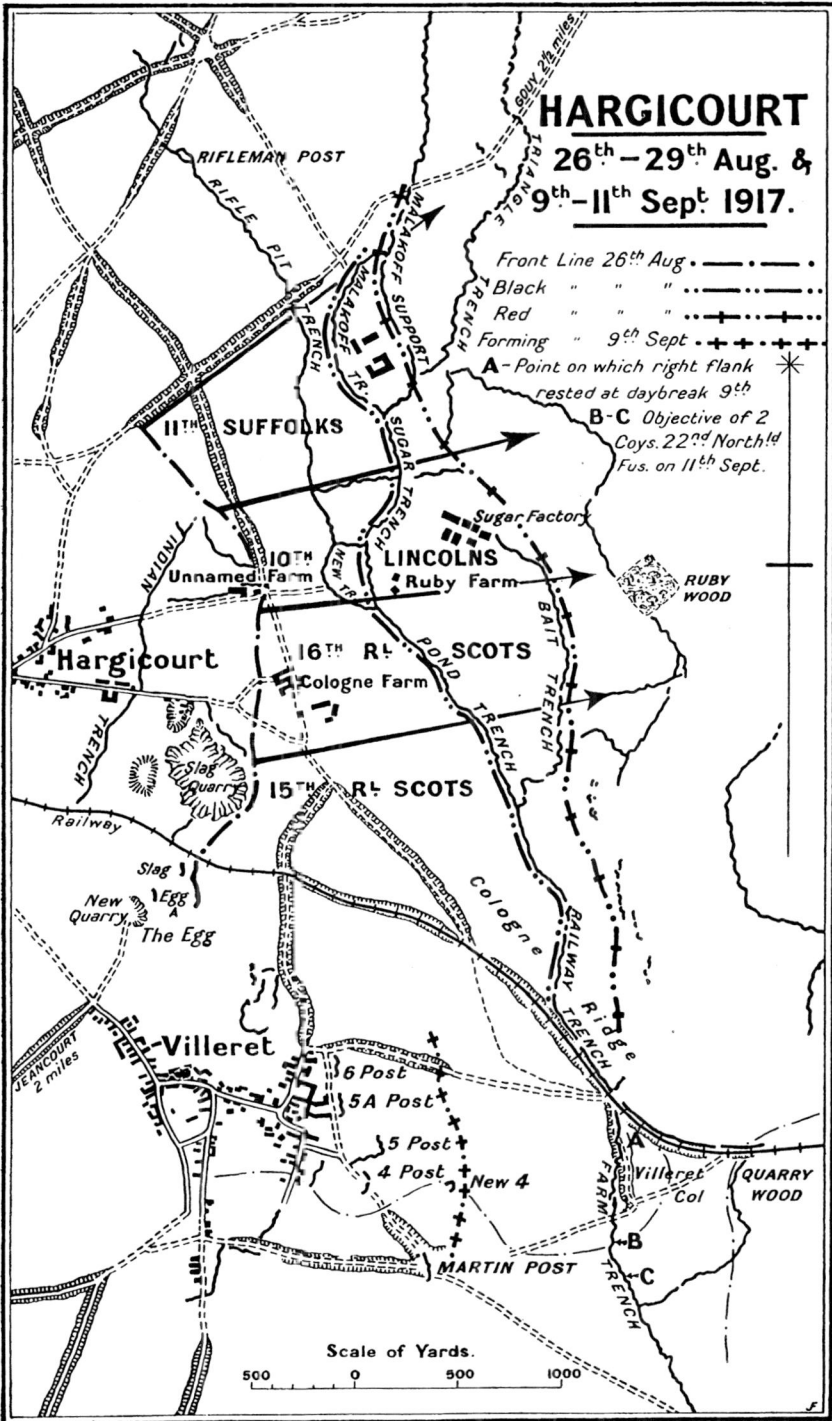

RIFLEMAN POST

SOUY 2½ miles

RIFLE PIT

TRIANGLE TRENCH

MALAKOFF SUPPORT TR.

MALAKOFF TRENCH

SUGAR TRENCH

11TH SUFFOLKS

INDIAN TRENCH

NEW TR.

Sugar Factory

10TH
Unnamed Farm

LINCOLNS
Ruby Farm

RUBY WOOD

BAIT TRENCH

Hargicourt

16TH Rl SCOTS
Cologne Farm

POND TRENCH

Slag Quarry

15TH Rl SCOTS

Cologne Trench

RAILWAY TRENCH

Railway

Slag Egg A

New Quarry
The Egg

Railway Ridge

JEANCOURT 2 miles

Villeret

6 Post
5A Post
5 Post
4 Post   New 4

Villeret Col

QUARRY WOOD

FARM TRENCH

MARTIN POST

B
C

Scale of Yards.
500   0   500   1000

Our casualties amounted to twenty-nine officers and three hundred and seventy-four other ranks, by no means excessive.   Divided as follows :

	Officers	Other ranks
20th Northumberlands	4	93
21st Northumberlands	9	93
22nd Northumberlands	2	37
23rd Northumberlands	13	138
102nd M. G. Company	0	6
102nd L. T. M. Battery	1	7
TOTAL	29	374

It was estimated that eighty-nine per cent of these casualties were caused by shell fire after the termination of the assault. General Thomson comments on the rapidity and excellence of the consolidation work, which he attributes to the instruction given by the officer of the 207th Field Company. The valuable assistance given by the Stoke's mortars during the defence, when they got off six hundred and fifty-five rounds, is also commented on. Captain R. R. Telford died of his wounds, Second-Lieutenants J. P. Henderson, H. H. H. Hoard, F. Hardy, and two officers of 23rd Northumberlands were killed.

During the rest of our stay in these parts we carried out no offensive operations, but patrolling went on regularly, and there were frequent scraps between patrols. On the night of the 21st/22nd six patrols were out, and they captured four Germans, and recaptured a prisoner of war who was escaping. One of the prisoners gave useful information of an attack which he thought was to come off shortly, so that when the Huns, at five a.m. on 23rd, under cover of a heavy bombardment, and in a thick mist, attacked Farm trench, the company of Suffolks holding it beat them off without difficulty. The response to the S.O.S. was particularly prompt, the guns concerned opening fire within a minute, and, in addition, sixteen Vicker's guns, covering the brigade, opened at once, and the sixteen covering the centre brigade switched over within four minutes, and all fired at their maximum pace for ten minutes, then slower for another ten, getting off four thousand three hundred rounds. The Stoke's guns on the front attacked were also busy, and the garrison made good use of its Lewis guns and rifles. Therefore it is not surprising to hear that few Huns got anywhere near the line. At daylight, some unfortunates were seen hiding in shell holes, and attempting to get away, and were dealt with by the rifles of the Suffolks.

The Huns continued to be very troublesome, shelling all parts of our position, and causing many casualties.

General Pulteney, commanding the 3rd Corps, paid us three visits during September, inspecting the brigades concerned in our two little battles, and bestowing medal ribbons on those who had earned them.

The wastage during the months June to September, inclusive, had been heavy. We had lost in killed, thirty-eight officers and four hundred and seventy-eight other ranks, and from all other causes, two hundred and thirty-eight officers and four thousand and forty-five other ranks. Until the last week of September the reinforcements received had not been sufficient to make good, to any considerable extent, the original deficiency, with which, as has already been stated, we started the month of June; in fact, in August our losses exceeded the reinforcements received. During the last week of September, how-ever, we received fifty-two officers and two thousand eight hundred and sixty-seven other ranks.

The new drafts contained very many men of only a few months' service, who were naturally but imperfectly trained; some, in fact, had never fired their rifles, and the value of those who had seen service was diminished by the fact that, in accordance with the system already commented on, few of them had ever served in the units to which they were now sent. If only all our old men could have returned each to his own unit how different things would have been!

The relief of the Division commenced on 27th September, and was completed on 29th, when, at ten a.m., General Nicholson handed over command of the line to General Daly, commanding the 24th Division.

Our gunners came with us, much to our joy. Their weapons required a thorough overhauling, and had to be sent direct to Inspector Ordinance Machinery as they were relieved.

Divisional Headquarters went to Basseux, about seven miles south-west of Arras, where they were housed in a dirty château in a dirtier village. The three Infantry Brigades had their quarters at Pommier, Bailleuval, and Blaireville. Training began at once, but was rudely interrupted by an order, received on 2nd October, to move to 5th Army area on 7th. This we duly did, and by the 9th we were all in and round Proven, in the infamous " Wipers " salient.

CHAPTER IX

THE first party to move north was the 101st Brigade and the three Field Companies which were to be employed on road making. A nasty job in the forward area, carried out under the worst weather conditions, and under almost continual shell fire.

Colonel Dobson considerably lessened the difficulties by the careful preparations he made. Sketch maps and duplicate notes on repairs of roads were distributed beforehand, and the orders were so clear and complete that, as a Field Company Commander states, "parties started work with very complete knowledge of what they had to do."

Although the work only lasted three days, it was severe and unpleasant, but it had its humorous side, for those lucky enough to be able to enjoy it. "Our first job was making roads (from Martin's Mill to Langemarck) ahead of the gunners during the advance, with results that surprised the Boche as much as ourselves. My company had a couple of thousand infantry as a working party for this job, and the sappers were engaged most of the time sprinting up and down dissuading people from following their natural inclination to make mud pies. The great thing is to get a solid foundation (a whole general service wagon was used to make a bottom in one shell hole), and to finish off with a good layer of road metal on top. One weary old soldier came staggering along with a sack full of something that

154

he had collected under very heavy fire among adjacent
ruins, and dumped on the road all the Boche bully
beef tins and household pots and pans he had been
able to find. ' What on earth is that for ? ' ' Orficer
told me to fetch all the *metal* I could find. ' '' The
writer's Field Company and his two thousand infantry
in the three days accomplished two thousand yards
of road, and had about one hundred casualties.
'' Shell fire pretty heavy all the time, but shooting
not good.''

The Division detrained at and near Proven (one
of the stations being appropriately named Hop-outre).
By the 9th October all units had arrived, and those
not on road work were training.

Our Pioneers had been in this unpleasant region
since early in July, and we found them encamped by
'' Dawson's Corner,'' near to Brielen, working on a
sixty centimetre railway, which had, since the beginning of the last offensive, on 31st July, been pushed
on from the canal bank, near Bridge Four, to St
Julien, with many branches stretching far and wide.
They had been much worried with long range shelling at the commencement of the offensive, and later
by nightly bombing raids, and had suffered a good
many casualties (forty horses were killed by one
bomb), but on the whole they said they had been
lucky.

For some time after our arrival the general
situation might be described as obscure, and what
we were to do, and when and where we were to do it,
was the subject of numerous contradictory orders,
the fact being that our fate depended on the success
or reverse of operations then pending, in which the
Boche had a good deal to say.

We now joined the 14th Corps, under Lord
Cavan, in the 5th Army, commanded by General Sir
Hubert Gough.

On the 12th October there was an attack on a
considerable scale, in which we had no part. The

result of the day's fighting in the waste of mud and
shell holes was that the 14th Corps got all its objectives except on its right, where the 4th Division had
to refuse its right flank owing to the 18th Division not
having succeeded in taking Poelcapelle. It was our
fate to relieve the 4th Division and take our share in
the next attempt at an advance. The 103rd Brigade
moved up to Stray Farm, east of Pilkem, during the
12th, and tried to relieve two battalions 4th Division
in the battle front at night. Owing to bad weather
and pitch darkness, this was only partly carried out,
but was completed during the following day and night.

General Nicholson took over command from
General Matheson at ten a.m. on 14th October, his
headquarters being in dug-outs in the Yser canal
bank, near to Bridge Four. He was no stranger in
these parts, having commanded the 16th Brigade, 6th
Division, for thirteen months in the Ypres salient.
Since then times had changed, and we no longer sat
patiently in waterlogged trenches, suffering whatever the Boche chose to send over, our gunners not
having enough ammunition to reply efficiently.

The operations which commenced on 31st July
had pushed the Boche so far back that it was a good
two hours' walk, mostly through what was Boche
territory, on 30th July, to the headquarters of the
103rd Brigade, in Alouette, on the outskirts of
Langemarck. The walk was over country which was
a mass of shell craters, salvage, guns, and men.
The ground surface being impossible, all walking
had to be done on duckboard tracks, which went to
within about one thousand to one thousand five
hundred yards of the front line, and were prolonged
nightly. The pill-box in which General Trevor's
headquarters were located was in one of the Boche
barrage lines, which made it rather uncomfortable,
and when the 102nd Brigade relieved the 103rd on
the night of 16th/17th, the Brigade Headquarters
was moved to another pill-box, Au Bon Gite, close

to the Pilkem-Langemarck road, also an unhealthy spot.

On its way up to carry out this relief, the 102nd Brigade was very unlucky, the 23rd and 21st Northumberlands being bombed by aeroplanes about one p.m., just after they had reached Malakoff camp. The former had two officers and six other ranks wounded, and the latter lost one officer and eight other ranks killed, and an officer and sixty-six other ranks wounded.

On the relief of the 103rd Brigade the divisional front was extended considerably, the 34th taking over the whole of the 17th Divisional front on its left, and on the night of 18th/19th it took over a further two hundred and fifty yards on this flank from the 35th Division.

On 17th October Divisional Headquarters moved back from the canal bank, which was only an advanced abode, to Welsh Farm, a camp near Elverdinghe, but moved up again on 21st for the coming attack. On the 19th the 101st Brigade moved in to the left of the front line, relieving the battalions of the 102nd Brigade in the left subsector. On this day we received a warning order that we should be relieved on the night of the 23rd/24th. We certainly did not receive the warning with regret. It may safely be asserted that no division ever left the Ypres salient with regret. Conditions there, even at the best of times, were such that life was sheer misery for all in the line. A correspondent writing from near our front line at this time says: "I won't attempt to describe the conditions under which the infantry have been existing; for one thing, it is rather recent history, and for another I know of no words to describe them. One outstanding feature, however, is the extraordinary endurance of the men—an endurance, under impossible conditions, which is almost superhuman."

On the 20th October the 15th and 16th Royal

Scots relieved the 10th Lincolns and 11th Suffolks in the 101st Brigade front line.   Both battalions lost their commanding officers on this day, Lieutenant-Colonels Guard and Stephenson both being gassed while reconnoitring.   Both recovered and rejoined us later, but their loss just at this moment was very unfortunate, as the operation before their battalions was a difficult one.   Not only was the state of the ground such as to make any attack most difficult, but, owing to reasons which were unknown to us, the line of our opening barrage did not conform to our front line, but was so arranged that the left company of the 15th and right company of the 15th Royal Scots had to form up some two hundred yards behind the string of connected shell holes, which in this part represented the front line.   In the absence of any landmarks in the waste of mud, it was a very difficult task to form up a battalion on such a line on a dark wet night, and the difficulty was increased by the heavy shell fire under which the assembling had to be done.   The 16th Royal Scots were on the left, next to the 23rd Manchesters of the 35th Division. The 15th Royal Scots were next to them, each with two companies in front, and two in support.   Both battalions suffered many casualties from heavy shell fire on their way up, and during the day and night previous to the attack.   Their front was Aden House to Gravel Farm, about a thousand yards, and they had, in the attack, to pivot on the right of the 15th, swinging the line round till the left of the 16th, in touch with the 23rd Manchesters, rested on the Six Roads.   This entailed the left flank advancing about one thousand one hundred yards.

On the right of the 15th Royal Scots, a company of the 20th Northumberland Fusiliers held about three hundred and fifty yards to Bower House.   This company was to stand fast, keeping the enemy on its front and flanks under fire, and thus assisting the troops on its right and left.   The attack on the 102nd

POELCAPELLE.

From an Air Photograph taken on 17th August, 1917. Two months before the attack by the 34th Division.

Brigade front was to be carried out by the 24th/27th Northumberlands, who were placed under the G.O.C. 102nd Brigade for this purpose. Previous to the battalion going up to the front line, General Nicholson inspected it, and explained what he wanted them to do, which was to keep in touch with and cover the flank of the 18th Division on their right. The left flank of the two companies, which held the front line, rested on Bower House, and in the attack this flank was to remain fixed, while the right swung forward, keeping pace with the left battalion of the 18th Division, till it reached a point some six hundred yards northeast of Poelcapelle, and about one hundred yards north of the Poelcapelle-Stadenreef road. The 18th Division troops were to sweep well north of the village in their attack, and capture and hold Requete Farm, which was really in the 34th Division area, but was allotted as part of the 18th Division objective.

The task of the 24th/27th was easier than that of the Royal Scots battalions. The commanding officer evidently believes that brevity is the soul of diary writing, and records only : " 22nd October, advanced against the enemy in conjunction with the 18th Division on our right. All objectives gained. Casualties light. Held line till midnight 24th, relieved, and moved back to Stray Farm. Billeted there." Fortunately I have General Nicholson's authority for stating that they did a bit more. In the advance the right Company Commander noticed that the left battalion of the 18th Division had overlooked Requete Farm, and captured it, lining up with the Norfolks on the outskirts of Poelcapelle.

The two battalions of the Royal Scots had a bad day. For particulars of the former battalion's doings I have to thank Major C. Anderson, who was Second-in-Command, from whose account I take extracts.

" Our positions were simply a line of shell holes full of water. The conditions were past speaking

about, mud and filth up to the neck." Owing to the
peculiarity in the barrage line already mentioned the
assaulting waves only just got into position in time.
" The attack commenced, zero being five-thirty-five
a.m., and we advanced on a two company front, ' A '
on the right, ' B ' on the left, ' C ' in support, and
' D ' in reserve. The enemy put down a heavy
barrage, but our right company I find in the battalion
war diary the following entry : " At six a.m. about
one hundred of the enemy, led by an officer, advanced
towards an officer and thirteen men of the right
company, ' A.' The German officer called upon
our officer to surrender. The British officer shot the
German officer, and the thirteen men opened fire.
Only one of the one hundred men was seen to return
to his lines." Major Anderson thinks that this
officer was Second-Lieutenant Simpson, who was
killed later in the day. " The left company reached a
point near their objective, which was a line of concrete pill-boxes, which had appeared to be deserted,
but which were found to be occupied by enemy
machine gunners, who had an easy target at our men
floundering about in the mud, and only very few of
this company came back, fourteen in all, and no
officers. ' C ' Company was ordered up to support,
but was unable to cross the Brombeek, which was in
flood and heavily barraged. The company in
reserve, ' D,' was at Taube Farm, and could move
neither one way nor the other, owing to terrific
barrage all round. The whole affair was a disaster
as far as we were concerned ; communication was
broken between headquarters and the companies, and
between companies themselves. Battalion Headquarters was at Olga House, and when we got into it,
it was wellnigh impossible to get out, owing to the
barrage, and runners could not come near it for hours
at a time."

When Lieutenant-Colonel Guard was gassed,
Major Selby took command of the 15th Royal Scots,

but he was taken seriously ill at Olga House, and it was with difficulty that he was got back when the battalion was relieved.

The casualties of the battalion are recorded in the war diary as seven officers and two hundred and eighty-eight other ranks.

The 16th Royal Scots fared no better. While forming up they were heavily shelled by the enemy, and also coming under our own barrage (due to the difficulty in forming up correctly already alluded to), suffered such heavy casualties that only enough men remained for one wave, but these advanced at zero, in line with the Manchesters of the 35th Division, and the left companies, "C" and "D", reached the final objective—the pill-boxes about Six Roads—where they came under heavy machine gun fire. Thence they covered with rifle fire the advance of the Manchesters, who tried to get round the left of the pill-boxes, but were held up by wire. A Lewis gun crew of the 16th pushed on and captured a pill-box, taking six prisoners, but trace of them was afterwards lost. At seven a.m. the enemy made a strong counter-attack, but the rifles of the Scots were used with deadly effect, and the attack failed.

For some time the gallant little party of Manchester men and Scots held on, but they suffered heavily, and at last the survivors had to give way, retiring sullenly to a position east of Egypt house, where they took up a position under Second-Lieutenant Cruickshank.

The right companies were held up by heavy machine gun fire from the same huts that cost the 15th Battalion so dearly. Many of their rifles were so clogged with mud as to be useless, and they were driven back by a counter-attack. Second-Lieutenant J. H. Hope and twenty men were last seen near some huts north-east of Turenne Crossing.

It was an anxious day for all in command. News from the front was scarce. It had been impos-

L

sible to bury cables, and the state of the ground made the progress of the best of runners painfully slow. The enemy shelled the whole of the battle area severely throughout the day, and sent over many gas shells. The 103rd Brigade Headquarters, in Stray Farm, got such a dose of this, that Lieutenant-Colonel Moulton Barrett was placed in command of all the troops east of Marsouin Farm, with Captain Rotherford and Lieutenant Black as his Staff Officers. During the night of the 22nd/23rd the remnants of the 15th and 16th Royal Scots were relieved by the 10th Lincolns and 11th Suffolks. It was a most difficult operation, owing to the impossibility of the depleted and disorganised battalions sending guides to meet the relieving troops. However, the relief was completed without any accidents, and though the position remained somewhat obscure, a line was formed, and the night and the next day passed without any attack being made by the enemy, though he shelled us very freely.

When General Nicholson inspected the 101st Brigade a few days later, he summed up the action of the 22nd October thus :

"General Gore ; Officers, Non-Commissioned Officers, and Men of the 101st Brigade, I had you out here this morning just to see how you looked after this last rather strenuous time in the trenches, or rather shell holes. I am very glad to see how well you look. You have been through a great deal, and have done extraordinarily well. This morning I have had handed to me your Brigadier's report on the operations, and am going to read you a little of it, because it exactly expresses what I intended to say : ' In view of the enormous difficulties encountered, it is greatly to the credit of the attacking battalions (that is to say, the 15th and 16th Royal Scots) that succeeded in forming up, though in greatly diminished numbers, and in making so gallant an attempt to carry out the task allotted to them, and it was through no fault of theirs that they were unable to hold what they had gained. . . . Great credit is also due to the 10th Lincolnshire Regiment and 11th Suffolk Regiment, in taking over the line, without a hitch, on the night of the 22nd/23rd, without guides and under a harassing fire.'

"Those remarks put the whole thing in a nutshell. The behaviour of the two attacking battalions, as brought out in the detailed report which has been sent me, is beyond all praise, and as regards the 10th Lincolnshires and 11th Suffolks, although they had no actual attacking to do, I always look upon a relief on the night of an action, under most favourable circumstances, as a most difficult operation, and on this particular night the difficulties were increased a hundredfold.

"Now, this brigade has been over the top four times this year. Everything that you had to do has been done to the utmost of your ability. On two occasions out of four you have done everything that you were asked to do, and done it well, and the failure on the remaining two occasions was no fault of yours in either case.

"I can say nothing more, except to congratulate you again on your magnificent behaviour, and to say that I am more than proud to have such a brigade under my command."

The following telegram was received from the 5th Army, dated 25th October : "The 34th Division has shown the greatest pluck during its short stay in the 5th Army. Ill fortune and bad weather have prevented its operations being rewarded with complete success, but, despite this, the Division has contributed to the successful course of the great battle now in progress. Not the least of its achievements has been the fine work of its Pioneer Battalion on light railway construction. I wish all ranks good luck in the future."

During the month of October, of which only sixteen days were spent in the forward area, our casualties amounted to :

	Killed	Wounded	Missing	Total
Officers .	16	76	11	103
Other ranks	287	1013	394	1694
	303	1089	405	1797

During the period 10th to 27th October, thirty-four officers and eight hundred and forty-six men were evacuated sick.

On the 23rd October orders were received that the Division, less artillery, would be relieved by the 50th and 57th Divisions, and proceed to another area. A welcome order; both men and officers were done to a turn. The conditions of ground and shell fire were the worst we ever experienced. The relief began on the 24th, and was completed by four a.m. the next day. The wearied troops were given two days in the back area, and then moved by rail to the 6th Corps area, and on 31st the 103rd Brigade was in the front line again in the new area. Our Pioneer Battalion rejoined us before we left " The Salient."

The Divisional Artillery did not rejoin us till the 11th November. They had a very rough time in the muddy margins of the Broembeek, and they lost heavily, but they did right good service. The 152nd Brigade covered our front on the fatal 22nd, and fired seven thousand eight hundred and fifty-eight rounds on that day. An ordinary day's shooting was about two thousand three hundred rounds. After our departure they covered the fronts of the divisions that relieved us, and on the 26th they took their share in the attack by the 14th, 18th Corps and the French Army.

We now joined the 3rd Army, commanded by Lieutenant-General Sir Julian Byng, and were in the 6th Corps, Lieutenant-General J. A. Haldane. The 102nd and 103rd Brigades took over the right and left subsectors of the left division front, and the 101st

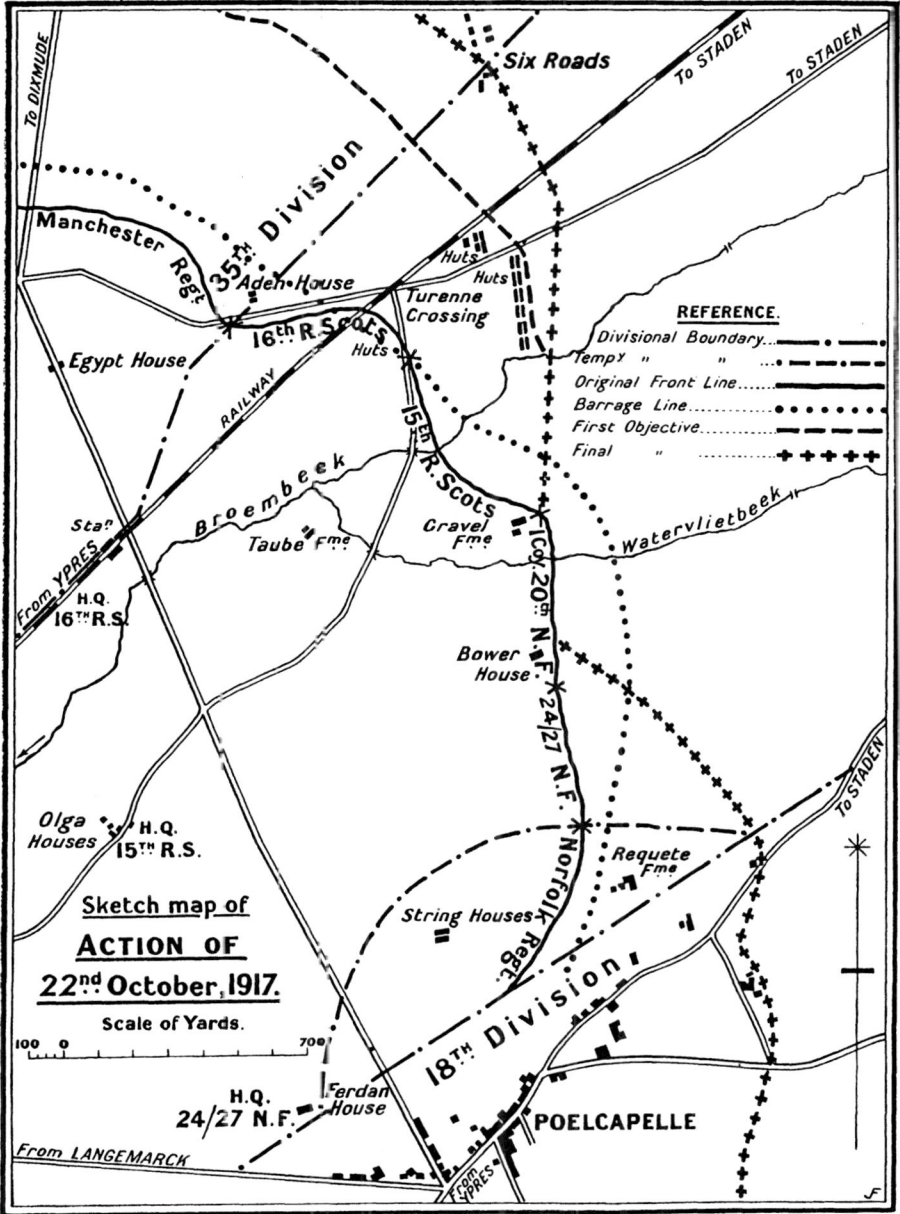

To DIXMUDE

To STADEN
To STADEN

Six Roads

35TH Division

Manchester Regt

Aden House

Huts

Turenne Crossing

Huts

16TH R.Scots

Egypt House

Huts

RAILWAY

15TH R.Scots

REFERENCE.

Divisional Boundary..........
Tempy   "   "..........
Original Front Line..........
Barrage Line..........
First Objective..........
Final   "   ....

Broembeek

Stan

From YPRES

Taube Fme

Gravel Fme

I Coy. 20TH N.F.

Watervlietbeek

H.Q.
16TH R.S.

Bower House

24/27 N.F.

Olga Houses

H.Q.
15TH R.S.

Requete Fme

To STADEN

Sketch map of

ACTION OF

22nd October, 1917.

Scale of Yards.

100   0   700

String Houses

Norfolk Regt.

18TH Division

POELCAPELLE

H.Q.
24/27 N.F.

Ferdan House

From LANGEMARCK

From YPRES

were in reserve. The relief was completed without incident by ten a.m. on 2nd November, when General Harper, commanding 51st Division, gave over command to General Nicholson. We had the 16th Division on our right and the 4th Division, 17th Corps, on our left. Our front extended from opposite Fontaine les Croisilles on the right to the Arras-Cambrai road on the left. Divisional Headquarters was at Boisleux au Mont; the Reserve Brigade was in Durham Lines, Northumberland Lines, and Henin Camp. The headquarters of the two brigades in the line were respectively north-west and south-west of Wancourt. The divisional reinforcement camp, under command of Major Vignoles, 10th Lincolns, was established at Achiet le Petit. Major Vignoles had visited this site before our journey to Ypres, with a view to starting the camp. At that time the site was " a field of barbed wire and shell holes," but while we had been away some huts had been erected, and some progress made towards forming a decent camp, and under Vignoles' vigorous and skilled direction it soon became a model of all a training camp should be.

" All round this camp the country was deserted, covered with old trenches; every bank had gun pits or entrances to dug-outs in it, and the whole country was littered with dud shells, old dumps of ammunition and bombs . . . as wild and bleak as the highest moor in Yorkshire, whereas in peace time it was fertile and well planted with sugar beet." " Near the camp was a big casualty clearing station, and one day, when two of the charming nurses, escorted by two gallant officers of the R.A.M.C., were walking close by the bombing school, the bombing officer threw a bomb. He was well rewarded by seeing the nurses, in their fright, wildly clasp their respective officers ! and I expect the M.O.'s were very much obliged to him. What do you think ? "

Major Vignoles about this time was appointed to

command the 9th Northumberlands, much to the
sorrow of the Lincolnshire lads, but to the advantage
of the Division in general, and the 9th in particular.

We stayed in this section of the line till 29th
January, and from 27th December we had all three
brigades in the line, the Corps front being reorganised and held by two instead of three divisions. The
101st Brigade took over the front of the left Brigade
of the 40th Division. Our stay was peaceful, and
without any special incidents, as far as we personally
were concerned, but during November we prepared,
very completely, for the contingency of the Boche
opposite us retiring, as a consequence of a surprise
attack on the Cambrai front, which was made on 20th
of that month. Some of us witnessed a rehearsal,
carried out by a brigade of the 29th Division and
about fourteen tanks, without realising the great
event for which they were preparing.

Our Pioneers were taken from us to assist the
5th Corps in the laying of railways through the newly
captured territory, and were nearly captured themselves when the Boche made his great counter-
attack, which was stayed by the magnificent advance
of the Guards. The Cambrai attack not having been
as successful as was expected, the Pioneers returned
to us on 6th December.

Throughout this period patrols were active every
night, especially during November, when a retirement of the enemy was thought possible, and there
were many encounters, which generally ended
favourably for us. From prisoners taken in one of
these little affairs in January, we learnt that we had
opposite us the 41st I.R., 1st Reserve Ersatz
Regiment, 60th Reserve I.R., and 452nd I.R., of
which we caught an officer, who, on the completion
of his examination, inquired whether he was going
to be shot.

The 26th Northumberlands carried out a raid
on the night of 5th/6th December, for which four

officers and seventy-four other ranks trained for four days. Unfortunately it was not a success; Second-Lieutenant J. Jenkins and a small party got into the enemy's line, only to find it empty, and the other parties were met with very heavy machine gun fire, losing Second-Lieutenants D. Kinnaird and G. Laughton and three other ranks killed, and seven wounded.

In December indications pointed to the enemy being about to attack rather than retire, and vigilance was exercised and much energy expended in strengthening the line.

Christmas of 1917 was celebrated in comfort. Our versatile play-actors, the Chequers Company, put on Dick Whittington, a real good show. The Corps Commander, after witnessing the pantomime and dining at Divisional Headquarters, announced that it was the pleasantest evening he had spent during the war. It would be invidious to inquire which entertainment contributed most to this eminently satisfactory result. Shall we say, Honours easy?

During December Lieutenant-Colonel Braine handed over the duties of G.S.O.1 to Lieutenant-Colonel Sir T. A. A. M. Cunninghame, Bart., D.S.O., and joined the 29th Division in the same capacity.

Lieutenant-Colonel W. G. Thomson, D.S.O., who had commanded 152nd Brigade, F.R.A., since the start, also left us, to our loss, and to the gain of the 4th Division of which he became C.R.A.

The 103rd Brigade got a new commander, Lieutenant-Colonel J. G. Chaplin, Cameronians, being appointed Brigadier-General vice Trevor, whose health had succumbed to the rigours of The Salient.

Captain B. C. B. Tower, M.C., Royal Fusiliers, arrived at Divisional Headquarters in February, as G.S.O.2.

Our losses during 1917 were :

	Killed	Wounded	Missing	Sick	Totals	Reinforcements
Officers ...	129	392	56	210	787	806
Other ranks	1446	8262	2218	5796	17722	18577
Totals ...	1575	8654	2274	6006	18509	19383

Early in January we had bad weather, and after much snow had fallen, a rapid thaw on 15th made communication trenches in the 101st Brigade area almost impassable. Carrying parties had to move over the top, and there was difficulty in keeping up the supplies of the garrisons of the front line. On the 16th an inter-battalion relief was much interfered with by these conditions. A company of the 16th Royal Scots, after being relieved, was stuck in a communication trench till nightfall, when it struggled home over the top in a very exhausted state. It was cheering to know from reports of our airmen that the Boche were in a similar plight.

On 29th January we were relieved by the 3rd Division, and went back to the Gommiécourt area to train, our gunners, as usual, remaining in the line, and our Pioneers and 208th Field Company, after one day out, marching back to Henin Camp to work for the Corps.

During February, the infantry, pioneers, and machine gunners of the Division were reorganised. Northumberland, from which nine of our original battalions came, is by no means one of the most populous counties, and the response to the bugle call was so ready that by January, 1916, twenty-five battalions of the old Fighting Fifth were overseas, and these were followed by several more of the second line Territorials. The population of the county was inadequate to keep so many battalions supplied with recruits, and therefore some of the battalions had to be struck out of the army list. Thus we lost the 20th, 21st, 24th, 26th, and 27th from our 102nd and 103rd Brigades, and the three remaining of our original Northumberland Infantry units were grouped together into the 102nd Brigade. The number of battalions in a brigade was now reduced from four to three. The 103rd Brigade was made up by taking the 10th Lincolns from the 101st and bringing the 1st East Lancashire (this the first regular unit of any arm in the Division). The brigades at the end of the first week of February stood thus: 101st Brigade, 15th and 16th Royal Scots, and 11th Suffolks; 102nd Brigade, 22nd, 23rd, and 25th Northumberlands; 103rd Brigade, 9th Northumberland Fusiliers, 10th Lincolns, and 1st East Lancashire.

At the same time all Pioneer Battalions were reorganised on a three company basis, and the machine gunners were formed into battalions. Our three Machine Gun Companies expanded, by the inclusion of 240th Machine Gun Company and by volunteers from the infantry into the 34th Machine Gun Battalion, with four companies and a complete staff under the command of Lieutenant-Colonel E. H. Kendrick, who had long commanded the 11th Suffolks.

On the 10th February we moved farther back into General Headquarters reserve, our Divisional Headquarters being at Le Cauroy, and about the same time our gunners, much to their own surprise, found themselves beyond the reach of the Boche guns in the same neighbourhood.

Training went on all the time, combined with recreation. The Divisional League Football final was won by the 16th Royal Scots, and the tug-of-war by the 22nd Northumberlands. Our quarters were distinctly comfortable; the General in the château cemented the *entente cordiale* by an interchange of hospitalities with his host, the Count and Countess Kergohlay. Humbler folk enjoyed themselves also: " Then followed a short and peaceful period in a little red and white French village, where the only tiles off had been removed by the wind, the only broken windows had been smashed by small boys. Here we fattened on hen's eggs and cow's butter, and played at tin soldiers—forming fours and sloping arms just as if there was no war on."

CHAPTER X

IN a heavy gale, and showers of snow, we took over the centre sector of the 6th Corps front. The 101st and 102nd Brigades went in on the 1st and 2nd March, the former being on the left, where it had the troops of the 3rd Division on its left, the junction line being east of the top of Henin Hill at Pug Avenue; thence the front line inclined south-south-east across the valley of the Sensée River, and up to the summit of the Hendecourt-Bullecourt-Longatte ridge. Bullecourt, the scene of much heavy fighting in 1917, was held by the 59th Division, the dividing line being at Pelican 'Avenue. The line between our right and left brigades was at Juno Lane, leading back into Factory Lane. The 103rd was Reserve Brigade, with its headquarters in Hamelincourt, where also was the 10th Lincolns, the 9th Northumberlands and 1st East Lancashires being in Ervillers. Divisional Headquarters were in Gommiécourt Château, one of the few buildings remaining in this land of ruins. By the 5th the relief was complete, the Machine Gun Battalion and the Divisional Artillery having taken over from their opposite numbers, and the high winds and snow showers having given place to bright spring weather. The Boche was unusually quiet, and to us in the line all things looked as if we were in for a pleasant time, but among those higher up on the military ladder, appearances were held to be deceitful, and from information received from prisoners,

171

deserters, and other sources, it soon began to be generally known that another offensive was in preparation, but on this occasion the offender was to be the Boche. On the night of the 9th/10th a deserter gave himself up to the 59th Division, and described more or less accurately what actually took place on the 21st March, but placed the date of the attack on 13th. He described accurately, in great detail, the rehearsals of the attack which his battalion had been practising.

From this it was possible to guess that the Boche meant to smash his way through the 59th Division line at Bullecourt, then wheel northwards, taking our right brigade in flank. Though information from such a source was open to suspicion, General Nicholson took precautions against such tactics, strengthening his flank defences along Pelican Avenue and Écoust Switch, and placing a company of the battalion of the Divisional Reserve at disposal of the Brigadier of the right brigade for use on this flank.

On the night 12th/13th our guns put down counter-preparation, i.e., every sort of gun we had blazed away on what we hoped were the assembly positions and lines of communications of the enemy. The 13th passed quietly, perhaps in consequence of our bombardment. Those not in the know began to think that all the talk of the Boche offensive had been a blind, and that it was we that were about to attack. We moved up into battle positions and waited. The Boche did nothing; he was quieter than usual, not a gun registered. Night after night our guns blazed away. Work was carried on as usual, but always under the disadvantage that everyone had to be ready at any moment to get to his battle position. Days went by, and nothing happened. Every morning the patrols pushed out and examined the front, right up to the Boche lines, and on their return telegrams were sent to report the results of their explorations.

Those in the line undoubtedly took the situation

more quietly than those behind; they knew less, and
" where ignorance, etc.," there was a tendency to
accuse those farther back of being unnecessarily
anxious, and one battalion's morning report read :
" Patrols report all clear, General Headquarters can
stand down."

On the 14th reports were received from the 5th
Army, on our right, that prisoners gave 15th or 16th
as the probable date of the attack. On the 15th we
noted that the Boche opposite had cut gaps in his
own wire. On 18th a prisoner, taken by the Corps
on our left, gave the 18th or 19th as the date of the
assault. One could not help wondering whether these
communicative gentry were not being sent over,
" according to plan," to upset our nerves, or by constant cries of " Wolf " render us careless.

On the 19th the 102nd Brigade, which had been
relieved by the 103rd on 7th again, took over the right
sub-sector. The 103rd now had its three battalions
disposed close up, one behind each flank and one in
rear of the centre. (Note.—Battle dispositions are
shown on Map, and descriptions of them are omitted
to save space.)

The 40th Division, which was in Corps reserve,
was brought up closer, but a time came when we
wished its units had been closer still.

From the 5th the weather had been fine, warm,
and almost summerlike. On 19th heavy rain fell,
and the morning of the 20th was wet, but in the
afternoon it cleared up and the sun came out. Truly
the stars in their courses fought for the Hun, for the
result of this rain, followed by warm sun, was a misty
morning on 21st March, a date that most of those in
the 3rd and 5th Armies will never forget.

The usual morning and periodic reports recorded
in the divisional diary of that day show nothing to
excite suspicion : " two-forty a.m., patrols report
all clear. Two-thirty-five a.m., right brigade reports
enemy patrol driven back; no sign of attack." So

the reports went on : " Five-twenty-six, 3rd Division morning report, situation quiet." Then, " Five-thirty-three a.m., 102nd Brigade. Left battalion reports heavy enemy artillery fire and intense gas shelling all along front. No S.O.S. sent up." From this time onwards the messages all tell of war, but with varying intensity. " Five-fifty a.m., Brigade-Major, 34th R.A. Shelling slight on left front. Heaviest on right group R.F.A., whose forward lines to infantry are all gone. Shelling on St Leger and Croisilles."

This early cutting of the telegraph lines had serious results. At six a.m. General Chaplin was directed to move his headquarters to the same line of shelters on the Henin-St Leger road which sheltered General Gore and his staff, and at one-fifteen p.m. a further move to the 102nd Brigade Headquarters was ordered, so as to be nearer the storm centre. The airmen at this time reported, " No massing of enemy in trenches of Cherisy and Fontaine." Six-forty a.m. the G.S.O.1 of 59th Division reports : " Fire mostly on Bullecourt, but some also on right brigade. No S.O.S. raised yet. Fire generally slackening." Five minutes later 102nd Brigade reports : " No communications with battalions since six a.m. Lines down. Mist prevents visual signalling. Fire seems less. 176th Brigade (left brigade of 59th Division) reports heaviest fire on their left. No S.O.S. anywhere." About an hour later G.S.O.1 of the 59th Division sends : " We are through to all our battalions. No one sent up S.O.S. Shelling mostly H.E.," but a few minutes later, seven-fifty-eight a.m., the 59th Division wires : " Shelling. Gas replacing H.E. No S.O.S. Right brigade headquarters communication cut off from its battalions." Now suddenly the interest shifts to the other flank, for at eight-ten a.m. 160th Brigade, R.F.A., suddenly informs Divisional Headquarters that " Enemy are in our front line, between Rotten trench and First

Avenue " (i.e., extreme right of 3rd Division). When asked, 3rd Division say they know nothing of this, but add that they are out of touch by telephone. At eight-thirty 3rd Division admits the accuracy of 160th observer, but adds that enemy has been ejected by 9th Brigade. This was evidently a feint to attempt to deceive us as to the real point of attack. To increase our bewilderment the fire on the left decreased about this time. At nine a.m. 102nd Brigade wired that it was in touch with 176th Brigade, and no attack had been made. At nine-thirty comes a message from 23rd Northumberlands, telling of heavy destructive fire, especially on Tiger trench; " from information from wounded officers, they seem to be having a very bad time. We have not seen the S.O.S. go up. Runners from this end are casualties. Nothing able to cross hostile barrage."

Very early Gommiécourt was heavily shelled, which made General Nicholson sure the blow was going to fall, and though the 59th Division still reported no change in situation, he felt that the deserter had spoken the truth, and warned General Thomson to be ready to make use of a company of the 1st East Lancashires should he need it to relieve a company of the 25th Northumberlands, in brigade reserve, in railway reserve trench. 102nd Brigade telegrams, timed eight-fifty, received at Divisional Headquarters at nine-fifty-two, says, " Right battalion (22nd Northumberlands) heavy barraged, but all right."

At ten-six a.m. the G.O.C. 59th Division telephones : " Left battalion, left brigade, 59th Division, reports, nine-fifty-five a.m. enemy now advancing." And four minutes later he adds, " 59th left sector attacked enemy through front line, but not certain how far they have got. Right brigade not attacked."

So the blow had fallen, and in the expected spot.

At ten-thirty Divisional Headquarters heard from the 6th Corps that the attack had developed from

just right (south) of Lagnicourt to just north of
Bullecourt. "Bombardment extends Bullecourt to
Rheims."

Nothing further is heard from the 59th for some
time. At eleven-fifty a.m. the 102nd Brigade
reports that no attack has yet been made on its front.
Shelling still severe on first and second system, and
patrols are being sent from reserve battalion (25th
Northumberland Fusiliers) to try and clear up situation on right. At twelve-fifteen p.m. comes a
dramatic telephone message from 59th Division,
pregnant with evil : " 34th Division right holds on.
Apparently 59th line runs down Pelican Avenue to
U.27.c, thence to C.4. Situation farther south
obscure, but situation of right of 59th Division and
left of 6th Division believed critical."

This meant that the right flank of the 102nd
Brigade troops holding the first system was completely uncovered.

On receipt of this bad news the 6th Corps, at
twelve-ten p.m., ordered up the 40th Division, the
120th Brigade being directed into the third line
system in the 59th Division area, the 121st Brigade
from Blaireville to Hamelincourt, and the 119th
Brigade, after some delay, was placed at the disposal
of the 34th Division. The distances that these
reinforcements had to travel caused them to arrive
rather later than the hard-pressed troops in the front
system would have liked.

So far we have watched matters from Divisional
Headquarters, now we must get nearer the front.
The diary of the 22nd Northumberlands, which held
the right of the line, tells of the enemy breaking in
to the battalion on his right and forcing back his
right company as far as Gollywog trench. Reinforcements were hurried to the spot, and the enemy were
held for the time. This battalion had been under
very heavy fire since five-thirty a.m. Gas masks
had been worn for three and a half hours, and an

officer who went into Tiger trench, the support trench, about noon found it blown in and most of the garrison killed and partly buried. A company of the 25th Northumberlands was sent to the assistance of the 22nd, and was employed to form a defensive flank to the right along Ecoust Switch, but the progress of the enemy was too rapid to allow of this being held. By a quarter to one the ruins of Ecoust were occupied, and the position was getting very critical. With a view to helping the 59th Division, in whose area most of the trouble was, General Nicholson sent Lieutenant-Colonel Earle, commanding the 1st East Lancashires, the right battalion of his reserve brigade, to see the Brigadier of the 176th Brigade, 59th Division, at his headquarters at l'Homme Mort, with a view to arranging for a combined counter-attack to recover Ecoust, but this attack never came off. The 176th Brigade troops were all heavily engaged, and one company of the 1st East Lancashires had already been sent to aid the 22nd and 25th Northumberlands in their efforts to defend their right flank, and another was detained by Colonel Vignoles to aid the 9th Northumberlands in the defence of the third system, so that Colonel Earle could only get hold of two companies, but with these he did invaluable service, pushing forward about four p.m., just in time to forestall the Boche in his attempt to seize the firing line of the third system to the left of the Ecoust-Mory road, thus protecting the headquarters of the 175th and 176th Brigades at l'Homme Mort.

With a view to meeting the danger on the right flank, the three remaining companies of the 25th Northumberlands had, as early as noon, been ordered to move to the south and form a line facing south-south-west, with the left at the junction of Bunhill Row and Pelican. The first company to get the order was under Captain T. McLachlan, M.C., who at once sent two platoons, under Second-Lieutenant Bowmer, along Bunhill Row towards Pelican, while

M

he went with the rest of the company along the Croisilles-Ecoust road to the top of the spur known as the Hog's back. As soon as he got over the crest he came under the fire of masses of the enemy, several battalions strong, on his right rear, and had to retire rapidly, till he came to the support line of the second system, where he was joined by " A " Company of the battalion, under Second-Lieutenant Vipond. McLachlan tried to hold this line, though it was faced the wrong way for the present position of the enemy, who continued to outflank him, and he continued his retirement till he reached the railway embankment, and lined it from the bend south-east of Croisilles, to the cross-roads some seven hundred yards along the line towards St Leger, which he states was at about two p.m. He also pushed men down the sunken road to the south-west. He held on to this position till dark, being joined, shortly after arriving at the railway, by " B " Company of his battalion, which had come down the Sensée Valley from its stand-to position in the second system, and by men of various battalions, who had got separated from their units.

When McLachlan's little party was driven in a north-westerly direction from the Hog's back, the enemy, which pursued him, passed in rear of Bunhill Row, in which trench were the headquarters of the three battalions of the 102nd Brigade. What happened here was long a matter of conjecture, but full details are now available, and I have been allowed the use of an account written by Lieutenant W. G. Mitchell, of 160th Brigade, R.F.A., who was on duty with these headquarters on that fatal day, and have also met other officers who were present.

When the bombardment started it was at first thought to be retaliation for our " shoot " of 12/13th, but it was soon realised that a general action had commenced. The headquarters were shelled with H.E. and gas by guns of all calibres, and when Colonel Charlton asked Lieutenant Mitchell to put down the

S.O.S. it was found that all the lines were broken.
In a very short time communication on both sides
was interrupted not only on the artillery but also on
the infantry lines. As soon as it was light, efforts
were made to mend the artillery line, but this proved
impossible, on account of the severity of the barrage.
Rockets were fired, and carrier pigeons were released.
The buried cable was restored at intervals, but communication was only possible for short periods.
Lieutenant Mitchell then went to Pelican to try to
open visual signalling, but the mist was too thick.
All this time efforts were being made from Brigade
Headquarters to restore communications; mounted
men were sent out, but the return of riderless horses
told the tale of failure. Lieutenant W. Drake and
Sergeant G. E. Mills, with some others of the Signal
Company, set out to attempt to put matters right,
and in spite of the barrage which Sergeant Mills
describes thus, "but what a barrage! such a
beauty!" the party reached Battalion Headquarters
and restored communication, and then set out on its
return journey. Before the arrival of this party,
rumours of the progress of the enemy round their
flanks had reached the three commanding officers,
and there had been talk of shifting to a safer spot, but
it was now decided to hold on.

Suddenly Lieutenant Drake, Sergeant Mills, and
one man returned with the news that the enemy was
right round the rear of the position. As the party,
numbering about ten, was returning, a shell fell
almost on them. Drake was hurled into some barbed
wire, and Mills was wounded, but went to the help
of his officer, who, without this help, could not have
extricated himself. Having extricated their officer
the party went on, but suddenly found itself, much
to its surprise, surrounded by Germans coming from
the rear, who had broken through on the right and
wheeled to the north. Lieutenant Drake at once
realised that the headquarters of the three battalions

in Bunhill Row were in a very precarious position, and determined to do his best to warn them. He asked Sergeant Mills whether he would make a dash for it. Mills at once agreed, and told the rest of the party to be ready. Just then some of the German officers were wounded, and this caused some confusion, of which Drake and Mills took advantage, and the whole party made a bolt for it. They had over four hundred yards to go, and only three of them reached their destination. Thus were the troops in Bunhill Row warned of the enemy being in their rear.

Communication was still open, and at three p.m. a message was received from the brigade to the effect that the 40th Division was about to counter-attack, and that they would be relieved in an hour. So all preparations were made to stand a siege. All papers were burnt, then the three headquarters were organised for defence. Captain McKellen, Adjutant of the 25th Northumberland Fusiliers, Captain Kirkup of the same regiment, Regimental Sergeant-Major W. Peterkin, Sherwood Foresters, attached to the 23rd Northumberland Fusiliers, are all mentioned for the skill and bravery with which they organised and cheered up the personnel of the headquarters. Sergeant A. E. Collins, of the 23rd, though wounded in the arm, lead two counter-attacks, which held back the enemy for some time. Communication with the brigade was broken; no sign of relief came, but the little party fought on. When their outposts had been driven in they organised bombing and rifle grenade parties, and made sallies which drove back too adventurous foes. The single Lewis gun of the 25th, with a solitary pan, was kept going, largely through the Adjutant's coolness and skill. But in spite of all they could do the enemy closed round, and all hope of relief or escape seemed gone.

At about five p.m. Lieutenant-Colonel Acklom decided to attempt to fight his way out with his head-quarter party. He was killed in the attempt, but some, including Lieutenant and Adjutant Moyes, reached the headquarters of 102nd Brigade. The rest of the garrison still held out till about five-thirty p.m., when, to quote Lieutenant Mitchell, " The Boche shouted a message intimating that we had three minutes in which to surrender, and that at the end of that time he would blow us all to blazes with his Minnies if we refused. The two infantry Colonels decided, on account of the wounded and the hopelessness of the position, to surrender. It was the bitterest moment of our lives, and I shall never forget the look of anguish on everybody's face. The troops that actually took us were quite chivalrous towards us; one of them bound up my left hand, which had been wounded earlier on, and another gave me some water." So ended a very gallant defence. Most of the defenders were badly gassed, and many had been wounded, and none of them had had a bite or sup since the previous evening, yet they fought on till the enemy were within a few yards of them and all hope of rescue was gone.

Though unsuccessful, their stout resistance was of much value in delaying the encircling hostile movement which threatened the troops in the front and support lines. Guns 36 and 37 of " C " Company Machine Gun Battalion, near the headquarters of 25th Northumberlands, were knocked out early in the day, and of six more guns stationed farther down the valley only two were got away during the night to the third system. All these guns did great execution before they were put out of action. " B " Company had two guns near Pelican Avenue, of which one was blown to pieces, the officer in charge being wounded; the other was got away by the non-commissioned officer, and eventually joined " C " till relieved. Four guns of " B," in Maida Vale, numbers 32, 33, 34, 35, under Second-Lieutenant J. E. Lord, did their best to stem the Hun onrush, firing into the masses at about six hundred yards. Lord ordered two guns back under

Sergeant Foster. These got away, but of Lord and the other two nothing was heard, save that Lord was wounded.

While their headquarters were going through such trying times the troops of the 22nd and 23rd Northumberlands, holding the front line, were fighting desperately against crowds of eager Huns advancing from the south against their right flank. The additional defences, prudently constructed along Pelican Avenue, after the deserter had given us warning, and the company of 25th Northumberland Fusiliers, sent up earlier in the day, enabled them to put up a better fight than would otherwise have been possible, but were gradually forced northwards. Each communication trench in turn became a front line; Golliwog, Jove, and Mars Lane were each held in turn. At the last a prolonged stand was made, till by an attack from the east, on the original front line, the enemy turned the left flank of the defence, and drove remnants of the 22nd Northumberlands into the support line about Queen's Lane, a little to the south of which a block was established in conjunction with the remnants of the right company of the 23rd Northumberlands. All the officers of this company had been killed or wounded early in the day, but the Company Sergeant-Major, A. S. Harle, rose to the occasion, and under his cheery leadership the company put up a great fight.

At this block the enemy was held up for some time by rifle and Lewis gunfire, but gradually our men were forced back along Stray Reserve and Burg Support, to the line of Factory Avenue, where they came on the right flank of the 15th Royal Scots, which had been thrown back as soon as the direction of the coming blow was known. Blocks were established in Burg and Tunnel trenches, south of Juno Lane, and the two battalions tried to hold Juno and Factory. The aid post of the 23rd Northumberlands was in Stray Reserve, and the Medical Officer carried on to the last, only leaving when all the wounded had been evacuated.

The Machine Gun Battalion had two guns of "A" and eight of "C" Company in this portion of the first system. The sole survivors of teams C/40, 41, in Valley Support, were Second-Lieutenant Percy and a Private, who carried his severely wounded officer to the aid post. Nothing was ever heard of Second-Lieutenant Lloyd and the teams of C/42, 43 in Camouflage trench. The teams of C/44, 45 were last seen under Second-Lieutenant Stanson, constructing a bombing block in Queen's Lane, the enemy being in Tiger trench behind them. Sergeant Browning, in command of guns C/46, 47, fired till the enemy were within bombing distance. One team was overpowered; the other, reduced to three men, got their gun away to Factory, but lost it there in a hand-to-hand scrap. Guns A/48, 49, in Hump Support, were buried by a shell in the morning, but were dug out and were in action by two p.m. A little later the enemy suddenly appeared on the parados, and number two of 48 was shot. The guns were got away to Factory Avenue, whence they did execution on masses of the enemy in the valley south of Croisilles. Later they went with the Royal Scots to the second system and did splendid work. On 22nd, gun 49 was blown to pieces by a shell, and Second-Lieutenant Paton and gun 48, with its team, was last seen fighting somewhere in the second system.

As far as can be ascertained, the remnants of the 22nd and 23rd Northumberlands reached Juno Lane and Factory Avenue about three-thirty p.m. If this is correct one cannot but admire the skilful design and exact execution of the Boche plans, for just now, when his right flank was being driven in by an attack from the south, General Gore found his left flank assailed. Between three and three-thirty p.m. the front of the left of 101st Brigade, and whole of right brigade, 3rd Division (the 9th Brigade), was subjected to an intense bombardment by artillery and trench mortars, and then wave after wave of Huns crossed the front of " C " Company, 11th Suffolks, to attack the 1st Northumberlands, which was the right battalion of the 9th Brigade, and was commanded by Lieutenant-Colonel E. M. Moulton-Barrett, D.S.O., who had lately been transferred to it from our 25th Battalion of the same regiment. " C " Company, at close range, and " B " Company and the personnel of the 11th Suffolks Headquarters, at about one thousand yards range, took heavy toll of the Huns as they crossed their front, but they made good their attack for all that, breaking through the front line at the junction of the two divisions, and penetrating some distance. There was fierce fighting round this corner, and it was not till six p.m. that the Suffolks and Northumberlands ejected the enemy and restored their front.

To meet the incursion of the Huns from the south, General Nicholson determined to hold the firing line of the third system, from his right to its junction with the Croisilles Switch; thence the line was to run along that trench and Factory Avenue, to the front line. In order to carry out this plan General Gore directed the 16th Royal Scots to man the Croisilles Switch, and placed a Composite Company, made up of detachments of infantry who had been working with Royal Engineers, astride the Croisilles-St Leger road. Lieutenant-Colonel Stephenson had already prepared for this action by sending Second-Lieutenant Inglis, with two platoons to man the railway south of Croisilles. Inglis was killed almost at once, but the platoons went on, and eventually got in touch with Captain McLachlan and the remnants of the 25th Northumberlands, whose retreat from the Hog's back has already been described.

The 10th Lincolns were placed at General Gore's disposal. He posted one company on Henin Hill, and, with the remainder, closed the gap between

Croisilles and St Leger. From this point the firing
line of the third system was occupied by the 9th
Northumberlands, who had been ordered up, when at
one-ten p.m. General Nicholson ordered Colonel Earle
to take the 1st East Lancashires to help the 176th
Brigade.

The Lincolns and Northumberlands arrived only
just in time to stop the enemy breaking clean
through; in fact, it was a race between the Boche and
the men from the Tyne which would first reach the
firing line third system, west of St Leger Wood.
The Northumberlands won, and the situation was
saved, but, though their commanding officer, Colonel
Vignoles, kept one of the East Lancashire companies
to aid in the defence of this line, a small pocket of
Boches established itself in the line farther along,
just on the divisional boundary, and stayed there till
the next day. Odds and ends of troops were hurried
up to stem the rush. "J" Special Company Royal
Engineers, and the 102nd Brigade Pioneer Company,
joined Colonel Vignoles, and in this way, between
five and six p.m., some sort of line was formed, from
the right divisional boundary, and connection established with Captain McLachlan's party of the 25th
Northumberlands, which we heard of last on the railway and in the sunken road south of Croisilles at about
two p.m.

This little force formed a connecting link between
troops under the command of General Thomson, and
those under that of General Gore, being in touch with
the 9th Northumberlands in the firing line of the third
system, and with the Royal Scots in Croisilles Switch.

Shortly after six p.m. the troops south of
Croisilles were withdrawn into the village, but with
this exception the line was held intact until after
nightfall, when fresh orders were received from 6th
Corps. The arrival of the 9th Northumberlands and
East Lancashires, coupled with the gallant and skilful
handling of the three companies of the 25th North-

umberland Fusiliers by Captain McLachlan, had averted the danger of a break through between St Leger and Croisilles, and consequent envelopment of the 101st Brigade, but the position on the extreme right of the division was very critical. The enemy was pressing very hard at the point of junction of 34th and 59th Divisions, where he had already forced back our forces to their third system of defence. If this could not be held they had only a single line of trench—the Army line—to fall back on. Into this trench Divisional Headquarters ordered the Pioneers and three Field Companies, its last reserve. It really became a question whether our line could hold out till the troops of the 40th Division, hurrying up from the rear, could come into action. The enemy seemed determined to win through. Lieutenant-Colonel Vignoles, from St Leger Wood, saw wave after wave of grey figures advancing over the Hog's back, undismayed by the heavy losses inflicted on them by the guns of B/160, firing over open sights, the machine guns of " D " Battery, and the Lewis guns and rifles of all infantry within range. Though many fell, many got through, and gradually a large force collected in some dead ground not far from the firing line third system, whence they surged forward as far as the wire, only to be beaten back. About five-thirty p.m. Second-Lieutenant C. H. Walker and No. 1 Platoon of the 9th Northumberlands made a dash out of the south-east corner of the wood and captured two machine guns, killing some twenty Boche and establishing themselves on the Croisilles-l'Homme Mort road, whence this dead ground could be commanded. So the fight swayed backwards and forwards, and it must have been with considerable relief that General Nicholson heard that the 12th Suffolks, the leading battalion of the 120th Brigade, 40th Division, had reported to the 103rd Brigade at six-thirty p.m., and been pushed forward to fill gaps in the third system. Other troops followed, and with dusk falling quickly, the General felt that the day was saved.

The necessity of attempting to blend the varying accounts of the different incidents of this eventful day into one continuous narrative has led to the omission of almost all reference to the doings of our gunners, and to them I must now devote some space, for indeed there is much to tell.

The 160th Brigade Royal Field Artillery gun positions on the 21st lay very much in the storm area; in fact, those of " A " and " D " Batteries lay right in its track. The tale of " D " Battery is soon told. By eleven-thirty a.m. all its guns were disabled, and Major Young and his men joined " B " Battery, where the officers helped direct the guns, and the men carried ammunition.

" A " Battery had two guns, under Second-Lieutenant Bird, just in front of Bunhill Row, close to the Northumberland Battalions' Headquarters. The last news received from this detachment was a note by a runner, received about twelve-thirty a.m., stating that the position was being heavily shelled, the ammunition and camouflage were on fire. No enemy in sight yet, but should any appear they would be suitably dealt with. The remaining guns, in the main position, fired on the enemy advancing on Ecoust.

About twelve-twenty p.m. Major Hodges and a telephonist went forward to observe, and were both wounded, the command of the battery devolving on Captain E. C. Charlton. The enemy worked round, and about one p.m. appeared close on the right flank of the battery. It being impossible to get the guns round to bear on them, the breach blocks and sights were removed, and the personnel retired and joined the infantry, with whom they fought, doing good service, the anti-aircraft Lewis guns being especially useful.

" C " Battery, commanded by that cheery fire-eater, Major G. O. S. Smyth, won great glory. By eight-thirty a.m. both the guns of the advanced section in Croisilles were out of action, Second-Lieutenant T. E. Talbot, who had done uncommonly good work, being killed by a shell while trying to repair some damage. The personnel was withdrawn to the main position, bringing with them the breach blocks, etc. To quote the war diary : " eight-thirty a.m., No. 4 gun hit, and ammunition on fire. Gun sent down to wagon lines. Noon, battery shelled with eleven inch H.V. Withdrew personnel for an hour. Two p.m., masses of enemy moving from Ecoust towards Croisilles, and also up to the ridge to Mory Copse. Pulled guns out of their pits into the open, swung them round, and commenced fire at two-fifteen p.m. (Those who knew Smyth will appreciate how he was enjoying himself at this time.) Fired till dark without stopping them for more than a few minutes at a time. Four p.m., heard three new guns had arrived at wagon lines. Sent Lieutenant A. P. Humble to take them over and come into action, which he did at seven p.m. Five p.m., Lieutenant W. P. Walker sent to rescue his guns (from Croisilles), got them both away under heavy fire of rifles and machine guns. (Major Smyth omits to mention that he went with this party, and that he used two teams of *greys*, which happened to come up just then with ammunition.) Eleven p.m., ordered to withdraw to a position at T.26.a.5.3." And about time too, the Boche being then only about five hundred yards away.

" B " Battery, one thousand two hundred yards south of St Leger, silent till 21st. Major Towell went forward to direct the fire, all wires forward being cut. Fire was opened on Ecoust, when the Boche occupied that place, and later, about one-thirty p.m., the guns were run out of their pits and fired over open sights at the approaching Huns, till about six-thirty p.m., by which time four of them were out of action, and the hostile rifle and machine gun fire was so intense that the position was abandoned, the breach blocks, etc., being removed, and the maps and documents burnt. After dark all the guns were withdrawn one by one, by hand, to a position where their teams could be harnessed in, and taken back to the wagon lines, damages repaired, and they were back in action the next day. Major Towell was wounded early in the day, but carried on for some time. When he could do so no longer Major Young, of " D " Battery, took command. Thus at the end of the day only " C " of the battery of 160th Brigade was in action, and that had had three guns knocked out, but had replaced them during the day.

The 152nd Brigade had less exciting experiences, being farther removed from the flank assailed, but it had a busy time, and suffered some casualties, losing Major H. A. M. Johnstone.

Although the opportune arrival of the 120th Brigade had considerably eased the pressure on the right flank, the situation was still most critical. The extreme urgency of the case had caused reinforcements to be pushed into the fighting line in any order, just as they came up, so that reorganisation was urgently needed. About one thousand yards of the firing line of the third system, on the edge of St Leger Wood, from the railway southwards, were held by " J " Special Company Royal Engineers, two platoons 12th Suffolks (120th Brigade), two platoons " A " Company, one platoon " C " Company 9th Northumberlands, one company 13th Yorkshires (120th Brigade), on the right of whom were the Boche, beyond whom again were Colonel Earle's East Lancashire men and details of the 176th Brigade, units of three British and one Boche Division. A similar state of affairs existed more or less all along the front, even to the extreme left, where, during the night, one hundred men of the 22nd Northumberlands reported to Colonel Tuck, and were located in the second system, in support of the 11th Suffolks.

At nine p.m. orders timed eight-forty-five p.m. were received at Divisional Headquarters from 6th Corps, in accordance with which the reorganisation of the line was carried out before daylight on 22nd.

The new line, which the division had to take up during the night, was as follows : 103rd Brigade, from south-east corner of St Leger Wood, along firing line of third system to the southern end of Croisilles Switch North, whence the 102nd Brigade, now formed into a mixed battalion, under Major Neaves, carried on the line along that switch, skirting the north-western side of Croisilles to the second system firing line, when the 101st Brigade took up the defence along a line of old works known as " A " Posts to the Sensée Reserve, along which the line ran to Hind support and Farmer's Lane, and thus to the 3rd Division right flank.

The 119th Brigade, 40th Division, placed at the disposal of 34th Division, and disposed from four p.m. on and in rear of Henin Hill, was directed to revert to its own division and move into the Sensée Switch (west of St Leger) as soon as the 101st Brigade had taken up its new position.

These orders involved considerable readjustment. On the left, portions of the 101st Brigade, had to withdraw from positions they had all day. Throughout the line the fortuitous mixture of units would have made the operation a difficult one at any time, and to accomplish it at night, in close contact with an enterprising enemy, flushed with victory, and in greatly superior numbers, was a supreme test for the tired troops of the 34th Division, after the severe punishment they had suffered from the enemy's artillery and heavy hand-to-hand fighting of the last sixteen hours. But the enemy, apparently, had suffered enough to make him a little cautious, and the necessary movements were carried out without much interference, except on the extreme left, where the 11th Suffolks were attacked in the middle of their retirement, but, thanks to the excellence of Colonel Tuck's arrangements, completed it successfully, and in the centre, where an attack on Croisilles was defeated by Captain McLachlan's mixed command at about seven p.m., shortly before it retired.

The adventures of Second-Lieutenant Cowan and his platoon of the 16th Royal Scots are worthy of being recorded. Three platoons of this battalion had been in Sensée Reserve all day. During the night 21st/22nd, orders were sent to them to withdraw and join the battalion. These orders failed to reach Cowan, so about eleven p.m. he went to the Battalion Headquarters at Quarry, but found the place empty, and so he remained in Sensée Reserve. In the morning he sent out patrols, one of which met a party of Huns coming along on either side of Sensée Reserve, and drove it off with rifle and Lewis gun fire. Cowan and his platoon were unmolested all the day by the Boche, but he was rather worried by the barrage which our own heavies put down in that part of the battle-field, so that after dark on 22nd he found his way into Hind Support, and reported to the 9th Brigade, and in due course rejoined his battalion in Armagh camp on the 23rd.

General Gore makes special mention of the good work done during the night of 21st/22nd by 207th Field Company, which, working double tasks under machine gun fire, dug a trench from the south end of Hill Switch to the Sunken road to the west, thus providing a covered approach to a dangerous flank, where previously all reinforcements had to pass in the open on the skyline under machine gun fire.

Divisional Headquarters remained at Gommiécourt, to which place also the 103rd Brigade Headquarters were moved. General Thomson established the 102nd Brigade Headquarters in the Sensée Valley, in rear of St Leger, and General Gore moved back to Henin.

The morning of the 22nd found a thick mist

lying all over the battle-field, which considerably aided the enemy in his perparations for renewing his attack. At eight a.m. the 9th Northumberlands, on the right, in St Leger Wood, were attacked. Lieutenant Walker allowed the enemy to reach the wire, and then opened such a hot fire that the attack collapsed. About the same time Captain McLachlan was vigorously attacked, and the enemy broke through astride of the Croisilles-Boyelles road, but were at once counter-attacked by parties under Second-Lieutenants Vipond, Coleby, and Bowman, and driven back whence they came. Shortly after this the enemy renewed his attack with more success, effecting an entry between the troops of the 102nd and 101st Brigades. The 25th Northumberlands, in withdrawing to avoid being taken in rear, lost Second-Lieutenant Peckston and a few men who were surrounded. The 15th Royal Scots were attacked in rear with bombs, rifle grenades, and rifle fire, and they withdrew along the support line of the second system towards Hill Switch. The enemy pressed his advantage and attacked a portion of the 16th Royal Scots in Hill Switch in support of the 15th. Unfortunately, this trench was incomplete and unsuited for defence, giving little cover and being very difficult to fire out of. The enemy's gunners, informed by an air scout, put down a crushing barrage, chiefly of 5·9 inch and eight inch shells, added to which the enemy attacked from Croisilles. Under these trying circumstances the right flank and centre of 101st Brigade began to give way, and a general retirement took place some time early in the afternoon, which was not stopped till the third line system, in front of Boiry Becquerelle, was reached, in which were the 207th and 209th Field Companies and two companies of the 18th Northumberlands, on which the shaken troops of the 101st Brigade were rallied.

This retirement had opened a wide gap between the 11th Suffolks and the 102nd Brigade. As soon

as General Thomson heard of its commencement he
sent up "B" Company, 18th Northumberlands,
which all this while he had held in reserve, to prolong
the left flank of the details of 102nd Brigade; but
even when thus reinforced they were not sufficient to
fill the gap, and throughout the day the Suffolks were
fighting hard, and only escaped being annihilated by
their own efficiency and bravery and the skilful
handling of Colonel Tuck and his officers.

For this battalion the day commenced with a
heavy bombardment. "B" and "D" Companies
formed the outpost line, the former on the right connecting with the Royal Scots, the latter on the left
with the 1st Northumberlands, 3rd Division. "A"
and "C" were the second system in rear. Colonel
Tuck placed his headquarters in post C.9. About
eight-forty-five a.m. the enemy attacked along Hind
trench on "D" Company's front, but was driven off,
Captain G. F. Reid being wounded in the fight. Two
other attacks in the same neighbourhood were also
beaten off. Later, the battalion was shelled heavily,
and when about one p.m. the Royal Scots, on its
right, retired, the enemy began to attack from the
direction of Croisilles. They were beaten off, at first
by rifle and Lewis gun fire, but later a bombing post
was constructed in the second system and held by a
party under Lieutenant W. R. Hall, M.C., who
repulsed several attacks with great coolness. He was
wounded and later on killed in this strenuous struggle.

The enemy continued working round the right.
First "B" and then "D" Companies were forced
to retire. Battalion Headquarters turned out to the
last man. The enemy cut in between "D" and the
remainder of the battalion, and about five-fifteen p.m.
"D" had to withdraw northwards into Hind trench.
A little later the enemy launched another attack from
the south, and "C" and part of "A" became
detached, and retreated also into Hind, covered by
some of "B" with a Lewis gun. In this fight

N

Lieutenant Wood was killed after doing good service. The remainder, to avoid being surrounded, retired to a bank south-east of Martin sur Cojeul, whence, about eight-fifteen p.m., Lieutenant-Colonel Tuck, with the remnants of Battalion Headquarters and two platoons of "A," made good his retreat in the dark to the third system, in front of Boyelles. His Adjutant, Captain J. H. Brett, remained at Crucifix Corner with some details to cover the flank of the 9th Brigade, and did not rejoin him till two-thirty a.m. on 23rd.

The parties which had been driven into Hind trench joined the 3rd Division troops in the defence of that trench till ordered to return to their battalion, which they did about eight-thirty a.m. on 23rd. During their retreat into Hind trench on the evening of 22nd, "C" Company came on a party of eight Boche with five British prisoners. The captors were killed, and the captives released.

The machine guns in this area belonged to "A" Company, Machine Gun Battalion. They fully upheld the good name that this very new unit made for itself on this day. Gun 49 was captured by a German officer, but he was killed and the gun recovered, and finally got back through the 3rd Division area. Guns 44 and 45, after being knocked out on 21st, were patched up at Company Headquarters and did good service the next day in "G" Battery.

To return to the right. After the repulse of his attack on the 9th Northumberlands the enemy remained quiet for some time, and about eleven-forty-five a.m. after a bombardment by our heavies, a company of the 13th Yorkshires ejected the Boche from the portion of the third system, which he had been holding since the day before. From noon onwards the enemy renewed his attacks under cover of a very intense barrage. Assisted by the machine guns of Batteries "D" and "E," the 9th Northumberlands defeated all these efforts decisively, and held the enemy off till four p.m.

During this time the 10th Lincolns, on the left of the 9th Northumberlands, gradually became seriously involved in the fighting on their left, where the remnant[1] of the 102nd Brigade, under Major Neaves and Captain McLachlan, were being constantly outflanked by the enemy, who were pushing through the gap left by the retirement of the Royal Scots. To their assistance, shortly after one-thirty p.m., there came three companies of the 1st East Lancashires, who had been ordered up from their position in brigade reserve as soon as the news of the enemy's success had reached Divisional Headquarters, but while they were able to hold off the enemy on their own front, they had to be constantly throwing back their left flank farther and farther, so that the centre of the line in front of St Leger became a very vulnerable salient. Just at this moment the enemy made a very strong attack on the 9th Northumberlands and the 13th Yorkshires on their right. There was hand-to-hand fighting, and Lieutenant H. S. Rowe, of the Northumberlands, leading some Yorkshire men, had a scrap with a strong party of the Boche who had broken into the front trench, killing four himself, and clearing the trench, but though he repeated this operation with Corporal Watson and some bombers of " B " Company of his battalion, the Boche were not to be denied, and gradually made good their hold in the firing line of the third system, our lads retiring

---

[1] In addition to the troops under Major Neaves, about fifty men of 22nd and 23rd Northumberlands, under Captain A. W. D. Mark, D.S.O., M.C., joined the 10th Lincolns about three a.m. on 22nd, and fought with them until the retirement in the afternoon, when they withdrew to the third line system in front of Boiry Becquerelle, where they remained till ten p.m. on 23rd, when Captain Mark received orders to rejoin his Brigade, which he did at five a.m. on 24th. His party was then reduced to about thirty. Captain Mark and his party, which at one time numbered nearly two hundred men of various units, after fighting all day in the front line system, and in Juno and Factory with the Royal Scots, was entirely cut off by the enemy on the night of 21st/22nd, but by skill and daring he found his way between the hostile groups.

into the support line. During this fighting Second-Lieutenant W. L. Brown, with Sergeant Campbell, Private Neil, and a few others of his platoon, made a smart counter-attack and killed about twenty Huns, temporarily regaining a portion of the front line, but it could not be held. In these encounters the enemy suffered severely, and when our guns, in response to a call for help, shelled that portion of the trench in which he had gained a footing, he retired suffering heavily from our rifles and Lewis guns. Colonel Vignoles wished to follow up the enemy, but had not enough men to allow of his doing so.

Though held off by the 9th, the enemy got forward on the right, in the 59th Division area. The Lincolnshires and three companies of 1st East Lancashires, on the left of the 9th Northumberlands, had been holding out stoutly all the afternoon, constantly stretching back to their left rear as the enemy got farther round that flank, and when the Northumberland and Yorkshire men were compelled to retire to the support line the Lincolnshire and Lancashire seemed likely to be attacked on both flanks. Touch was lost with the 9th Northumberlands, and a withdrawal to the third system, north-west of St Leger, was ordered, and successfully carried out by seven p.m.

Lieutenant-Colonel Vignoles was thus left quite isolated with his own battalion and one company of the East Lancashires, which had not moved with the battalion. The Yorkshires, on his right, had been ordered to fall back, but his communications with the 103rd Brigade had been cut for some time, and when, thanks to the efforts of Sergeant Rising of the Signal Company, they were restored, about eight-fifteen p.m., General Chaplin expressed his surprise at the battalion being still in St Leger, and directed its immediate withdrawal. This operation was successfully carried out, in spite of great difficulties, not the least of which was dodging the fire of our own troops, who did not know that any British troops were still so far forward. It was between nine and ten p.m. when St Leger was evacuated, and a Lewis gun party, covering the movement, did not come away till nearly midnight.

Lieutenant-Colonel Vignoles speaks with admiration and gratitude of a Major and a Subaltern of the R.F.A., whose names he never knew, who all day, in a very exposed position, directed the fire of the guns and ensured his getting efficient support when it was most needed.

By this time the troops of the 31st Division were arriving to relieve the 34th, and as soon as Lieutenant-Colonel Vignoles could get into communication with Divisional Headquarters he received permission to take his wearied men to huts in Hamelincourt, which were reached before daylight, and where, thanks to the kindly foresight of the Staff Captain and Quartermaster, every one got some hot tea and a bite or two before turning in, weary but cheerful, conscious of having done right well.

About noon General Nicholson heard that the 2nd Guards Brigade was on its way by bus, and would take over the third system north of the Boyelles-Croisilles road, and later he received news of the approach of the 31st Division to take over the rest of his front.

At nightfall the situation was very obscure. Divisional Headquarters knew the whereabouts of its own troops, but the situation on the right, where the 40th Division had relieved the remnants of the 59th on the night of the 21st/22nd, was very imperfectly known, and it was rumoured that the 3rd Division, on the left, was about to retire west of the Cojeul. Accordingly, as soon as the relief began, between seven and eight p.m., the bulk of Divisional Headquarters was sent back to Ayette, and was followed about midnight by the remainder. Later, it was ascertained that for some hours before the last party left, there had been no British troops between Gommiécourt and the Boches in Mory.

The relief was carried out without contretemps, save that, owing to an order miscarrying, the 1st East Lancashires had an extra twenty-four hours in the line.

The line on which the division was relieved by the 31st Division on the night of 22nd/23rd from left to right was : Front line of third system from just south of Henin to the junction with the St Leger Switch, thence along the switch to the army line, two thousand yards north-east of Ervillers, thence along the army line for about one thousand two hundred yards to the left flank of 40th Division.

Thus, after two days of being heavily shelled and continuously attacked in flank, the division, though driven back about five thousand yards, still held the third system of the defences and presented an unbroken front. No bad record.

Our casualties for March, most of the battle casualties of which may be safely attributed to the great fight on 21st and 22nd, were :

	Killed	Wounded	Missing	Sick	Total
Officers	20	56	62	22	160
Other ranks	192	1005	1844	687	3728
Total	212	1061	1906	709	3888

Battle casualties, 3179.

Action of
21st and 22nd March, 1918.

Line at 6 pm 21st March
Line taken up during night 21st/22nd
Final line 22nd March.

Scale of Yards
1000   500   0   1000   2000

3rd Division Area

GERMAN

BRITISH

FONTAINE les Croisilles

BULLECOURT

Longatte

Ecoust

FIRST   OUTPOST   LINE

TUNNEL TRENCH

SPREE SUPPORT

SPREE RESERVE

OUTPOST LINE

11th Suffolks   15th R¹ Scots

SECOND   SYSTEM

152 Bde

152 Bde

152 Bde

HILL SWITCH

CROISILLES

103 Bde

101st Bde

10th Lincolns   9th North⁴ Fus.

THIRD   SYSTEM

Vale

Maida

THE HOGS BACK

C/160

A 40th DIV.

201st Bde.

A 176th BDE.

59th Division Area

L'Homme Mort.

HENIN

BOIRY Becquerelle

103 Lincolns

BOYELLES

THIRD   SYSTEM

9th North⁴ Fusiliers

1st East Lancs

Judas Farm

SENSEE RIVER

SENSEE SWITCH

COJEUL RIVER

BOISLEUX St Marc

from ARRAS

from BOIS

HAMELINCOURT

RES. BDE.   LINE

ARMY

ERVILLERS

2300 Yds.

34TH DIVISION H.Q.
at GOMIECOURT

CHAPTER XI

THE GREAT GERMAN OFFENSIVE—II

WHEN the division came out of the line on 23rd March, its destination was uncertain. The first orders were to join the 1st Army. The brigades marched to the Le Cauroy area, and prepared to entrain on 25th, but on that date the orders were cancelled, and the division was told to march to Auxi-le-Château on 26th. While on this march, when nearing their destinations, the troops had an opportunity of showing that the rough handling and heavy casualties they had suffered on 21st and 22nd had not disheartened them.

Shortly after his arrival at Auxi-le-Château, the General met an excited despatch rider, who told a wonderful tale of the 3rd Army being in full flight through Doullens. Having put the man in the guard-room for spreading false rumours, General Nicholson proceeded to take necessary precautions, in case any portion of his tale should turn out to be true, and the three brigades were met at various points by the General himself or Staff Officers, and directed to positions covering the Auxi-le-Château-Doullens road. The troops, though tired, were very cheery, and took up their positions readily, quite keen at the thought of another battle. However, news soon came that the General had correctly gauged the value of the rumour, and the march to billets was resumed. Subsequently, the cause of the alarm was ascertained to have been some motor agricultural implements making strategic movements to the rear, which an excited imagination had transformed into armoured cars, and some of our own gunner patrols returning from reconnaissances, which timorous ones took for Uhlans.

This alarm over, the General was greeted with an order to entrain next day at Doullens for 1st Army, but by prudent and persuasive use of the telephone he got the order modified, so that the troops entrained at Frevent and Petit Houvin, which saved his tired men some four or five miles marching, which was welcome, for the division had covered about forty miles since the 23rd.

The start on 28th was somewhat delayed by the Boche airman, who, during the preceding night, bombed the line near St Pol, but by ten a.m. all were off, and by the next evening we were back in our old haunts, Erquinghem, Neuf Berquin, and Merville.

On 30th the 101st went into the line, relieving the left brigade of the 38th Division, and the next day the 103rd took over the right sector, relieving a brigade of the 57th Division, while the 102nd Brigade went into billets in Erquinghem. The same day General Nicholson took over command of the left sector, 15th Corps, from Major-General Blackadder, commanding 38th Division.

From our two previous sojourns in these parts many of us knew a good deal of the geography, though not many remained of the happy, inquisitive crowd of greenhorns which had explored these trenches with wondering eyes in the spring of 1916.

There were, however, many changes, and not for the better. The trench system seemed rather decayed. The continuous front line had given place to a series of posts, disconnected, lightly held, and badly wired, the main line of resistance being the subsidiary line, known to the old hands as the B.G. (Bois Grenier) Line.

During the summer of 1917 Armentières had

been heavily bombarded with H.E. and gas, and all the civilians had left. As we tramped through its empty, echoing streets we missed the *pâtisseries* and *estaminets*, with their charming, smiling occupants, who had lightened our leisure hours during our previous spells of service in these parts. Erquinghem had escaped, and was much as it used to be. The big factory was still working, and we recognised many old friends.

The sector held by the division extended from the River Lys on the left, in a southerly and south-westerly direction, some eight thousand yards, to just beyond the Rue du Bois salient on the right.

The 25th Division held the line on our left from the north bank of the Lys, and we had the 40th Division on our right, and beyond them were our oldest allies, the Portuguese. Both the 25th and 40th Divisions had shared with us the fighting farther south, and, like us, had suffered heavily.

Our artillery had not arrived, and our front was covered by the gunners of the 38th Division. Our Field Companies and Pioneers, after working some days improving the new line in our old area, had marched up at the rate of fifteen miles a day, arriving just after the brigades.

Divisional Headquarters was in Steenwerck; that of the right brigade in La Rolanderie, as of old; that of the left in the Jute factory, east of the railway bridge, on the south bank of the Lys. The 102nd Brigade had its headquarters in Erquinghem, and was in Corps reserve.

The gaps in our ranks, caused by the fighting of 21st/23rd, had been filled up, but there had been no time to test or train the drafts, for the two brigades in the line were fully employed repairing and strengthening the defences, and the training of the reserve brigade was also broken in on by urgent work. As our infantry had lost eighty-seven officers and two thousand six hundred and fifty-four other ranks, the battalions were largely composed of these new drafts. The 102nd Brigade had suffered most, having lost all its Commanding Officers and seven Company Commanders, besides forty-four other officers and one thousand four hundred and twenty-two other ranks. The division was therefore heavily handicapped when it entered on its next battle.

The position which General Nicholson had to hold was not without its drawbacks. The River Lys, unfordable, and crossed by only seven bridges, ran so close along its rear, especially on the left, that there was danger of the troops being forced back into the river, should the enemy achieve even a temporary success, and a successful flank attack from the right would certainly end in the left brigade being penned between the front line and the river, over which, in its immediate rear, there were only two bridges, very difficult of approach.

The town of Armentières, behind this section, was also a cause of difficulty, owing to the danger of gas bombardments, the poisonous stuff hanging for days among the houses.

In both sections, switch systems of defence, although projected, were still incomplete. With the exception of some lines of wire, perpendicular to the front, breastworks and obstacles alike were designed to meet frontal attacks only.

On 1st April the Corps Commander, Lieutenant-General Sir J. Ducane, held a conference, at which various alterations in the trench systems were discussed, and the Corps Commander laid down his policy, which might be summed up in the words *j'y suis, j'y reste*—until ordered to move.

The disadvantage of having the river in our rear was lessened as far as possible by the Field Companies and Pioneers constructing many temporary bridges, which were moored along the bank, ready to be swung into position when needed, and carefully camouflaged, thus to some extent preparing for the heavy bombardment of the permanent bridges and their approaches, which was sure to take place should the anticipated attack come off.

The first six days of our sojourn were uneventful. The enemy, imitating the tactics of Brer Fox, lay low and waited. Our patrols could find no trace of him in No-Man's-Land, save on one occasion, when on the night of the 3rd Company Sergeant-Major Mellor and twenty men of the 15th Royal Scots came on a party of the 32nd I.R. of the German 32nd Division, of whom they killed four and brought in one unwounded, supplying a much needed identification. From this prisoner we learnt that the German order of battle from north to south was 255th R.I.R. 49th Division, 102nd I.R. and 177th I.R., both of 32nd Division. The prisoner would not admit knowledge of any preparations for an attack, but information from other sources made it very certain that trouble was brewing, and on 6th deserters who gave themselves up to troops on our left indicated the Portuguese front as the probable point of attack. We did all that was possible in the way of improving our flank defences, but the Hun gave us little time.

After a peaceful day, at about eight-thirty p.m. on 7th the Hun began to bombard Armentières with gas shells (yellow cross) from all calibres up to 15 c.m. howitzers. This went on incessantly till seven a.m. on 8th, the estimated number of shells fired varying from twenty-five to forty thousand.

The wind was blowing gently from the west, i.e., from us to the Boche. With great care and forethought he let his deadly shower fall on the town, so that the gas, carried along by the breeze, might expend its full force on our side of No-Man's-Land; in fact, so careful was he that his own troops should not suffer, that its effects were but little felt by the troops in our front line, but the troops in town, and just east of it, suffered very severely. In all, we had about nine hundred casualties. Two companies of 25th Northumberlands, which were in reserve in asylum buildings, on the south-eastern edge of Armentières, and in Nouvel Houplines, were practically all gassed, and had to be replaced by two companies of the 15th Royal Scots from the 101st Brigade, which was in Corps reserve. The 207th Field Company suffered severely, and Major Glendenning's record is worthy of reproduction : " 7th and 8th. Gas shell bombardment (yellow cross). The gas gradually filtered through the gas protectors of the cellars. (The company was in Armentières.) It was impossible to clear the gas, as the whole atmosphere of the town was permeated with it."

" B " Company of the Pioneers was in " the blue factory," on the north-western edge of the town, its officers being in houses a few hundred yards to the south. All the officers, with supernumeraries, amounting to ten, and about forty men, were sent to hospital by eight a.m. on 8th, and within the next thirty-six hours the casualties had reached one hundred.

The efficacy of the gas used was due to the cumulative effect of many whiffs inhaled as the shells fell, no one of which, singly, produced any feeling of discomfort, and therefore the need of wearing masks was not realised till violent vomiting made it impossible to do so.

The rest of the 8th was very quiet, and before we begin to deal with the events of the stormy period that follows we better glance at the position of the units of the division.

The 34th Divisional Artillery arrived in the back area from the Arras front on 7th, and on 8th one section of each battery moved up and relieved its opposite number of the 38th Division during the night. Therefore, when the bombardment, which heralded the great attack, commenced at four-fifteen a.m. on 9th April, our gunners were in the uncomfortable position of being neither in nor out. However, there was no delay or confusion. The personnel of the sections of the 38th Divisional Artillery, who had already gone back to their wagon lines, taking their guns with them, quickly returned to the battery positions without their guns, and took over those of the 34th Division, which were already in action, and the personnel of the 34th hastened back to the wagon lines, picked up the guns of the 38th, and hurried off to their own batteries, with which they went into action at three p.m. the same afternoon, north of Estaires, covering the 50th Division. Their doings during the " push " will be dealt with later. General Nicholson was very lucky in this matter. No General would, for choice, go into action with strange artillery, but even his own gallant gunners could not have done him better ; as General Nicholson told their C.R.A., Brigadier-General T. E. Topping, C.B., C.M.G., D.S.O., when the time came for them to part company.

The line commencing from the left was held by the 102nd Brigade, which had relieved the 101st on 5th. All three battalions were in line, in the following order from left : 22nd, 23rd, 25th Northumberland Fusiliers, the left of the first named resting on the Lys, on far side of which the British line was carried on by the 25th Division, but there was a gap of one thousand yards of ground, which was thought too marshy for movement. The right sector was held by the 103rd Brigade, which had all three battalions in the front line ; the 1st East Lancashires with " B " Company on the left, and " A " on the right, their front extending from the Armentières-Lille railway to the Lille road. Their reserve and support companies were very far back, and suffered about seventy casualties in the gas bombardment.

From the Lille road to Salop Avenue the line was held by 10th Lincolns, with " C " and " D " in front, and " A " in the brickfields, " B " in Spring post, on Rue Fleurie.

The 9th Northumberlands were, on the right, disposed as follows: "A" and "C" in front line, each with two platoons in front posts, two in subsidiary line; "B" in the posts along Rue Fleurie, from La Vesée northwards, available for counter-attack—in this line also was No. 2 Section, "D" Company, Machine Gun Battalion—"D" as a permanent garrison of l'Armée switch from Streaky Bacon Farm to Half-way house, with No. 4 Section, "D" Company, Machine Gun Battalion, in pill-boxes near l'Armée and Streaky Bacon Farm.

On the right of the Northumberlands, across Park Row, was the 13th Yorkshire Regiment, and on its right the 20th Middlesex; both of these belonged to the 40th Division.

The 101st Brigade was in reserve, but it was not at General Nicholson's unfettered disposal, being the Corps reserve, there being no 3rd Division, under General Ducane's orders. The battalions were billeted: 15th Royal Scots, less the two companies sent to reinforce the 102nd Brigade, at the laundries to the west of Erquinghem; 16th Royal Scots in Erquinghem, where General Gore also had his headquarters. The 11th Suffolks was at La Rolanderie. The 12th Battalion of the same regiment, 40th Division, was not far off, at Fleurbaix, being in support to the 13th Yorks and 20th Middlesex. Thus we were again alongside of the 120th Brigade, with which we had come in touch at St Leger on the 22nd March. Beyond the 40th Division came the 2nd Portuguese Division, which had been in the line for a long time, and needed rest. Its relief was fixed for the 10th April. To the south of the forces of our most ancient ally was the 55th Division.

After a quiet day and night, at four-fifteen a.m. on the 9th April, the Boche guns to the south of our position spoke in an unmistakable manner. The volume of sound was so great that it could only portend an attack on a considerable scale, and as the

hours passed and there was no cessation in the din,
we all realised that yet another " day " had arrived,
and all units and parties " stood to." The bombardment did not affect our front line, but our back areas
got more than usual shelling, Erquinghem especially
being made almost untenable. Still there was no
sign of any attack on our front, but as early as five-
fifteen a.m. an S.O.S. rocket went up from the right
of the 40th Division line. Orders were issued at
about six a.m. for the Field Companies and Pioneers
to be ready to swing the emergency bridges into
position, and shortly after this the Pioneers, and the
details attached to them, and 1st and 2nd Sections,
" A " Company, Machine Gun Battalion, were ordered
to man the bridge head defences. At eight-five the
101st was ordered to stand to; a little later half a company of the Machine Gun Battalion joined the brigade,
and orders came to be ready to move to Nouveau
Monde, beyond Sailly-sur-Lys.

Still no activity on our front. We knew the 50th
Division was on the move towards Estaires. Some
thought the attack, which was evidently some way
from our front, would very probably be stopped, without our being much inconvenienced. However,
rumours of all sorts soon began to fly about. The
Boche was reported in many places on our right flank
and rear.

Early on 9th No. 3 Section, " A " Company,
34th Machine Gun Battalion, was sent to Bac St
Maur. The mules having been stampeded by the
bombardment of Erquinghem, the guns and gear had
to be man-handled all the way to a position south of
the Lys, covering the pontoon bridge. Here they
did great execution, temporarily delaying the enemy's
advance, but finding both his flanks in danger Second-
Lieutenant Lee withdrew his guns across the river.
Here he remained busily engaged till early on the
10th, when his ammunition was all expended, and
he found his guns five hundred yards in front of

our infantry. Only one gun was got away, which, having replenished its ammunition supply, was in action at Trois Arbes on the next day.

At nine a.m. General Nicholson heard from the 40th Division that the enemy were in the front line on their right flank. An hour later came an order for the 101st Brigade to march to the south of Bac St Maur, and to act under orders of 40th Division, as the Portuguese front had been broken and the enemy was in the battle zone of the 40th Division. Owing to heavy shelling, communication forward of Divisional Headquarters was very difficult, and this order does not appear to have reached the 101st Brigade till eleven-twenty. The 16th Royal Scots, being close to Brigade Headquarters received this order at eleven-twenty-five, and started for the spot indicated, followed by two companies of the 15th Royal Scots, which were attached to them. Major A. E. Warr, Second-in-Command, was in command of the leading two companies, and on nearing Bac St Maur he found the enemy already in possession of the village, so that it was impossible to reach the objective given him. On Lieutenant-Colonel Stephenson coming up with the remainder of the battalion, a position was taken up near Fort Rompu, facing west and south-west, and although two of his companies were sent across the Lys by orders of the G.O.C. 119th Brigade, 40th Division, this position eventually became the pivot on which a defensive flank facing south and south-west was formed.

While these events were taking place, the Corps Commander paid a visit to General Nicholson, and, after discussing the changes which had occurred in the situation, replaced the 101st Brigade at his disposal to repel this attack on his flank. Major Bertie Tower, G.S.O.2, was at once sent to get hold of the brigade, but it was too late. When he arrived, the leading troops were already engaged, and the Bac St Maur bridge was blown up just after Major

Tower had crossed. He found the Royal Scots, and joyously joined in the fray.[1]

In this curious way did the division go into action; if not backwards, certainly crab fashion—sideways. Surely there are not many instances of the reserve going into action first, and bearing the brunt of the first attack.

The enemy, having broken through the Portuguese front line, pushed vigorously forward, and then out to either flank. Thus the 12th Suffolks, 40th Division, in Fleurbaix, in support of the left brigade front of the 40th Division, came in contact with the enemy by ten a.m. They occupied a line from the west of that village, round its southern edge, and as far eastwards as Canteen Farm. The headquarters were at Port a Clous Farm, about one thousand yards north of Fleurbaix. The enemy, making a vigorous attack, cut off the C.O., Colonel Lloyd, from the companies of his battalion, and he, with some sixty men of the Battalion Headquarters and stragglers, fought a rear-guard action, retiring slowly

[1] Major Tower spent an interesting day. He crossed the Lys at Bac St Maur, just before the bridge was blown up by the retreating 40th Division. Proceeding eastwards, he met Major Warr, and explained the new order to him, and then went to Brigade Headquarters in Erquinghem, whither his car had preceded him by the north bank road. Filling up his car with S.A.A., Major Tower returned to the Royal Scots, who by now were heavily engaged, and spent the rest of the afternoon assisting the Royal Scots officers, and taking a hand in the fighting as opportunity offered. Eventually he returned to Divisional Headquarters with a complete account of the situation, remarking that he had had the time of his life. Major Warr, in a letter describing the events of that day, says: " The sight of a Staff Officer at such a time was worth a whole battalion." Throughout these operations Major Tower, in spite of severe physical disabilities, worked unceasingly. His high spirits and absolute confidence in our final victory infected all with whom he came in contact. Whether in the front line, where he was to be found whenever he could get there, or at Divisional Headquarters, where his tactical skill and excellent reports were invaluable to the Divisional Commander, Major Tower did great work all through those anxious days. Major Tower was killed commanding a battalion of his regiment, the Royal Fusiliers, in August, 1918, when the tide of victory was in flood. The loss to the Army was great, and to his friends (he had no enemies) irreparable. To one of these, whom he served with all his heart and soul for many months in 1915, 1916, and 1918, he will always be the perfect knight *sans peur et sans reproche.*

O

to a position west of Fort Rompu, which he maintained for some time, and then joined the Royal Scots on the east of that place, taking post on Lieutenant-Colonel Stephenson's right, on the south bank of the Lys. The 12th Suffolk Companies, being attacked in front, and with both flanks unsupported, retired slowly northwards, disputing every yard of the ground, till their right came on to the left of the Royal Scots, south-west of Fort Rompu, and their left on the right of the 11th Suffolks, advancing with three companies in line, and one in support, from La Rolanderie, in accordance with orders which Colonel Tuck had received from General Gore. Lieutenant-Colonel Tuck's left was close to Streaky Bacon Farm, where he soon got in touch with the 103rd Brigade.

The 121st Brigade Field Artillery had its guns in the neighbourhood now assailed, and about noon they were ordered to withdraw across the Lys. "A" and "D" Batteries limbered up under heavy machine gun fire at close range, the others followed, and by three p.m. all the guns were in action again in previously selected positions north of the Lys, except two howitzers, which had been damaged by shell fire and had to be abandoned in La Vesée.

The enemy's western thrust was so successful that by noon the 40th Division front was shattered, except on the extreme left. Half of the left company of the 20th Middlesex made a stout stand in Moat Farm Avenue, and Lieutenant-Colonel F. Misken, M.C., commanding 13th Yorkshire Regiment, in conjunction with Lieutenant-Colonel Vignoles, prepared to meet the attack on their right flank. Early in the afternoon a line, though rather a thin one, had been formed from the original front line at Pharm Street to the south bank of the River Lys, east of Fort Rompu.

The constituents of this line were various. On the south bank of the Lys was Colonel Lloyd and his

small party of 12th Suffolks; then came Royal Scots
and Australian Tunnellers, under Lieutenant-Colonel
Stephenson; then two companies of 12th Scots, with
one in support. This brought the line to the Rue
Delpierre, about a mile south of Erquinghem, whence,
to the vicinity of Streaky Bacon Farm, were the 11th
Suffolks with remnants of a company of the 12th.
Here also was No. 4 Section, "A" Company, 34th
Machine Gun Battalion. At the farm itself was a
company of East Lancashires, hurried across by
General Chaplin from the left of his line, and two
guns, four sections "D" Company, 34th Machine
Gun Battalion in a pill-box. Thence to Gunner
Post was "D" Company, 10th Lincolns, with "B,"
9th Northumberlands, carrying on the line through
La Vesée to Ration Farm, where two platoons of
"C" Company held a strong point. Two platoons
of "A" Company carried on the defence up Park
Row to the front line.

The 13th Yorks, with remnants of 20th
Middlesex, held the front line as far as Pharm Street,
and also lined Shaftesbury and Tramway Avenues
with posts, connecting them with La Vesée.

About noon the enemy made a most determined
attack on the Yorkshires, just at the angle formed by
the old and new lines, and there was some stiff fighting. The enemy was driven off, and, though he made
four subsequent attempts, he made no impression on
the Tikes.

On the extreme right, near the Lys, the Boche
was very active. On our side of the river he achieved
no great success, though he pushed our right back
a little, but north of the river he was more successful,
and Lieutenant-Colonel Stephenson was annoyed by
rifle and machine gun fire from Jesus Farm, well in
his rear. Four Vicker's guns of 34th Machine Gun
Battalion, which were sent him, were employed in
dealing with these troublesome pests.

Before leaving the south bank of the Lys it is

well to consider the actual state of affairs on that side of the river, on the proper front of the 34th Division. This front had not been attacked, save by shelling, but, in order to protect its flank, the whole of the reserve brigade, and nearly all the supports of the right brigade, had been used up. The original front of that brigade, about three thousand five hundred yards, was held by six weak companies, with only two in support. The left brigade certainly had not been attacked, but had suffered so heavily in the gas attack that it had absorbed two companies of the reserve brigade.

The other forces of his own division, at General Nicholson's disposal, were the three Field Companies and the 18th Northumberlands. The 207th Field Company was practically out of action from gas casualties, and the Pioneers had lost about one hundred from the same cause; the remainder were needed as bridge head garrisons. The two remaining Field Companies were standing to, ready to swing emergency bridges and demolish the permanent ones. Therefore, one cannot help rejoicing that the Boche did not attack the left brigade that evening, nor shut one's eyes to the fact that on the night of 9th/10th the chances of all those south of Lys making a free trip to Germany were rather good.

The fighting north of the Lys must now be dealt with. The enemy having crossed the Lys at Bac St Maur, about three p.m., close on the heels of the troops of the 40th Division, pushed on to Croix du Bac and Sussex Post. His numbers rapidly increased, and he swept aside the remnants of the 40th Division and our two companies of Royal Scots who were digging in there. Had his course not been stayed this chapter would have been a short and dismal one.

However, at one-thirty p.m. on this very critical day the 74th Brigade was placed at General Nicholson's disposal. It consisted of the 9th Loyal North

Lancashire Regiment, 11th Lancashire Fusiliers, and 3rd Worcestershire Regiment, and was commanded by Brigadier-General H. M. Craigie Halkett, D.S.O. As part of the 25th Division it had taken part in the recent operation farther south. It had just come out of the Le Touquet Sector, and on the morning of the 9th was training. One battalion was at the baths, and several companies were at the ranges. At one p.m. an order was received to proceed to Steenwerck and report to 34th Division. Without any delay, the battalions were set in motion, each marching independently as far as the rendezvous, Steenwerck Church. The Brigadier reported himself to General Nicholson, and received orders to counter-attack and drive the Huns back over the river. At three-forty-five p.m. General Craigie Halkett met his commanding officers in front of Steenwerck Church, and briefly gave them their orders for the advance towards Croix du Bac. The Loyal North Lancashires were on the right, the 11th Lancashire Fusiliers in the centre, and 3rd Worcesters on the left. At that time it was far from certain where the enemy would be encountered, so the movement was covered by strong patrols.

At Sequemeau General Craigie Halkett found the Commander of the 119th Brigade, 40th Division, and learned that the enemy, at least a battalion strong, was in Croix du Bac. The 11th Lancashire Fusiliers, picking up some one hundred and fifty details of 119th Brigade, 40th Division, and with four guns 25th Battalion Machine Gun Company, deployed and advanced with their right flank on the Le Sequemeau-Croix du Bac road and parallel to the Croix du Bac-Hallobeau road. The two flank battalions were ordered to push on, and while keeping touch with the Fusiliers to try to reach the river, and secure the bridges. The Loyal North Lancashires were held up on the west of Croix du Bac by machine guns in a house south-west of that place. Their right was covered by some of the Pioneers of the 40th Division. At six-thirty their Commanding Officer, Lieutenant-Colonel W. H. M. Wienholt, D.S.O., rode into the village and escaped with difficulty, with serious injuries to his knee, his horse being shot under him. Major E. P. Nares took command. The Worcesters on the other flank had pushed through Hallobeau, and made good the river bank from Lancashire Post to Erquinghem. At eight-thirty the Lancashire Fusiliers attacked, and got almost through the Croix du Bac. Some of the 16th Royal Scots filled in a gap between the Fusiliers and the Worcesters. At two a.m. on 10th a fresh attack was launched, which carried the line through the village in the centre, and right down to the river on the right, and on the left the Worcesters and Royal Scots also advanced along the river bank. At four-ten a.m. the Fusiliers were reinforced with four more guns of the 25th Machine Gun Battalion, and at six a.m. by the 74th Trench Mortar Battery. Shortly after this, the right and centre of the line was compelled to withdraw, as in the dark parties of the enemy had either been overlooked or had penetrated round the flanks. At eight a.m. another attack was made, and was making good progress when, at nine-thirty, the Boche launched a tremendous blow down the Bac St Maur-Croix du Bac road, and broke in between the Fusiliers and the Loyal North Lancashires. While ordering everyone to hold on, General Craigie Halkett specified the line Pt Vanuxeem-Le Sequemeau-l'Hallobeau as that on which he meant to stand if he were compelled to retire, and cautioned the Worcesters on the left not to lose touch of the 101st Brigade. The enemy pushed his attack with much force, and gradually, paying heavily for every yard he gained, he forced the weary, much reduced but still stiff-necked brigade back from one position to another, till Steenwerck was reached. Throughout this movement the enemy, while keeping up the pressure in its front, continually pushed round the brigade's right flank, forcing the whole line to retire.

In this retirement the bulk of the Loyal North Lancashires got too far to the right, and a gap was created on the right of the Fusiliers, which was partially filled by some Royal Engineers of 40th Division. In Steenwerck there was hand-to-hand fighting, in which Lieutenant-Colonel E. C. de R. Martin, D.S.O., M.C., commanding the 11th Lancashire Fusiliers, was wounded and reported missing, with Second-Lieutenant A. Marchant. This was at three-thirty p.m., 10th, and affairs were very critical, as, if a new line could not be formed at once, the enemy would be right through the line towards Le Creche. Captains R. K. Beswick, M.C., and G. H. Stead, M.C., collected a few men from headquarters and stragglers, and formed a line between the Carbaret du Saule and the Still Becque. Behind this screen the Brigadier formed a new line, with elements of Lancashire Fusiliers and Loyal North Lancashires, from Pont de Pierre as far as Steenwerck Station, and thence south-east along the railway till touch was established with Major Cook and his 209th Field Company.

It is necessary now to leave this hard-pressed but unbeaten brigade and return to the south side of the Lys. The night, save for shelling, was uneventful. General Gore reinforced Lieutenant-Colonel Stephenson with two Vicker's guns and one hundred and fifty infantry, collected from all sources. Lieutenant-Colonel Tuck declined, as unnecessary, a similar reinforcement. The 101st and 103rd Brigade Headquarters were removed to Waterlands before daylight, and Divisional Headquarters, being under machine gun fire, also shifted back to the cross-roads, about a mile from Outtersteene on the Bailleul Road, at four-thirty a.m.

About seven a.m. two attacks in great strength were launched by the enemy, northwards from

Fleurbaix and eastwards from Fort Rompu, the result being that the composite line of Royal Scots and Suffolks was attacked on both fronts of the right-angled bend in the line south-west or west of Fort Rompu, the full weight of the attack falling on "the point of the bend," and here, by sheer weight of numbers, the enemy penetrated the line north of Fleurbaix. Major A. E. Warr, who was in command about Rue Dormoire, was captured with some six or seven others. The Royal Scots suffered very heavily in this attack. Probably most of those shown as "Missing" on this day were killed at this time.

Lieutenant-Colonel Tuck at once hurried up his reserve, and counter-attacked so effectively that by eight-forty-five he had re-established touch with the troops under Lieutenant-Colonel Stephenson. The success of the 74th Brigade on the previous evening had eased the situation on the extreme right, but after the retirement already recorded, the enemy on the north of the river again became troublesome, and Lieutenant-Colonel Stephenson had to detach Vicker's guns and riflemen, whom he could ill spare, to try to keep down his fire. As the enemy kept on pressing him hard, his line was gradually driven back, the Suffolks on his left also retiring, so that the line was unbroken. The 13th Yorks were also attacked. At about eleven a.m. a heavy trench mortar from Moat Farm planted a shell at the junction of Shaftesbury Avenue and the subsidiary line, annihilating the garrison of the blocking post. About one p.m. a desperate assault was made from Emma Post on the junction of the old and new lines. The assailants got through as far as Haymarket, but Percy Post and Jocks Joy held on, and the intruders were expelled, leaving some dead, which identified them as belonging to the 22nd and 369th Regiments.

About this time the centre and right of the Suffolks was attacked in great force, and the situation became very critical. The enemy succeeded in reaching the western edge of Erquinghem, and his machine guns swept the main street. The centre of the Suffolks was temporarily breached, and the remnant of No. 4 Section, "A" Company, Machine Gun Battalion, was overwhelmed, only three men escaping. Its commander, Second-Lieutenant Aston, had been wounded the day before. Second-Lieutenant Hancock and two teams of "D" Company, Machine Gun Battalion, appear to have been overwhelmed about this time. When last heard of they were defending stoutly the l'Armée pill-box.

Just at this moment, when once more it seemed as if success was to crown the Boche's efforts, the situation was changed by the appearance on the scene of the 1/4th Duke of Wellington's Regiment, "B" Company, which, under Captain Farrar, quickly pushed through the village and, supported by "A," held the western end from Rue du Moulin to the Lys. "C" Company, under Captain Luty, supported by "D," pushed out to the south and lined the railway. These positions were gallantly held until orders to withdraw were received five hours later. The enemy made constant attacks, and about one p.m. enfiladed "C" Company at close range. The losses were very heavy. A platoon of "A" Company, which pushed forward to fill a gap, was almost destroyed, and the few survivors were surrounded and captured. But the enemy was kept out of Erquinghem. All round and in this village the fighting was very fierce. The buildings which, till the morning of the 9th, had suffered but little, though for three and a half years they had lain within easy reach of the Boche's guns, were by this time mere ruins, on fire in several places, and there were many sad scenes; for the inhabitants had clung to their beloved homes, and even now were loathe to quit them, and kept returning amid the shells and bullets to save some specially valued article.

The hard-pressed troops knew nothing of what

was happening elsewhere. Since midnight all wires had been cut. They were very weary, but they held on doggedly, and in the meantime events were taking place farther north which had an important bearing on the situation on our front.

The enemy had made a successful attack on the troops on our left, and by midday on 10th had gained Ploegstreet Village and Messines. Thus at that hour General Nicholson's forces were in the grip of a pair of pincers, one point of which was at Ploegstreet and the other close to Steenwerck; only a little more than five miles apart; the bulk of them still being south of the Lys, and two whole brigades in the front line over five miles in an air line from the line joining the pincer's points. Truly a precarious situation.

News of the commencement of the attack reached Divisional Headquarters at about eight a.m. on 10th, and it became clear that a retirement to the north bank of the Lys had become imperative. This retirement had been suggested to Corps Headquarters the previous evening, but the suggestion was not accepted, and it was not until ten a.m. on 10th that orders to withdraw the division were received at Divisional Headquarters. The plan elaborated beforehand was at once put in motion, and, communication being difficult, timed to start at three p.m. The original plan could not be followed completely, owing to reserves having been used up and to the pressure on the 101st Brigade south of the Lys.

The orders, though transmitted as rapidly as possible, took a long time to reach the different units. The 102nd Brigade, the headquarters of which were still in the Jute Factory, close to the railway bridge on Armentières-Bailleul line, got the order at eleven-forty a.m., and by six-twenty p.m. the whole brigade was on the north bank, holding a line from the railway on its right, via Manchester post to Burnley post, and thence north-west towards the Nieppe system. "B," 34th Machine Gun Battalion, withdrew with the brigade and occupied posts in the new line.   The troops crossed by the railway bridge and bridges to the north, all of which were under shell fire, and some under that of machine guns.

The next troops to receive the order seem to have been those in and round Erquinghem, who got it between two-forty-five and three-twenty p.m., and to them it must have come as an immense relief.   The 101st Brigade had been fighting continuously since early the previous day, and the Duke of Wellington's Regiment, though it had but recently entered the fight, had been on the move since midnight. Although weary and sore pressed, no move was made till plans had been arranged with the troops on their left holding the old front line.

The order seems to have reached the 13th Yorks (now under General Chaplin's orders), 9th Northumberlands, and 10th Lincolns about three p.m., and the Colonels of these battalions quickly agreed on the method in which it was to be carried out, and asked Lieutenant-Colonel Tuck on their right to hold on for two hours to allow them to get their battalions away.

In accordance with this wish the Suffolks, Duke of Wellington's, Royal Scots, and "C" Company of the 18th Northumberlands, which was bridgehead guard, held on, though sorely pressed, till after five p.m., and then began to withdraw to the north bank. The masonry bridge had been blown up, and the last crossings were made by emergency foot-bridges. "C" Companies of the 18th Northumberland Fusiliers and 1/4th Duke of Wellington's were the rear-guard, but the Boche came along the north bank so quickly that to save the bridges falling into his hands they had to be destroyed before all were over, and about a platoon of each battalion fell into the enemies hands.   Both companies suffered heavily, "C" Company of the 1/4th Duke of Wellington's losing about three-fourths of their numbers.   Private

A. Poulter of this company won the Victoria Cross for his great gallantry in dressing the wounded and carrying many of them across the river under heavy fire.[1]

The 101st Brigade took up a position north of the Lys, the Duke of Wellington's and Northumberlands going to Nieppe. The withdrawal of the battalions of the 103rd Brigade was a difficult and ticklish matter. It will be remembered that about one o'clock the Yorkshires had ejected some intruders from the Haymarket. The enemy was seen massing in preparation for another onslaught, and Lieutenant-Colonel Misken was just preparing to counter-attack them when he was summoned to arrange for the withdrawal. This caused the abandonment of the counter-attack. By the plan agreed on the retirement was to be made from right to left, in order 13th Yorks, 9th Northumberlands, each covered by its own rear-guard, the 10th Lincolns moving independently, the 1st East Lancashires having already moved off.

The movement was to begin at four-thirty p.m. Just as this had all been settled, a message was received from Lieutenant-Colonel Tuck, telling of the difficulty he was having in holding on, and, to increase the trouble, the enemy rushed Shaftesbury Avenue. The remnant of its garrison fell back to Tramway Avenue. It was a bitter disappointment to the gallant Yorkshires that they should lose this line which they held so stoutly, but they had the satisfac-

---

[1] " 24016 Private Arthur Poulter, West Riding Regiment (Wortley, Leeds). For conspicuous bravery when acting as a stretcher-bearer. On ten occasions Private Poulter carried badly wounded men on his back to a safer locality, through a particularly heavy artillery and machine gun barrage. Two of these were hit a second time while on his back. Again, after a withdrawal over the river had been ordered, Private Poulter returned in full view of the enemy, who were advancing, and carried back another man who had been left behind wounded. He bandaged up over forty men under fire, and his conduct throughout the whole day was a magnificent example to all ranks. This very gallant soldier was subsequently seriously wounded when attempting another rescue in the face of the enemy."—*Supplement to the " London Gazette,"* *28th June,* 1918.

tion of knowing that they had held it till the order
to withdraw had been duly received.

The retirement of the four battalions was carried
out successfully.   The enemy detected the first movement to the rear, and attacked at once, so that the
Northumberlands and Lincolns were entangled in a
mêlée in the front line trench.   Fortunately a heavy
mist fell, which aided our poor weary fellows, but
even so it was a difficult and dangerous job which
would never have been accomplished but for the
steadiness of all ranks and the skilful leading of the
officers.   The two battalions in rear fought a series
of gallant rear-guard actions all the way up Rue
Fleurie, and all three battalions had to ward off
attacks from the west.   To have stood and beaten off
their foes would have been simple, but to retire
sufficiently rapidly to avoid being cut off, and yet to
maintain unbroken order, was truly difficult.

Several patrols were encountered in Armentières
with which there were scraps.   Rue Marle was
already burning and being heavily shelled when the
Yorkshires passed, so, hearing that the railway bridge
had been already blown up, Lieutenant-Colonel
Misken led his battalion through the echoing streets
of Armentières to the Pont de Nieppe.   In the middle
of the town the leading platoon of " D " Company had
a scrap with a party of Boche, of whom the officer was
killed.   Lieutenant-Colonel Vignoles, with his headquarters and " A " Company, had a sharp encounter
with the enemy, who barred his approach to the
timber bridge near the railway, and, in forcing his
way through, some casualties occurred.   The bridge
had been destroyed, but the party contrived to get
over with the aid of some ingenuity and planks.

There were many wounded in the aid post in the
Jute Factory, and, as it seemed impossible to get them
across the river, Captain K. D. C. MacRae,
R.A.M.C., and Captain J. F. Jollands, C.F., stayed
with them.   The enemy, however, did not press

forward, and with the help of four men of the R.A.M.C. all the wounded were successfully brought away.

The rest of the force, hearing the sound of the scrap, turned off and crossed by the Pont de Nieppe, the last of the column being the headquarters of the 10th Lincolns, which left the bridge at eight-twenty-seven p.m. That this bridge remained available for the remnants of the 103rd Brigade was due to the cool patience and foresight of Major Russel, commanding the 208th Field Company, who had been authorised to destroy it as early as six-thirty p.m., the last of the 102nd Brigade having then passed over, but decided to wait and see. Captain Clements threw out outposts of the bridgehead guard, which was composed of " B " Company, 18th Northumberlands, towards the right flank where the Boche was already much in evidence. The railway and adjacent timber bridge was destroyed at six-forty-five p.m., and the garrison of Pont de Nieppe came under machine gun fire from both flanks, and a very considerable amount of shelling.

However, they waited patiently and were rewarded, for it was undoubtedly due to this delay that the bulk of the 103rd Brigade got away just when the Germans thought they had got them.[1]

[1] It is necessary to explain briefly the dramatic and very opportune appearance of the 4th Duke of Wellington's at Erquinghem earlier in the day.

On 9th April, the 147th Brigade, 25th Division, after a march in the morning, paraded in the afternoon, near Reninghelst, for the presentation of medal ribbons by General Plumer commanding 2nd Army. The various units were just settling down for the night when an order came for them to embus for the Armentières front. Between midnight and four a.m. on 10th, they got off from their various camps, and, debusing at De Seule, they marched to the neighbourhood of Le Veau, where they dumped their packs, had tea, and an easy. About nine a.m. they were off again to l'Epinette.

General Nicholson had been informed, in advance, of the movement of the brigade, and selected l'Epinette as its point of assembly, as from there the brigade could act effectively either with the 101st or the 74th Brigade. Thus the timely entry of the 4th Duke of Wellington's became possible.

Just when the arrival of this welcome reinforcement was reported to him, General Nicholson heard the unpleasant news that Messines

The various units of the 34th Division as they crossed the river were collected and reorganised. This was a long and difficult undertaking, but by midnight 10th/11th a line was built up parallel to the northern bank of the river, though some of the weary troops did not reach their final positions till close on dawn on 11th. In the dark considerable intermingling of units occurred, and many men lost their units. These stragglers were, on the next day, collected and attached temporarily to the 207th and 208th Field Companies, and this composite force, under Majors Glendenning and Cook, did good service in closing a gap on the right of the 74th Brigade.

The touch with the 101st on his left, which General Craigie Halkett had so frequently instilled to the 3rd Worcesters as they were forced back, was a counsel of perfection that could not, under the circumstances, be fully carried out, and parties of Boches had intruded and made themselves very unpleasant with machine gun and rifle fire north of Waterlands, as far as Le Veau, threatening to cut our line of retreat from the river along the Bailleul road. Against these adventurous gentry went a mixed force, the bulk of which was the companies of the 4th Duke of Wellington's, which had just come out of the Erquinghem fight, but with them were odds and ends of the headquarters of 102nd Brigade, remains of two sections of 208th Field Company, and various men of other units. The enemy were driven out, leaving behind a machine gun and some dead of 371st Regiment. The 209th Field Company arrived and connected up with the left of the 3rd Worcesters, but shortly were relieved by the 1/2nd Monmouths,

had fallen, and the 15th Corps added a hint to be sparing in the use of reserves. Therefore, though otherwise the General might have been tempted to use some of the 147th Brigade to aid the 74th in their gallant struggle, he felt obliged, after ordering the 4th Duke of Wellington's to Erquinghem, to keep the remaining battalions intact near l'Epinette till eleven a.m., when they were ordered to occupy the Nieppe system to protect the left flank of the division in its retirement, which was done early in the afternoon.

Pioneers of 29th Division, who had arrived on the scene with the 88th Brigade, which had left St Jan-ter-Biezen on the previous afternoon and hurried up by bus and marching, arriving about seven p.m., and thus for the third time was the Boche held up when a break through seemed imminent.

The companies of the 18th Northumberlands, as they arrived, were disposed west of Nieppe in support.

Many very strange sights were to be seen in Nieppe this afternoon; comedy and tragedy were strangely mixed. The parties of refugees flocking down the road: "Grandmother in armchair on wheelbarrow, pushed by grandson; mother, with sack of cooking gear, leading cow; small girl with calf; old man pushing a bicycle, used as a sort of pack animal, carrying two beds; small boy bearing family clock. All dressed in best Sunday black. Devoted but perspiring swain carrying off a hefty young lady sitting side saddle on the top bar of the cycle he is riding." A poor old chap quite mad with grief went raging to and fro. Wounded came streaming through, and weary, dirty men searching for their units. Every now and then shells dropped among the buildings and on the road, and bullets from the adventurous machine gun intruders whistled by. Through this pandemonium, sedately, as if on his way to a mother's meeting, Padre Hinchcliffe trundled a barrow load of S.A.A. to a company of the 1st East Lancashires. The three brigades of the 34th Division and the 147th Brigade had their headquarters in Nieppe that night.[1]

---

[1] The following incident must have occurred on the 9th or 10th April: The Germans were held up in one place by a single machine gun. Try as they would, they could not get on, so deadly was its fire. At last an officer hoisted a white flag, and went forward to ask the gun team to surrender. To his astonishment, he found only one man alive. Him he promised the best treatment and all kinds of things to chuck up, but the lad said no he would die with his comrades. The German officer went back, and the lad fought on till he was killed.

A German officer related the story to Professor Brice, of Lille University, saying that it was splendid, and had much impressed

The enemy was fairly quiet during the night, the fog of war probably lying densely over our movements. Early on the 11th, however, the attack was renewed, its weight falling on the 102nd Brigade and various teams of " A," " B," and " C " Companies of the Machine Gun Battalion, which, during the withdrawal, had taken up positions in the line held by that brigade.

The brigade held the railway near the Lys, and thence down the river to Burnley Post, with the left thrown back to the Nieppe system, where it was in touch with the 147th Brigade, the left of which was in touch with the right of the 25th Division, whose line passed through Oosthove Farm. The 22nd Northumberlands were on the left, the 23rd in the centre, and next to them the 25th, whose right flank rested on a post on the railway in which were two guns of " A " Company, Machine Gun Battalion, under Lieutenant Sims. This post was in touch with the left of the 1st East Lancashires.

The enemy pressed his attack very hard, and gradually forced the Northumberlands back. The chief pressure was on the left, and " C " Company of the 22nd Battalion, which was acting as rear-guard, failed to get away, " practically the whole company becoming casualties." 'At about noon the enemy managed to obtain a lodgment in Pont Nieppe, where, after close fighting with the 23rd Battalion, he forced our men out of Burnley Post into the northern end of Pont Nieppe village. This drove a wedge into our line, exposing the left flank of the 25th Battalion, and forced it to retire. In this area several guns of the " B," " C," and " D " Companies, Machine Gun Battalion, under Second-Lieutenants Mathieson, Craig, Stevens, and Lieutenant Begg seem to have

the German troops. Professor Brice told the tale to Major Whirrell, R.A.M.C., who had served with the 40th Division in the fighting round Armentières. Major Whirrell felt convinced that the heroic machine gunner must have belonged to the 34th Battalion M.G.C., and communicated the story to General Nicholson, who read it to the 34th Battalion M.G.C. on Armistice day.

P

been cut off with their teams. The attack gradually involved the left of the 1st East Lancs, where, about three p.m., " C " Company lost heavily, being taken in enfilade by machine gun fire, and a few were captured. This incursion between the East Lancashires and 25th Northumberlands penetrated to the north of Les Tilleuls right up to the Headquarters of " A " Company, Machine Gun Battalion, the commander of which, Captain Dumaresq, organised a counter-attack with " Duke of Wellington's, Royal Scots, and machine gunners, and the situation was restored, but it was found that Captain Dumaresq, M.C., was missing. In his counter-attack many Boche were killed, and one unwounded prisoner captured."

Thus the front line troops were gradually forced back into the Nieppe system, which was occupied by the 147th Brigade, and on this line the Boche could make no impression, although the brigade was hard pressed till evening.

While this severe pressure was being exercised from the south, the attacks on the 25th Division from the east were having some disagreeable results, and about two p.m. a party of the enemy appeared in the rear of the 101st, and on the left rear of 147th Brigade, about La Rue du Sac and Pabot, whence they were ejected with some loss by a vigorous attack made by a composite battalion attached to 103rd Brigade, which had been made up of the elements of the 13th Yorkshires, 12th Suffolks, and 20th Middlesex, and some Australian Engineers, with a company of the 18th Northumberlands, the whole being under command of Lieutenant-Colonel C. E. M. Richards, M.C., 20th Middlesex. The chief work seemed to fall to the 12th Suffolk contingent, who had about seventy casualties. Throughout the fighting on this flank, the guns of 122nd Brigade R.F.A., particularly two batteries detached north-west of Nieppe, did great work.

The fronts of the 103rd and 101st Brigades were otherwise what at those times we termed quiet. The 74th Brigade was reinforced during the night 10th/11th by the 5th York and Lancashire Regiment, the 9th Loyal North Lancashires being temporarily with the 40th Division. With a view to easing the pressure on the right flank, General Craigie Halkett was ordered to make an attempt to push back the Boche and make good the outskirts of Steenwerck. The front held by this brigade at dark on 10th, as already stated, was from Pont de Pierre to Steenwerck Station, and then along the railway. The 1/5th York and Lancs, on arrival at four a.m. on 11th, was ordered to prolong the line south-westwards. Its right rested on a track some three hundred yards west of the hamlet Cabaret du Saule, where it was in touch with some Royal Engineer details of the 40th Division, beyond whom were the remains of the Loyal North Lancashires.

A determined attack was made by the whole brigade, but the new arrivals seem to have been most heavily engaged. The enemy were found in strength in Cabaret du Saule, and his machine guns were numerous, and, of course, well posted and well served. The attack, supported by 121st Brigade Royal Field Artillery, succeeded in pushing the Huns back to the outskirts of Steenwerck, and the fight was kept up all day, swaying backwards and forwards, both sides suffering many casualties, but the advantage lay with the brigade, especially in the York and Lancs area, till a strong attack on the troops on that battalion's right forced them back, and the Brigadier ordered a retirement to the line of the southern branch of the Stilbecque, and a defensive flank was thrown back on the right, north of the stream.

The 3rd Worcester casualties in this day are not given, but the 11th East Lancashires lost Second-Lieutenant J. V. Blackwell killed, and had over fifty other casualties, while the York and Lancs battalion lost seventeen officers, Lieutenant-Colonel Rhodes and four others alone remaining at duty, and the casualties in the ranks were in proportion.

In spite of these losses the attack was a distinct tactical success, in that it prevented another attempt to turn the 34th Division's right, and enabled the division to pivot on the 74th Brigade in the retirement which soon became necessary.

To quote the Commander-in-Chief's despatch : " Owing to the progress made by the enemy in the Ploegstreet sector, the position of the 34th at Nieppe, where they had beaten off a determined attack during the morning, became untenable. Accordingly, in the early part of the night our troops at Nieppe fell back, under orders, to the neighbourhood of Pont d'Achelles."

How simple it sounds ! But I don't think that anyone who was concerned in that night's operation will ever forget it. The troops had been engaged heavily for three days and nights, and had suffered heavy losses. The night was very dark, detailed maps were scarce, the positions alike of friends and foes were very uncertain and were constantly changing.

The plan of retirement was for the 101st, 102nd, and 103rd Brigades to retire by the 'Armentières-Bailleul railway and road covered by the 147th Brigade as rear-guard. The four brigades were to pass through the 88th and 74th Brigades to assembly positions in rear. The artillery were ordered back to positions about the Mont de Lille and Ravelsberg, east of Bailleul. The enemy evidently suspected some such movement, and barraged the railway so heavily that the troops had to leave it and find their way across country in small parties. Steenwerck Station, assigned as the rendezvous of the 103rd Brigade, was found in the hands of the Boche, and the Staff Captain had much difficulty in directing the scattered parties of his brigade to the new

Actions of
9TH, 10TH & 11TH APRIL, 1918.

REFERENCE

Position at midnight on 9th/10th . . . .
Round Erquinghem 10th . . . .
" " at midnight on 10th/11th . . . .
" " at midnight on 11th/12th . . . .

Scale of Yards.
1000   0   1000   2000   3000   4000

assembly position. "D" Company of the 1st
East Lancashires, was cut off, but fought its
way through. General Lewes handled his rear-
guard so well that the eager enemy was held off,
and, in fact, seems not fully to have realised what
we were doing.

The 74th Brigade was on the right in its old
position. Its relief by the 92nd Brigade of the 31st
Division, which was to have taken place during the
night, had proved impossible, but the 93rd Brigade,
of the same division, by a counter-attack had driven
back the enemy on what had been the 40th Division
front, on General Craigie Halkett's right. In rear
of the 74th, at the west end of La Creche, was the
101st, to which the 18th Northumberlands had been
attached, and 147th was still farther back, and slightly
to the west. On the left of the 74th was the 88th
Brigade, very much in the position it had held the
previous day, and in rear of it was the 103rd Brigade
in La Creche, with the 102nd one thousand yards
north of it. Thus the fortuitous line of the 11th,
the result of the enemy's furious attacks of the two
previous days, had been replaced by a well-established
line from close to Rue du Sac on the left, in touch
with 25th Division, to near Le Becque on the right,
in touch with 93rd Brigade of 31st Division, about
seven thousand yards held by two brigades, with four
others in rear. It must, however, be remembered
that, with the exception of the 88th Brigade, all these
formations had suffered many casualties.

The G.O.C. and advance Divisional Headquarters moved back to Le Grand Hazard under
Corps orders, and had a most unpleasant drive there
during the night, 11th/12th—no lights, roads
crammed with troops and vehicles; in one place they
drove through a bath of burning petrol. The whole
eastern sky was lit up by burning villages and petrol
dumps.

The enemy attacked our left flank early on 12th.

He appears not to have known that we had left Nieppe, for he made a " set piece " attack on the empty village. Large forces were then massed north of the village, and attacks were made on the 88th Brigade, all along the line which extended from the railway near Steenwerck Station to close to the west end of Rue du Sac, with a very pronounced salient at Pont d'Achelles, on which the weight of the attacks fell. This part of the line was held by the Monmouths, who maintained their position well, in spite of early in the attack losing four officers and seventy-five other ranks from trench mortar and machine gun fire. At one o'clock General Freyberg, 88th Brigade, is able to report that everything was satisfactory on his front, but later the enemy extended his operations and attacked the 75th Brigade, 25th Division, on his left, and at four p.m. the Boche attacked in great strength at Pont d'Achelles, and also on the left of the Monmouths, near Lampernisse, the line was broken, and eight officers and some four hundred men of the Monmouths, who refused to give ground, were cut off. The Newfoundland Battalion made a gallant counter-attack, in which a Lieutenant Moore and his platoon " fought to a finish, neither he nor his gallant platoon being seen again." The sacrifice, however, was not in vain, for it gave time for Lieutenant-Colonel Woodruffe, Newfoundland Battalion, to form a line with his headquarters and " C " Company, and with " A " Company fighting stoutly on his right to stem the Huns' onrush and to extricate some of the Monmouths, though Lieutenant-Colonel J. Evans records with regret that the total strength of the Monmouth Companies after the fight was only four officers and about one hundred and fifty other ranks. About six p.m. the remaining companies of the Newfoundlers came up, and made a brave but unsuccessful attempt to drive back the enemy on the left; their leader, Captain Strong, being mortally wounded. The situation was undoubtedly very critical for some time, till the dashing attack of Colonel Woodruffe's men had restored the situation.

The 23rd Northumberlands, which had been placed at General Freyberg's disposal, took up a position under cover of which the line was withdrawn, about six-thirty p.m., to the road junction at De Seule, where the 23rd Northumberlands and Newfoundlanders dug and wired a new trench line.

The line to the north of this was carried on by a single battalion of the 100th Brigade, beyond which there was a considerable gap to the right flank of the 75th Brigade, at the junction of the Kortepyp and Neuve Eglise road.

Now to turn to the right flank. About half-past ten on the morning of the 12th, General Craigie Halkett was told by the officer commanding a company of the 15th West Yorks, 93rd Brigade, that he had received orders to retire, and ten minutes later the enemy were seen entering Le Becque, and shortly after parties were seen about Blanche Maison.

To save the right flank from being enveloped General Gore sent the 11th Suffolks and 16th Royal Scots to form a line facing west from the junction of the Stilbecque and Becque de Flanche, along the line of the last stream, and this line was carried on as far as the railway, some three hundred yards from Bailleul Station by the 6th and 7th Duke of Wellington's of the 147th Brigade. No touch being obtained there with any British troops the 4th Duke of Wellington's was ordered to prolong this flank. A battalion of the 103rd was also held in readiness, if necessary, to carry the line on as far as Meteren. These precautions were taken because large forces of all arms of the enemy were seen about Nooteboom, and the trend of the movement seemed towards the valley between Meteren and Bailleul.

Although this flank was threatened thus early

no attack was made till the afternoon, and about three p.m. the 19th Brigade of 33rd Division was seen approaching on the east of Meteren. In the afternoon several attacks were made on the 16th Royal Scots, which were repulsed, four guns of " D " Company, Machine Gun Battalion, doing good service. About five-thirty p.m. an attack in force was launched against the Royal Scots, and there was heavy fighting, in which the Scotsmen were forced to give ground, but the line was quickly re-formed with the help of battalions of the 147th Brigade.

In order to further secure this flank, General Gore, who, as senior Brigadier on the spot, was allowed considerable independent action by the Divisional Commander, sent the 9th Northumberlands, 103rd Brigade, to prolong this flank as far as the St Jans Capelle road. Thus by midnight on the 12th/13th General Nicholson's command was disposed in a semicircle from De Seule to the north-western exits of Bailleul, the chord of the arc measuring about five thousand five hundred yards, the actual length of the line held being about nine thousand yards. The available reserves were the 103rd Brigade, of which the 10th Lincolns was behind the 101st Brigade, the 9th Northumberland Fusiliers in Bailleul, and the 1st East Lancashires about one thousand yards north of La Creche. The 98th Brigade, 33rd Division, had two battalions in the Bailleul lunatic asylum, and one near the Mont de Lille.

To cover this very long front there were only two brigades of the 38th Divisional Artillery, which remained in the positions they had taken up the night before. At five-fifty p.m. the division was transferred to the 9th Corps, and advanced headquarters were opened at Mont Noir.

The enemy, as usual, was fairly quiet during the night, but became active in the morning, and was reported opposite our centre and right. These concentrations were successfully dealt with by our artillery and machine guns, but in one instance the Huns penetrated a short distance into the 11th Lancashires' line, but, with the aid of the guns, were soon ejected. A serious attack was launched at about three-thirty p.m. It fell chiefly on the right of the 11th Suffolks, the 16th Royal Scots, and 6th and 7th Duke of Wellington's. For some time no impression was made, but finally weight of numbers told, and the line was forced back from two to five hundred yards. There was severe fighting, but finally a firm line was established.

On the left flank heavy fighting went on all day. About six a.m. a heavy attack was made on the 23rd Northumberlands and the troops of the 100th Brigade and 25th Division, farther north of them. Three assaults were beaten off, and severe losses inflicted on the enemy, but the gap already alluded to beyond the battalion of the 100th Brigade was enlarged to meet this encircling movement. The 25th Northumberlands, in brigade reserve, was moved into this area. About six o'clock in the evening the enemy made a desperate attack on the 22nd Northumberlands and two platoons of the Highland Light Infantry, which were holding De Seule. A single shell made casualties all the headquarter officers of the 22nd except the Signalling Officer, Colonel Studd and Captain R. L. Tate, R.C., U.S.A. Unit, medical officer, being killed.

The 23rd Northumberlands, a little farther north, was also involved, a very gallant fight being put up by Lieutenant Pigg, some eight hundred yards west of the De Seule-Neuve Eglise road. As the movement progressed, the 25th Northumberlands came into action, and eventually the line in this part was facing almost north. The garrison of De Seule was driven back fighting, and the Newfoundlanders, 88th Brigade reserve, were again hurried up. There was much mixed fighting. "D" Company, under

Captain Clift, caught a column of Huns in mass astride De Broeken road, and gave a good account of them; the other companies of the Newfoundland Battalion joined in the fray. A gap having occurred between "D" and "C" Companies, Captain Clift, calling to him men of the Northumberlands, closed it and held up the attack twenty-five yards from his line. Thus the advance of the enemy at this point was stayed at about nine p.m., and the efforts of the Boche to close the pincers in which he thought that he held General Nicholson's forces failed, and during the night they slipped away.

The situation on this flank had been growing more critical as the day advanced. General Chaplin, who watched the progress of the fight from the Ravelsberg, occupied the forward slopes of that hill by one of the battalions of his brigade. Critical as the situation was, the G.O.C. did not feel justified in ordering any withdrawal, as he had promises of relief by two brigades of the 59th Division, and was told that the 71st Brigade was hurrying up to close the gap between the 34th and 25th Divisions. About nine-thirty p.m. reports from the 102nd and 88th Brigades showed that, unless immediately withdrawn, the whole line south of the Armentières-Bailleul road would be turned. Accordingly, after ascertaining from Corps Headquarters that there was no hope of the 71st Brigade arriving in time, the G.O.C. ordered a withdrawal of the whole line to the position already laid out, pivoting on the section Steam Mill-Bailleul Station, which was carried out successfully, the Boche having been too severely mauled to attempt to interfere.

Just before the retirement commenced, General Gore and his Brigade Signalling Officer were killed by a shell, which also wounded Captain Gilbey, the Brigade-Major. This was a serious loss to the division, and especially to the 101st Brigade, which the General had commanded since its arrival in

France, and which had learnt to love him and admire his imperturbable coolness and bravery.

Lieutenant-Colonel Stephenson, of the 16th Royal Scots, took the General's place temporarily, the poor remnants of the 15th and 16th Royal Scots being amalgamated into one battalion, under command of Major Osborne, who was acting in command of the former.

The line to which the division and attached troops fell back had been prepared, to a certain extent, by the three Field Companies on 13th, and was partially garrisoned by a battalion of the Middlesex Regiment, placed at General Nicholson's disposal by the 33rd Division. The withdrawal was completed by two-thirty a.m. on 14th. The 102nd Brigade, now reduced to the strength of a weak battalion, marched to the neighbourhood of Hille, where it was reorganised as a Composite Battalion, under command of Lieutenant-Colonel H. S. Neaves, D.S.O., M.C., with a strength of four hundred and sixty-two all ranks, to whom were added ninety of the Motor Machine Gun Company and 34th Machine Gun Battalion with ten guns.

The 147th Brigade was on the right, extending from Steam Mill to Bailleul Station exclusive, about one thousand five hundred yards. Immediately on its right were some five hundred men of the Corps Reinforcement Battalion, only partially trained and organised, behind whom General Lewes thought it prudent to place three platoons of the 4th Duke of Wellington's. Beyond the reinforcements was the 19th Brigade, 33rd Division. From Bailleul Station inclusive to the western foot of the Mont de Lille, some seven hundred and fifty yards, came the remnant of the 101st Brigade, with which, since the 10th, the 18th Northumberlands had been leading a troublesome life, its companies being attached now to one, now to another battalion, as the exigencies of the battle required. Across the Mont de Lille, about one thousand one hundred yards, the line was held by the 74th Brigade; then came the 88th Brigade, holding one thousand one hundred yards to the little post of fifty men of the 102nd Brigade at Peuter Farm, beyond which the 103rd Brigade held the line which curved back to the vicinity of Crucifix Corner, a front of about one thousand six hundred yards. The 9th Northumberlands held the left of the line with " A " and " B " Companies, in posts round the south and east of the hill, on the summit of which stood the Crucifix, the left of " A " being nearly on the Neuve Eglise road. In this neighbourhood were some two hundred men of 9th Cheshires and Worcesters of 100th Brigade, and farther to the north came the 71st Brigade.

The troops of the 103rd had had little opportunity for rest in their new positions, when at about four-twenty a heavy bombardment warned them that an attack was imminent. Lieutenant-Colonel Vignoles quickly brought up his reserve companies and head-quarter personnel. The enemy advanced in great strength, and engaged the outposts vigorously. These fought fiercely, all in a post under Captain Davies, who died two days later, being either killed or wounded. Captain Patten was killed, and all the officers of " B " became casualties, but the remainder of the company, under Acting Company Sergeant-Major Hardman, at a third attempt drove off the Boche, deceiving them as to their numbers by their loud shouts. " A " Company, finding the Huns had got through the out posts, left their trenches, and, led by Lieutenant H. S. Rowe, after a sanguinary fight in some old bayonet fighting trenches, ousted the intruders, losing all their officers except Second-Lieutenant J. L. Baker.

The Huns, who got between the posts, moved up the hill, being met by the various units holding it, and a fierce mêlée was in progress when Lieutenant-Colonel Vignoles' party arrived at the crest, and turned the scale in our favour. The hill was quickly cleared, the enemy leaving many dead and a machine gun behind. By nine a.m. the position was completely re-established.

While this attack was in progress the enemy also assailed the 33rd Division on our right, and continued his assaults throughout the day. He also advanced and dug in in front of the 147th, 74th, and 101st Brigades, and made several local attacks. One of these, on the 74th Brigade front, was met and defeated, with the loss of about thirty killed and an officer and several other ranks and three machine guns, by a counter-attack made by the headquarters personnel of the York and Lancs Battalion and a party of the Loyal North Lancashires, under Second-Lieutenant Downing.

Hostile forces were also seen to be massing opposite the right of the division. As the bombardment was very heavy and a general attack seemed imminent, the last reserve, the poor remnant of the 102nd Brigade, was brought up, and permission asked of the 33rd Division to use the Middlesex battalion, which was in rear of the 74th Brigade, should he need its services. The attack on the 74th was, however, defeated by Lewis gun fire, and four machine guns were captured.

At twelve-fifty p.m. orders were received that the division would be relieved by the 176th and 178th Brigades of the 59th Division, which had been our next-door neighbours in the battle of 21st to 23rd March. The former was to relieve the 147th, 101st, and 74th Brigades, and the latter the 88th and 103rd. These brigades were nearly up to full strength, so they outnumbered the units they relieved.

'At two-fifteen a very intense barrage was put down on the Mont de Lille and Bailleul Station, and the enemy began massing troops opposite the front and right flank of the 147th Brigade, and a little after four a heavy attack was launched, the brunt of which fell on the right of the 4th Duke of Wellington's at Steam Mill, and the mixed body of Corps Reinforcements beyond them. The latter could not withstand it, and gave way, exposing the flank of the garrison of the Mill, which, after a very brave fight, was overpowered, practically all being either killed or wounded, Second-Lieutenant J. H. Kitson being among the former. Two companies of the 7th Battalion were hurried up, and three companies of the Middlesex were also moved to this flank. The line was restored, but the Mill was not recaptured, the divisional relief putting a stop to a counter-attack which had been organised. The casualties sustained by the 147th during the day amounted to about one hundred and thirty.

About five p.m. another intense barrage struck the left of the line, and a little later another attack was launched against the 9th Northumberlands, but the guns and machine guns played such havoc on their fivefold line that the Huns melted away, not one reaching our line.

At eight p.m., the 74th Brigade, by a counter-attack from a flank, defeated another attack, with severe loss to the enemy. Thus ended a fierce fight and a long day of heavy shelling, patiently endured by very weary troops, whom neither shell nor bayonet could move. A worthy end to six days of hard fighting under the most disadvantageous of circumstances.

The relief was carried out without any interference from the enemy, and the brigades reached their new positions by five-forty-five a.m. on 15th April. The 121st and 122nd Brigades, R.F.A., which, since the 11th, had been gradually retiring in accordance with the situation, remained to cover the 59th Division front, and five batteries of the 36th D.A. were added to General Topping's command on the morning of the 15th. Ever since the 9th April General

Topping's two brigades had been covering the whole of General Nicholson's very extended front, aided only by the heavies of the Corps. By rapid switching it had managed to stop many of the enemy's advances, and had dispersed many of his concentrations, but very little could be done in the way of counter-battery work, and consequently the losses inflicted by the various bombardments had been very severe.

Some readjustment of the line was made during the morning of the 15th, and by noon the troops were disposed in a curve some one thousand eight hundred to two thousand yards north of the northern edge of Bailleul, extending westwards from a point due south of St Jans Capelle. The 147th were on the right, then the 101st and 74th, and on the left the 103rd in touch with the 100th Brigade. The 88th and 102nd were in reserve west of Croix de Poperinghe. The line was not continuous, consisting of posts at wide intervals, and unprotected by any wire, but each unit dug in during the morning. For the first time for seven days we were out of the reach of bullets, and we all enjoyed ourselves, and the lucky ones got baths.

Advanced Divisional Headquarters joined Rear Divisional Headquarters at La Montagne, south-west of Boeschepe.

But our enjoyment was rudely put an end to by the enemy attacking the 59th Division in great force. At four-twenty-five p.m. all brigades stood to and manned the trenches in front of them, and the 102nd was brought up between the 74th and 103rd. At eight p.m. the 176th and 177th Brigades were seen to be withdrawing, and at nine-fifty-five p.m. orders were received that the 34th Division would push out posts to its front to cover this withdrawal. The enemy had attacked with fresh troops, taken Crucifix Hill, and then worked westwards along the Ravelsberg Ridge, taking the 59th Division in flank.

Two companies of the 9th Northumberlands on the left, where the situation was very obscure, were pushed forward some distance to meet the retiring troops, but the enemy did not press his advantage, though by eleven-twenty-five p.m. he had occupied Bailleul. The North Staffords of the 176th Brigade drew up on the right of the 147th Brigade, and the 33rd Division withdrew to the Meteren Switch, its left in touch with them; thus a new front line was formed, and we were in action again within sixteen hours of being relieved. The artillery of the 38th Division, and the five batteries of the 36th working with them, withdrew battery by battery, and took up new positions about Berthen.

The situation was far from pleasant. The strength and position of the enemy, as well as the lines on which he was advancing, were not known, and there had been no time to form an organised outpost line. Behind the 34th there were only two battalions of dismounted French cavalry between the enemy and the important ridges of Mont Noir and Boeschepe.

By midnight the 34th Division line was firmly established, and in order to give more depth to the defence, the 102nd Brigade was withdrawn and placed in reserve behind the 74th. At this time General Nicholson had only four thousand five hundred bayonets in the front line and two thousand five hundred in reserve.

Throughout the night the enemy's patrols were active on the left half of our line, and on that of the 100th Brigade, on our left. All the Brigade Headquarters were brought together at Mont Noir, in a large dug-out, in which General Nicholson established a report centre under a Staff Officer. By this means the Divisional Artillery was kept in such close touch with the infantry in the line that it achieved much success in dealing with hostile concentrations and in stopping attacks.

In view of the serious situation the 25th Division was asked to take up the organisation of the army second line, in which were the two battalions of dismounted French cavalry, and later, when the Composite Brigade, composed of the remaining elements of 7th and 75th Brigades, was placed at General Nicholson's disposal, it was directed to march to Wolfhoek in Divisional Reserve.

As the hostile movement seemed to be towards St Jans Capelle the 147th Brigade was strengthened by one hundred men, under Second-Lieutenant Viner, representing all that remained of the 23rd Northumberland Fusiliers. The remains of the two Pioneer Battalions, 18th Northumberland Fusiliers and 1/2nd Monmouthshires, with the rest of the 88th and 102nd Brigades, were placed in the army line behind the centre and left.

Every preparation was made to meet the coming attack. The front line troops dug and put up wire, while the Staffs prepared precise schemes for reinforcement and counter-attacks. General Nicholson called on his troops to hold on *coûte que coûte* till the arrival of French troops, which were hurrying up.

During the 16th the enemy put down several very severe barrages, and made several probing advances, which were dealt with by the artillery and machine guns; but it was not till four-twenty p.m. that a serious infantry attack was launched from the lunatic asylum against the 1/4th and 1/6th Duke of Wellington's, accompanied by a very intense barrage along the whole line.

The infantry attack was met by our counter-barrage from heavy and field artillery and machine guns, and being counter-attacked by the two battalions of Duke of Wellington's it failed completely. The enemy suffered very severely. Over one hundred bodies were subsequently counted on a very limited front. "A" Company, 6th Duke of Wellington's, took thirteen prisoners and three machine guns out of one of the buildings in a counter-attack.

According to the statements of prisoners, this attack was made by a complete regiment in two waves, and the attack was covered by the elements of another regiment on the right, which advanced against the 74th Brigade, but was also repulsed, the 74th capturing ten prisoners and a machine gun. The losses of the regiment which attacked the Duke of Wellington's were estimated to have reached fifty per cent.

While this assault was being made on our right, the Hun made a heavy onslaught on to the 2nd Worcesters, the right battalion of the 100th Brigade on the division's left flank. A call for help from that hardly pressed battalion was promptly responded to by three companies of the 9th Northumberlands, which made a gallant counter-attack, driving back the enemy with heavy losses to themselves, but inflicting heavy casualties on the Huns.

These successes greatly improved the situation, and, except for local attacks on our outpost line, no further attack was made, and the critical moment was safely passed.

The night of the 16th/17th passed quietly, but at six-thirty the enemy put down an intense bombardment on the 103rd Brigade area, shifting the barrage backwards and forwards, varying in severity, and at eight a.m. extended it to the 74th front. All preparations were made to receive an attack, but none was delivered, and information obtained from prisoners pointed to our artillery had saved us. The two brigades, however, had suffered severely, and, after having driven off two minor attacks, were relieved by the 88th and 102nd.

At this time the headquarters of all the brigades were in a tunnelled dug-out on Mont Noir, and they were joined there by the G.O.C. and G.S.O.1, as the heavy shelling made communication between Advance

Divisional Headquarters and Mont Noir almost impossible.

At noon the divisions on our flanks beat off strong attacks, and throughout the afternoon our artillery was engaged in breaking up attacks on our front.

During the morning and early afternoon, General Nicholson received further reinforcements, the 13th Tank Battalion, with forty-eight Lewis guns, and the 89th Infantry Brigade being placed at his disposal. The former was directed to allot half its guns to each of the 147th and 89th Brigades, and the latter brigade was ordered to relieve the 101st. At the same time the 88th relieved the 103rd, and the 102nd the 74th. The 74th Brigade, as soon as the relief was completed, was sent back to the 25th Division to reorganise. The 101st and 103rd Brigades had been so reduced in strength that they were formed into one Composite Brigade, under General Chaplin. The 153rd Brigade, R.F.A., joined the D.A., and covered the front of the right infantry brigade; five batteries of 36th D.A. covered the right centre, the 121st Brigade, R.F.A., the left centre, and the 122nd Brigade the left infantry brigade.

An attempt of the enemy to creep up against the centre and left was kept at a distance by our gunners. The reliefs were all safely completed by four-fifteen a.m., 18th April, and, except for some shelling, the front was quiet throughout the day. The 101st/103rd Brigade was moved back into the army second line, leaving two battalions north of it for immediate reinforcements. The 18th Northumberland Fusiliers were sent to Wolfhoek to work under the C.R.E.

A readjustment of the troops on the right set free the 19th Infantry Brigade of the 33rd Division, which was placed at General Nicholson's disposal, and sent to La Levrette area in reserve, and on the night 18th/19th relieved the 147th Brigade, which had been in the line since 10th April. The North

Staffords was relieved by the 98th Brigade and sent to Locre to rejoin the 59th Division.

The fighting now died down on our front, and during the next three days arrangements were completed and carried out for the relief of General Nicholson's force by the 133rd French Division. At eight a.m. on 21st our General handed over command, and moved his headquarters to Abeele. On the 22nd the division concentrated in the St Jan ter Biezen area.

" The Quarter-Master and transport met us with officers' valises and spare clothes, and we enjoyed the luxury of a bath and a change, after three weeks without taking our clothes off. Officers and men were, by this time, what the British soldier describes as ' chatty.' "

When relieved, the division had been in action for twelve days. Throughout this period, although frequently attacked heavily in front and on both flanks, the 34th Division had maintained an unbroken front, and it is no exaggeration to say that no unit, however small, ever retired until it was ordered to do so. At times, for hours together, control by Divisional Headquarters, Brigade, and even Battalion Commanders, was impossible, but the steadfastness and gallantry of the men, and the initiative of officers and non-commissioned officers, never failed. In this respect the operations may justly be called a " soldiers' battle." In speaking of the 34th Division I include, of course, the troops of other formations, which reinforced General Nicholson's original command, and rendered such gallant aid, without which the losses sustained by the infantry of the division would have made it impossible for it to remain in action.

On the 30th April a telegram was received by the General Officer Commanding from the Commander-in-Chief, thanking the division for its services, and this was communicated to all troops which had served under his command.

The following message from Sir Douglas Haig was much appreciated by all ranks :

" To 34th Division.
" My thanks are due to General Nicholson, to the 34th Division, and to the troops which, during the recent fighting, have been attached to General Nicholson's command for the many gallant actions fought by them round Armentières and Bailleul. The carrying out successfully of their withdrawal from Armentières in circumstances of exceptional difficulty and heavy fighting of the subsequent days called for a high standard of efficiency, discipline, and courage on the part of both officers and men. Please convey to General Nicholson and all ranks who served under him the expression of my appreciation."

General Nicholson's appreciation of the work done by the 38th Divisional Artillery was conveyed to General Topping in a letter, of which the following is a copy :

" C.R.A., 38th Division.
" Now that the infantry of the 34th Division is being withdrawn from the line, the G.O.C. wishes to record his appreciation of the services rendered by the artillery of the 38th Division and by the other artillery brigades which have gradually been attached to it.
" On the 9th April, the artillery of the 38th Division alone for some hours covered a front of nearly eighteen thousand yards, and by its steady accurate shooting enabled the infantry to preserve that front intact. This is an exploit of which the artillery of the 38th Division may well be proud.
" During the subsequent days the artillery of the 38th Division, supplemented by other brigades of artillery, have inspired ever-increasing confidence in the infantry of the division, have enabled them to beat off repeated hostile attacks, and on more than one

occasion have prevented hostile attacks from developing.

"It is not too much to say that throughout the period the conduct of the artillery has been beyond all praise."

To each of the three infantry brigades which had hastened to his assistance General Nicholson sent a letter of thanks, in which the special services of each brigade were briefly stated, the letter ending, " Throughout the period the steadiness, gallantry, and endurance of all ranks has been worthy of the highest traditions of British infantry, and the G.O.C. 34th Division is proud to have had such troops under his command."

Battle casualties suffered between noon 8th April, 1918, and noon 21st April, 1918, by the troops under General Nicholson's command :

	KILLED		WOUNDED		MISSING		TOTAL	
	O.	O.R.	O.	O.R.	O.	O.R.	O.	O.R.
34th Division	30	243	125	2105	40	2395	195	4743
74th Infantry Brigade ...	3	31	18	191	1	83	22	305
88th Infantry Brigade								
497th Field Co., R.E.	6	136	19	619	4	351	29	1106
1/2 Monmouths (Pioneers)								
89th Infantry Brigade ...	—	14	4	39	2	1	6	54
147th Infantry Brigade								
49th Battalion M.G.C.	10	109	35	463	1	195	46	767
57th Field Co., R.E.								
Tank Corps.	—	4	1	2	—	—	1	6
36th Division Artillery ...	—	—	2	5	—	—	2	5
38th Division Artillery ...	1	12	23	140	—	16	24	168
TOTALS ...	50	549	227	3564	48	3041	325	7154

The doings of our own gunners during the stirring times I have just described must now be dealt with, though space forbids me to tell the story as fully as I should like to do.

When the storm broke on the 9th April, Colonel Walthall was enjoying a brief easy at Merville. The brigades of his command had begun relieving their opposite numbers of the 38th Divisional Artillery, and his O.C. Signals, Captain Allcard, was at the 38th Divisional Headquarters; the Adjutants and Brigade Signal Officers were all in the forward area. The brigades, except one section per battery, which had gone into the line, were at Haverskirke. The D.A.C. was at the wagon lines of 38th Division, taking over. Three eighteen pounders and two 4·5 inch howitzers had been condemned and sent to the workshops on 7th. Altogether, the artillery were in about as bad a position for rapid movement as it could be. The day commenced by a heavy bombardment of Merville, during which a shell destroyed the R.A.H.Q. billet and all the kit of those there, so that the C.R.A. had to function for a time in slacks and minus his belts, but in spite of all these hindrances, by three p.m. the two brigades were ready for action with all their guns, personnel, and ammunition complete. And a quarter of an hour later 152nd Brigade was in its appointed position, ready to support 151st Infantry Brigade, 50th Division. A great morning's work. Neuf Berquin was the first Headquarters assigned to the C.R.A., but the rapid progress of the battle necessitated his moving to the White Château, north of Merville, where the Divisional Headquarters of the 50th Division, to which the 34th D.A. was attached, opened during the afternoon.

During the whole of this battle the question of maintaining communication between the guns, the R.A.H.Q., and the infantry was very difficult. It was only by dint of constant hard work, and the exercise of considerable ingenuity, that during the rapid changes of the next few days the Signal Officers managed to keep communications open.

Early on 10th April all guns were turned on Pont Levis (Estaires), which had fallen into the enemy's hands, and at first some success was achieved, the bridge being recaptured at eight-forty-five a.m. but there was fierce fighting in the town all day, and the 149th and 150th Infantry Brigades made many gallant efforts to keep back the Huns. The fight swayed to and fro, but by three-fifty p.m. the enemy was reported to have taken the whole of the town, and at six-fifteen p.m. he was bringing guns over Pont Levis. The enemy's progress continued during the 11th and 12th, and constant moves had to be made. The White Château on 11th came in for intense bombardment, and once more headquarters had to shift, first to Le Pont Tournant, an *estaminet*, in which Madame and her daughter bravely stayed and fed the troops, and later to La Motte. These constant moves gave much work to the hard-worked Signal Detachment, and men and mules were scarce able to keep going. La Motte at this time held the headquarters of the Corps and two divisions, but on the night of 12th the 50th Division moved to Le Grand Hazard, and the others elsewhere.

All this time the batteries were hotly engaged. On 12th 152nd Brigade engaged hostile guns in the open over open sights on more than one occasion. Our gunners were now supporting many brigades which had been hurried up. On the 11th and 12th they covered the 149th, 86th, 87th, 92nd, and the Guards Brigade. The 13th was a day of heavy fighting all along the front of the Nieppe Forest. The enemy made many attacks, but the rifle fire of the infantry and that of our gunners was too much for him, and his offensive was evidently losing its force, or perhaps our resistance was hardening. The 14th was another day of heavy fighting, in the morning about La Couronne, and in the afternoon about Verte Rue, but the line held everywhere. The 119th Brigade, R.F.A., came under General Walthall's orders on

Actions of
11TH TO 21ST APRIL, 1918.

Scale of Yards.

0   500   1000   2000   3000

Neuve Église

Kortepyp

75th Bde.

25th DIV.

25th DIV. about here

100th Bde.

Bn 100th Bde.

23rd N.F.

la Seule

Lampernisse

la Rue du Sac

Papot

Pont d'Achelles

Pont de Pierre

Papot

Tombelle

le Veau

STEENWERCK

88th Brigade

la Crèche

14th Bde.

le Pont de Pierre

Becq

York & Lancs.

A Coy. 18th N.F.

Becq de la Flèche

11th Suff.

16th R.S.

93rd Bde.

Counter-attack on 11th

Blanche Maison on 11th

Cabt-du Saule

la Becque

Nooke Boom

6th D. or W.

147th Station Bde.

4th D. or W.

Steen Mill

19th Bde. 33rd Div.

METEREN

From HAZEBROUCK

33rd BRit. Div.
4 133rd Fr. Div.

St. Jans Cappel

147th Bde.

74th Bde. on 17th

101st Bde. on 16th

89th & 102nd Bdes.

101st & 74th Bdes.

88th Bde. on 17th

102nd & 103rd Bdes.

103rd Bdes. on 17th

103rd Bde. on 16th

Croix de Poperinghe

ARMY LINE on 17th

Army Line on 16th

49th DIV.

16th & 100th Bde. on 17th

100th Bde. on 17th

148

27 Bde.

Crucifix Corner

49th & 103rd Bdes.

102nd & 103rd Bdes.

Pheuter Farm

88th Bde.

74th Bde. on 16th

Ravelsberg

Mt. de Lille

101st Bde.

BAILLEUL

Asylum

Hille

this day.   Our gunners were this day covering the
95th British and 2nd Australian Infantry Brigades.
The guns got no rest at night, as they were called on
for harassing on roads and probable assembly points.
Prisoners reported that severe casualties were caused
by this night fire.   By the 17th the enemy was
brought to a standstill, and no further attacks were
made on the front covered by General Walthall.   The
enemy's line between the 10th and 17th had advanced
about seven thousand yards.   Not much to show for
seven days' costly fighting.

Messages of thanks and appreciation of the work
done were received from the 11th Corps, 31st and 5th
Divisions, and from the G.O.C. 15th Corps Artillery,
who said : " We should have been in a parlous state
on the 9th April without your timely assistance, and
so would the 50th Division."

Our gunners served in various parts of the line,
and had but little rest.   They eventually rejoined the
division on its reconstruction in July, 1918.

CHAPTER XII

THE END OF THE FIRST 34TH DIVISION AND THE FORMATION OF THE SECOND

AFTER relief by the 133rd French Division, Advance Divisional Headquarters moved to Abeele, and later, on 21st April, to Vogeltje, where the whole Divisional Headquarters was united. At Abeele Lieutenant-General Sir A. Hamilton-Gordon, commanding 11th Corps, met as many Brigade Commanders as could be collected, and in warm words thanked and congratulated them on the magnificent work done by their brigades. The Army Commander also visited Abeele, and told the G.O.C. that, owing to lack of reinforcements, it had been decided that the infantry of the division must be reduced to cadres. This news, though accompanied by words of high praise for the conduct of the division, to use the General's own words, " fairly knocked the stuffing out of me."

From 21st April till early in May the division (less artillery) formed part of 8th Corps, Lieutenant-General Hunter-Weston. The artillery remained with the 5th Corps about Nieppe Forest. The division was employed in digging defence lines east and west of Poperinghe, but it was twice called on suddenly to stand to and prepare to defend the line it was digging. The first alarm was on the 26th April, when Kemmel Hill fell, and the second three days later when the Boche attacked and obtained a footing on the Sherpenberg-Mont Noir Ridge. On neither occasion were the services of the division actually required.

Lieutenant-Colonel Sir T. Cunninghame, G.S.O.1 was appointed Commandant, School of Instruction for the American Army, his place being taken by Lieutenant-Colonel Dooner, R.A. Major Tower, G.S.O.2, left us to become G.S.O.2 15th Corps, being replaced by Major J. Hunter, also a Royal Fusilier. The command of the 101st Brigade fell to Brigadier-General W. J. Woodcock, Lancashire Fusiliers, and Brigadier-General E. Hilliam came from the 15th Division and took command of the 102nd Brigade, exchanging commands with Brigadier-General N. Thomson.

The reduction to cadre strength was carried out in the middle of May. The artillery, three Field Companies, Machine Gun Battalion, and the 1st East Lancashire Regiment, 9th Northumberland Fusiliers, and 11th Suffolk Regiment were not included in the order of reduction. The Field Companies, under Colonel Dobson, continued working in the Poperinghe area. The Machine Gun Battalion departed temporarily to the 4th Army. The three infantry battalions went to the 61st Division. The 9th Northumberland Fusiliers and the 11th Suffolks saw the war out, not being broken up till after the Armistice. The remaining battalions were reduced to cadres, each consisting of ten officers and forty-five other ranks. The surplus personnel and transport were sent to the base and reposted to other battalions. The S.A.A. section of D.A.C. was disbanded, and the train reduced to cadre.

The headquarters of the division and brigades and the cadres of the battalions were moved to the Lumbres training area, and Divisional Headquarters was established at Nielles les Blequin on 17th May.

General Nicholson was now entrusted with supervising the training of American troops. An American Division consisted of two brigades, each of two regiments, each of which had three battalions; there were, therefore, twelve battalions in the division. To each brigade was affiliated the headquarters of an English brigade. To each regiment was affiliated a British battalion cadre, of which a company cadre was affiliated with each American battalion. This left one Brigade Headquarters spare, and each of the affiliated brigades had a battalion cadre spare, and each affiliated battalion cadre had a company cadre spare. These spare units were employed in assisting the others, supervising visits to the line, etc. The pioneer cadres was affiliated to the Engineer Battalion and the Machine Gun Battalion, and worked under the supervision of the 103rd Brigade Headquarters. An L.T.M. School was formed under Captain O. B. Palmer, 103rd L.T.B. The American troops were put through a very comprehensive course of instruction, drawn up by their own officers, who were given the benefit of our three and a half years' experience of the Hun and his ways, and how best to circumvent him.

The system worked well, and without any friction. This work occupied the division till 27th June, during which time it was associated with the 28th, 78th, and 80th American Divisions.

The cadres of the old battalions, when the training of the Americans was completed, were employed on similar work with British troops till the Armistice, and then on demobilisation work, and finally demobilised themselves, but before this each was presented with a King's Colour, which was carried back to England by a small party and found a resting-place in the local Cathedral or Church of the battalion's birthplace. Thus prosaically ended the original infantry of 34th Division which General Ingouville-Williams took to France early in 1916.

After the 27th June General Nicholson began the pleasant task of reconstructing the 34th Division. The artillery and Field Companies returned, and also the Machine Gun Battalion, but the infantry was all new, and some came from India, others had been employed in Gallipoli, Egypt, and Palestine, but had had no experience of war as waged in France.

The Brigades were constituted thus :

101st Brigade.—Brigadier-General W. J. Woodcock, D.S.O.
> 2nd/4th The Queen's.—Lieutenant-Colonel W. J. M. Hill, D.S.O.
> 4th Royal Sussex.—Major G. S. Constable, M.C.
> 2nd Loyal North Lancashire Regiment.—Lieutenant-Colonel C. S. A. Jourdain, D.S.O.

102nd Brigade.—Brigadier-General E. Hilliam, C.M.G., D.S.O. (who had taken over command from Brigadier-General Thomson, who took command of the 44th Brigade).
> 1/4th Cheshire Regiment.—Lieutenant-Colonel G. H. Swindells.
> 1/7th Cheshire Regiment.—Lieutenant-Colonel H. L. Moir.
> 1/1st Hereford Regiment.—Lieutenant-Colonel H. M. Lawrence, D.S.O.

103rd Brigade.—Brigadier-General J. G. Chaplin, D.S.O.
> 5th King's Own Scottish Borderers.—Lieutenant-Colonel R. N. Coulson.
> 8th Scottish Rifles.—Lieutenant-Colonel J. M. Findlay, D.S.O.
> 5th Argyll & Sutherland Highlanders.—Lieutenant-Colonel C. L. Barlow, D.S.O.
> Pioneers Battalion, 2/4th Somerset Light Infantry.—Lieutenant-Colonel E. B. Powell, D.S.O.

By the end of June the infantry battalions had arrived. Divisional Headquarters was at Bambecque, but shortly after moved to Couthove. Artillery, Machine Gun Battalion, and Field Companies arrived in the first week of July, and on the 11th the division passed into General Headquarters reserve. Until the 15th training and organisation occupied us. This was suddenly stopped by our being entrained on 16th at a few hours' notice for an unknown destination, which proved to be the Senlis area, where the division concentrated on 18th, and whence it marched, via Largny, to the Vivieres-Puisieux-Soucy-Longavesne area, and came, on 20th July, under General Penet, 30th Corps of the 10th French Army, commanded by General Mangin.

On the 18th July the 10th Army had attacked north of Soissons, and driven the enemy back some five miles, taking many prisoners and guns. The 34th was to take part in the exploitation of this victory.

On the 21st orders were received to relieve the 38th French Division in the line opposite Hartennes-et-Taux the next day, and before this was commenced came orders to take part in an attack early on the following day, 23rd July. Under the most favourable circumstances this would have been difficult for any troops, but for a newly constituted division, composed, as regards infantry, of troops which had not yet been in action in France, and which had just completed a trying move by rail, bus and route march, it was a very severe test. There was no time for reconnaissance. The country was entirely new; there were no organised trench systems on either side. The enemy's positions were never accurately known till they had been captured. To all these difficulties there were added those inseparable from acting for the first time with foreign troops.

The 101st Brigade was at Puisieux on 21st, whence at four a.m. on 22nd it marched for Villers-Helon, arriving about six-thirty a.m. The remaining brigades followed later, and took up positions of readiness in the valley and wood to the north of that village. While waiting for night to cover our move into the trenches, the scheme of operations for the next morning was explained to the artillery and infantry commanders, but the actual orders from the 30th Corps were not received till later.

As much reconnaissance as possible was carried out, but naturally it was not much, and the artillery had no opportunity of registering. The whole proceeding was rather unsatisfactory, but the state of affairs was such that a very little might induce the Hun to retire again, and it was worth risking a good deal.

The scheme of the attack had been prepared by the chef d'état-major of the 38th French Division, and was based on experience gained in previous actions, and General Nicholson determined to adopt it.

The general idea of the operations were that the 20th Corps on our left was to capture Tigny-Villemontoire and Taux, turn the wood north of Hartennes-et-Taux while the right of the 30th Corps, advancing through Le Plessier-Huleu on the Orme du Grand Rozoy, was to turn the Bois du Plessier and Bois de St Jean. The 34th Division and the French Divisions, 25th and 58th, on its immediate right and left, were to form the connection between the northern and southern turning movements, advancing due east to the high ground east of the Soissons-Château Thierry road. A most important point in the scheme was that the 34th was not to move till the 20th Corps on its left had advanced across the Soissons-Château Thierry road.

Besides his own artillery General Nicholson had the aid of the guns of the 32nd and 41st Regiments of French artillery, and also of twelve heavy 155 m.m. howitzers, the whole being under orders of Brigadier-General Walthall, who was assisted by Colonel Beranger, C.O., of 32nd Regiment.

The 152nd Brigade, R.F.A., was unable to get into position in time, but otherwise the relief was carried out without any hitch, and was complete, and the artillery in position by three a.m. on 23rd. The 101st Brigade relieved the 8th Tiraileurs in the right section, with the 2nd Loyal North Lancashires and 2nd/4th Queen's in the front line, the former on the right. The 2nd/4th Royal Sussex were in Brigade reserve.

The left section was taken over by the 102nd from the 4th Regiment, 38th Division, 1/1st Herefords being on the right, and 1/7th Cheshires on the left, the 1/4th Cheshires being in reserve.

The 103rd Brigade (less 5th King's Own Scottish Borderers) was taken from General Nicholson, and sent to the vicinity of Blanzy as Corps Reserve. The 5th King's Own Scottish Borderers and 2/4th Somersets were General Nicholson's reserve, and, with a half company of the Machine Gun Battalion, were stationed north of the Bois de Mauloy. The Field Companies were held in readiness to improve communications should our success make it necessary.

General Nicholson had, of course, been in close touch with the 38th Divisional Staff on 22nd and during the night, but he did not actually assume command of the section till seven a.m. on 23rd, and fifteen minutes later came the order for the 34th to advance. The 20th Division had not then crossed the Soissons-Château Thierry road, and it is doubtful whether they ever did so on that day, but in issuing the order the Corps Commander was, no doubt, only anticipating an event, which, on the information then available, seemed likely to take place very soon. The order to advance was issued by General Nicholson at seven-twenty a.m., and, according to the Operation Order, this meant that the infantry were to advance behind our barrage at seven-fifty, but unfortunately the French signal service took rather longer to transmit the orders than had been expected, so that the signal rockets went up a little late, and the lines to the 101st Brigade being broken, that brigade started some five minutes late.

The 102nd Brigade got off in time, and the 1/7th Cheshires and 1/1st Herefords advanced through high standing corn, which made control difficult, suffering from the very start from the fire of the enemy's machine gunners, but they got forward some twelve hundred yards to within three hundred yards of west edge of the Bois de Reugny, where they were stopped by the intensity of the

machine gun fire from that wood and from the village
of Tigny on the left and from the Bois de Chanois
on the right. Here they dug in, pending the advance
of the troops on their flanks. As this did not occur,
the line was consolidated with a defensive flank thrown
back facing Tigny till touch was obtained with the
French on the left and 101st Brigade on the right in
the G.M.P. (Gouvernement Militaire de Paris) line.
The losses in this operation were 1/7th Cheshires
about one hundred and eighty all ranks, and 1/1st
Herefords eight officers and two hundred and thirty
other ranks.

The 101st Brigade was unsuccessful. The
machine gun fire was so intense that on the right the
first wave, consisting of No. 12 Platoon, 2nd Loyal
North Lancs, was practically wiped out in the first
fifty yards, and the Commanding Officer stopped the
movement, but on the left " D " Company with " B "
Company of the Queen's, under Second-Lieutenant
R. M. Lessells, got across the Coutremain-Tigny
road, exterminating some machine gun posts, but
were counter-attacked and forced back. The company of the Loyal North Lancs lost Second-Lieutenant
R. J. Jones killed, and had some sixty other
casualties, including all its officers. Thus the only
result obtained was an advance of the line about a
thousand yards on the 102nd Brigade front. During
the night the 1/4th Cheshires relieved the 1/7th
Cheshires and 1/1st Herefords in the front line. One
and a half companies of the 34th Machine Gun
Battalion acted with each of the assaulting brigades.
Eight guns were attached to each attacking battalion
of the 102nd Brigade, the remainder being in reserve.
Owing to the short distance advanced by the infantry
the forward guns were not required to move forward.
When the advance was held up the guns were used to
cover the front and hold up any counter-attack.

The French, on our outer flanks, made no movement, and the next day the Corps Commander came

R

to General Nicholson with expressions of sympathy over his losses and pleasant messages from General Mangin.

All things considered, the new troops had done very well. As far as we were concerned, things were quiet till the 27th. During this period the 12th French Division took Villemontoire, but Tigny was not attacked. On the extreme right of the 30th Corps, and left of 6th Army, good progress was made, and there were indications of an approaching Hun retreat. On the night of 27th/28th the division was relieved by the French 25th Division and concentrated in the Bois de Nadon and Bois de Bœuf. This was preparatory to taking part in an attack on the Grand Rozoy Ridge on 30th July, but as the French took Fere en Tardenois on 27th, and indications of the enemy being about to retreat increased, it was decided to attack on 29th. The change of date was not communicated to the G.O.C. till the night of 27th/28th, but the C.R.A. and Brigadiers had already received details of the scheme. The troops did not reach the Bois de Nadon till the early hours of 28th, so there was but little time for reconnaissance of the routes to the jumping off line, near and south of the Bois de Baillette.

The distances to be traversed by the different units were from eight to ten miles, and in order that the movement might not be detected it had to be carried out in the night. The difficulties were considerably lessened by the provision of a guide to each platoon by the 5th French Division, which was holding the portion of the line from which the attack was to be made. This was arranged personally by General Nicholson, with the assistance of his liaison officer, Captain Beauchamp, of the 18th Dragoons, on the staff of 30th Corps, a cool-headed, cheery officer who throughout these operations was absolutely invaluable to Divisional Headquarters.

The 103rd Brigade was to be on the right, the

101st on the left. The divisional reserve consisted of the 102nd Brigade (less 1/4th Cheshires in Corps Reserve), headquarters and two companies of Machine Gun Battalion, and 2/4th Somerset Light Infantry, disposed in western end of Bois de Baillette and the three Field Companies disposed west of Geromenil Farm. Advanced Divisional Headquarters at Ferme. The attack was covered by our own artillery and three regiments of French seventy-five guns and three groups of 155 m.m. howitzers. Our guns managed to get one gun per battery into position early enough to register, but the French had no such opportunity.

The advance to the assembly line was not without incidents. Several units came under heavy shell fire in the wood, the 5th King's Own Scottish Borderers suffering considerably. Two companies lost touch, and the battalion was only got together just in time to advance at zero (four-ten a.m.), and in the hurry the reserve company went over with the rest.

The Royal Sussex was heavily shelled just after arrival at the position of assembly, and lost Captain A. N. H. Weekes, M.C., who was in command.

The battalions in the front line were, from right to left, 8th Scottish Rifles, 5th King's Own Scottish Borderers of 103rd Brigade, Royal Sussex, The Queen's of 101st Brigade. The advance started punctually close behind a heavy rolling barrage in dense fog, and the "Green line" was taken without any trouble. The battalions halted there and reorganised before pushing on at six a.m. So far everything had gone according to plan, and for some time the progress continued satisfactory. By seven a.m. the Beugneux-Grand Rozoy road had been cleared of the enemy, but his machine gunners were strongly posted and numerous in the rear of the wood, in Beugneux and on Hill 158. The 8th Scottish Rifles, in spite of heavy losses, pushed on as far as the foot of the Hill, and the 5th King's Own Scottish

Borderers passed round the north-west of Beugneux and got well up the slopes of Hill 189. Here they came in touch with " A " and part of " C " Companies of the 2nd Loyal North Lancs, under Captain G. P. Atkinson, who, though in support of the Royal Sussex, had, in the stress of battle, found their way through the woods and seized the crest of Hill 189 by seven-forty. Lieutenant-Colonel Jourdain, 2nd Loyal North Lancashires, was killed about this time. The Royal Sussex penetrated as far as the Courdoux-Beugneux road, but could get no farther. The Queen's also got some way up the slopes north of the Beugneux woods. Thus at about ten-twenty a.m. the situation was roughly as follows : The French had taken Grand Rozoy and pushed to the north-east of it, but not far ; then came some of the Queen's, stretching up the slope towards Point 189, but not in touch with Captain Atkinson and the small party of Loyal North Lancs and King's Own Scottish Borderers ; to the east of which were some of the Royal Sussex, who were also out of touch on their right. The rest of the King's Own Scottish Borderers and the 8th Scottish Rifles were held up in front of Beugneux and Hill 158, and not in touch with the French on their right. General Chaplin sent up the 5th Argyll and Sutherland Highlanders to reinforce his firing-line, and several attempts were unsuccessfully made to turn Hill 158 and the village from the south, but the fire, chiefly of machine guns, was too severe.

The 102nd Brigade, with 2/4th Somerset Light Infantry and a company of Machine Gun Battalion, was ordered up to counter-attack, but the Germans launched a heavy attack, the weight of which fell on the French on our left. The whole line fell back in sympathy, and before our counter-attack could materialise the line had fallen back to the G.M.P. line, where about two-thirty p.m. a new line was formed, and as the troops had become considerably mixed up they were reorganised; the order of battle being from right to left 103rd Brigade, 102nd Brigade, 101st Brigade.

The enemy was prevented from taking any advantage of our withdrawal by the heavy barrage put down on his positions by the artillery of both nations. At nightfall patrols were pushed forward and an outpost was established from the western foot of Hill 158 across to the Beugneux-Grand Rozoy road, and along it to the right of the French, and when the latter were forced out of Grand Rozoy a little later the 101st Brigade threw back a defensive flank towards the railway. The reserves of the brigades in the G.M.P. line, and the 2nd Loyal North Lancs was in divisional reserve near the Grand Rozoy station.

At six a.m. our allies on our left resumed possession of Grand Rozoy without opposition, and relieved the somewhat critical state of affairs on that flank. The 30th passed without any hostile action, the morning being unusually peaceful. The time was occupied in preparations for a further attack on 31st, but this was subsequently postponed to the 1st August. On the 31st Lieutenant-Colonel J. G. Dooner, G.S.O.1, was killed by a shell while returning from visiting the headquarters of the three brigades to explain the scheme of the next day's operations. The loss of such an officer at the eve of an important attack was a great blow, but fortunately General Nicholson had a very efficient substitute at hand, in the person of Lieutenant-Colonel R. Tyler, D.S.O., his A.A. and Q.M.G.[1]

---

[1] Lieutenant-Colonel Tyler had been Brigade-Major, 101st Brigade, during our early days at Sutton Veny, and in France. He had then transferred to the " O " side. He was a most competent and capable Staff Officer, who, in spite of very indifferent health, never shirked work, however hard. Throughout the whole of these operations Colonel Tyler had to run the line of communication's work, which, when the division was with our own troops, would have been done by Corps and Army Headquarters. Nothing ever went wrong, and fighting troops were never short of supplies. At

As the result of the operations of 29th July the 30th Corps line now ran from Bois de la terre d'or, inclusive, along the road to Grand Rozoy, round the northern edge of that village, and thence about one hundred yards south of the road to Beugneux as far as the eastern edge of the wood, and thence to some buildings at the station side of Hill 158, thence parallel to and south of the Beugneux-Cramaille road.

During the night 31st July/1st August the troops moved to their "jumping off" positions. Commencing on the right our front line troops were disposed thus: 103rd Brigade, with one company Machine Gun Battalion, 5th King's Own Scottish Borderers, 5th Argyll and Sutherland Highlanders, each with three companies in the front line—the inner flanks of these battalions were on the right divisional boundary. The King's Own Scottish Borderers were to turn Hill 158 from the South. Two companies of the Scottish Rifles were in close support, and two in brigade reserve. 101st Brigade, with one company Machine Gun Battalion. 4th Royal Sussex and 2/4th The Queen's, each with three companies in the front line. The 2nd Loyal North Lancs were in brigade reserve. The divisional reserve consisted of the 1/7th Cheshires, 2/4th Somerset Light Infantry, 34th Machine Gun Battalion (less two companies), and three Field Companies, all under command of the 102nd Brigadier. The other two battalions of this brigade had special missions on either flank.

One hundred and eight field guns and thirty-two howitzers covered the divisional front and prepared for the attack by harassing fire, which gradually developed into a heavy bombardment of the objective, which was the same as on the 29th July. This

the end of August, Lieutenant-Colonel Tyler was transferred as an instructor to the Staff School at Cambridge. He remained in that appointment till early in 1919, when he joined the 1st Division of the Rhine, and died a few days later.

bombardment lasted from four to four-forty-five a.m., and that hour the barrage commenced, and at four-forty-nine the troops moved forward behind it. The advance everywhere was successful, in fact the 1st August was a " good day." The Argyll and Sutherland Highlanders went into action with six officers and two hundred and sixty other ranks. Lieutenant Saunders was killed before Hill 158 was reached, and Lieutenant C. D. Robertson wounded on that Hill. Lieutenant Fleming lead the attack over the Hill, Lieutenant-Colonel Barlow with Lieutenant Thomson going round to the left. The Hill was taken at the second attempt, and a Battalion Commander and his Adjutant and two other officers with forty other ranks were taken prisoners with ten machine guns. Unfortunately Lieutenant-Colonel Barlow, R.S., Major Montieth, C.S., Major MacNab, and twenty more were killed in the fight. The remainder pushed on, and on the far side of the Hill came in touch with the headquarters of the King's Own Scottish Borderers, from whom they obtained the loan of Second-Lieutenants Gillespie and French, and pushed on and formed up on the right of the 101st Brigade troops. The King's Own Scottish Borderers, advancing through the aviation ground and woods to the east of Beugneux, swung round according to plan, and dug in on the right of the final objective, east of Point 189, where they were harassed by machine gun fire from Severnay, which ceased when the French took that place at nine-ten a.m. The 1/1st Herefords was intended to advance towards Bucy le Bras Ferme with the object of securing the high ground about Point 194, but it could make no progress, and dug in near 5th King's Own Scottish Borderers at eleven-thirty-five a.m. In its advance Major A. G. R. Whitehouse was killed by a " pocket " of the enemy, which had been overrun by the preceding troops.

In the meantime the 101st had been completely successful, overcoming considerable opposition in the woods north of the Grand Rozoy-Beugneux road, where there was fierce fighting with bayonets, and one section 101st L.T. Battery, under Lieutenant Archibald, M.C., did good work silencing machine guns, of which twelve were captured with five Boche, some fifty were killed, and the rest bolted and were chased by the Loyal North Lancs, who captured forty-one more. By six a.m. the Queen's Royal Sussex, and Loyal North Lancs were on the crest of the ridge near the objective " Brown line," but were enfiladed by machine guns from Hill 203, which was promptly cleared by Captain Atkinson, commanding the Loyal North Lancs, sending " D " Company of that battalion to form a defensive flank. This company was reinforced by 1/4th Cheshires, which had been allotted the special task of following the left flank of the attack, and then advancing towards the Le Mont Jour, to cover the advance of the 127th French Division. This task the battalion most gallantly carried out, its C.O., Colonel G. H. Swindells, being killed in the assault. At about nine a.m. the corn was set on fire by tracer bullets and anti-tank shells, and a German ammunition dump exploded, killing Captain and Adjutant J. Holding and several others. About eleven a.m. the line was handed over to the 127th French Division, and the battalion was withdrawn some two hundred yards into dead ground.

In this attack our C.R.A. had available one gun per fifteen yards of front, and was able to cover the advance with a double barrage, H.E. nearest to the infantry and timed shrapnel beyond the H.E. One battery of each of the 152nd and 160th Brigades limbered up, amid the cheers of the French artillery men, and drove up in close support of the infantry. The remainder of the artillery advanced, battery by battery, as soon as the barrage stopped, and came into action again three thousand to four thousand yards farther forward. The accurate shooting of the guns of both nations contributed largely to the success.

During the rest of the day the line remained stationary, but about five a.m. it became evident that the line was not far enough advanced to cover the valleys on either side of Hill 199, and that hostile action in the valley to the east of that Hill was causing trouble to the 68th French Division in Servenay. Therefore at seven p.m., under a creeping barrage, the line was pushed forward some three hundred to four hundred yards along the whole of the 34th Division and the left of the 68th Division front.

The night passed quietly, and we ascertained later from prisoners that the Huns sneaked away quietly about eleven p.m. under cover of a thick fog.

The next day, 2nd August, the 25th French Division passed through our depleted ranks and pursued the Boche, now in full retreat. Our average battalion strength was now less than two hundred and fifty, and the casualties among officers had been very heavy, so when we were told during the night of 2nd/ 3rd that we were to be withdrawn to the British area, though we felt annoyed that we were not to exploit the success we had done our full share in winning, we felt that under the circumstances it was the only thing to be done. The division had been in the line since the night of 22nd/23rd, and had in that time fought three general actions, two of which involved night advances to get into position, and attacking without knowledge of the ground. In the last and most successful action it went in with less than three hundred and fifty effectives per battalion, and achieved a very fine performance.

German orders, subsequently captured, confirmed what Generals Mangin and Penet told General Nicholson, that the capture by the 68th, 25th, and 127th French and 34th British Division of the ridge north of Grand Rozoy and Beugneux finally induced the Huns to retire to the Vasle. The position captured by the 34th was the key of that ridge. The new infantry of the division had fairly won their spurs.

Both Army and Corps Commanders issued complimentary orders, and with promptitude which fairly astonished the recipients a shower of French decorations descended upon us.

Our losses during the period were :

		Officers	Other Ranks
July 22nd to 28th inclusive—Killed	. . .	2	128
Wounded	. . .	43	1095
Missing	. . .	0	26
July 29th to 31st inclusive—Killed	. . .	16	206
Wounded	. . .	61	1356
Missing	. . .	0	136
August 1st to 3rd inclusive—Killed	. . .	12	138
Wounded	. . .	18	479
Missing	. . .	1	31

Making a total of one hundred and fifty-three casualties among officers, and three thousand six hundred and seventeen among the other ranks.

On 4th August we celebrated the fourth anniversary of the outbreak of the war by moving by bus and march back to the entraining area, whence we travelled in discomfort by train to the Bergues, where we had entrained three weeks earlier.

2nd August, 1918.
SPECIAL ORDER OF THE DAY

The Divisional Commander has received the following, and desires that they be read out to all ranks on parade.

By direction of General Mangin, Commanding 10th French Army.

"General Mangin, the Army Commander, has instructed me to convey to you his personal thanks for the magnificent results achieved by your division yesterday.

"The General says that yesterday's battle worked

out absolutely according to orders and times, and says that the general retreat taking place to-day is entirely due to the success of yesterday.

"The General has instructed me to tell you of his gratitude and appreciation for the splendid success achieved by the 34th Division yesterday.

"(Signed) B. V. JACKSON, *Major,*
"Liaison Officer,
" 18th French Army."

From General Penet, Commanding 30th French Corps.

" Au moment ou la 34ᵉ D.I. Britannique quitte le 30ᵉ C.A. Francais, le General Commandant le C.A. est heureux d'exprimer toute sa satisfaction, toute son admiration aux Etats-Majors, Officiers, Sous-Officiers et Hommes de troupe qui, au cours de la periode du 21 Juillet au 2 Aout, on fait preuve d'une energie, d'une bravure et d'une ardeur combatice veritablement remarquables.

"Tous ont rependu pleinement aux appels du Commandement qui a exige d'eux un effort consider-able, aussi bien dans l'execution de mouvements rapides de jour comme de nuit, que dans l'attaque et la defense des positions conquises.

"Le succes a couronne cet effort des Divisions Alliees; et le General Commandant le 30ᵉ C.A. est heureux de pouvoir affirmer que la 34ᵉ D.I. Britannique y a pris une tres grande part.

" (Signed) H. PENET."

ORDRE GENERAL, No. 343

(*Translation*)

" Officers, Non-Commissioned Officers, and Men of the 15th and 34th British Division,—You entered the battle at its fiercest moment. The enemy, already once vanquished, again brought up against us his best divisions, considerably outnumbering our own.

" You continued to advance step by step, in spite

of his desperate resistance, and you held the ground won in spite of his violent counter-attacks. Then, during the whole day of the 1st August, side by side with your French comrades, you stormed the ridge dominating the whole country between the Aisne and the Ourcq, which the defenders had received orders to hold at all cost.

" Having failed in his attempt to retake the ridge with his last reserves, the enemy had to beat a retreat, pursued and harassed for twelve kilometres.

" All of you, English and Scottish, young soldiers and veterans of Flanders and Palestine, you have shown the magnificent qualities of your race : courage and imperturbable tenacity.

" You have won ,the admiration of your companions in arms. Your country will be proud of you, for to your Chiefs and to you is due a large share in the victory that we have gained over the barbarous enemies of the free.

" I am happy to have fought at your head, and I thank you.

" MANGIN."

BEUGNEUX.

Operations of 28th July-4th Aug. 1918.

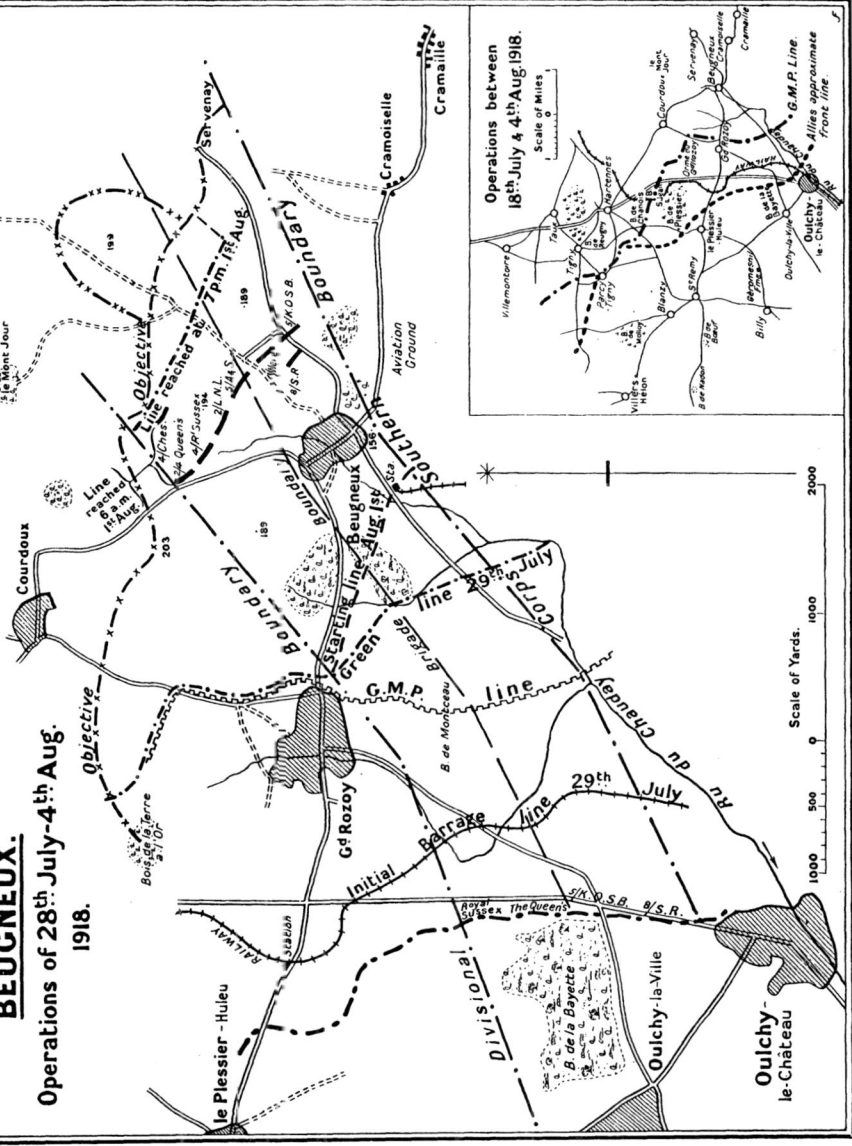

Bois le Bras Ferme

Servenay

Cramaiselle

Cramaille

le Mont Jour

S/K.O.S.B.

Line Objective at 7 p.m. 1st Aug.

Line reached at 8 a.m. 1st Aug.

192

189

4/R.Sussex

2/L.N.L.

1/4 Queens

1/4 Chess

4/R.P.Sussex

196

5/14th

4/S.R.

Boundary

Southern

Aviation Ground

Courdoux

203

189

Line reached 8 a.m. 1st Aug.

Beugneux

Aug. 1st

Starting line

Green line

Brigade

Boundary

G.M.P. line

B. de Monceau

Corps 29th July

Ru du Chaudy

Objective

Bois de la Terre a 1/'Or

Gd Rozoy

Barrage line

Initial

29th July

S/K.O.S.B. B/S.R.

Royal Sussex The Queens

RAILWAY

Stabäh

le Plessier - Huleu

Divisional

B. de la Bayette

Oulchy-la-Ville

Oulchy-le-Château

Scale of Yards.

1000 500 0 1000 2000

Scale of Yards.

Operations between 18th July & 4th Aug. 1918.

Scale of Miles

le Mont Jour

Courdoux

Servenay

Cramaiselle

Cramaille

G.M.P. Line

Allies approximate front line.

Villemontoire

Tigny

Hartennes

Bois de Reugny

Plessier

St Rémy

Blanzy

Beugneux

le Plessier Huleu

Grisonnay

Rozoy

Oulchy-le-Ville

Oulchy-le-Château

Villers Hélon

B. de Mauloy

B. des Bout

Billy

CHAPTER XIII

VICTORY

By 7th August, the infantry brigades were disposed in Bissesziele, Ziggers Cappel, and Wormhoudt areas; the artillery in Droglandt; Divisional Headquarters at Esquelbecq. From 8th to 16th we were hard at work refitting and training. On the 10th Lieutenant-Colonel B. C. Battye, D.S.O., R.E., took up his duties as G.S.O.1. The 101st Brigade went to Cormettes camp, and the Machine Gun Battalion to the Lumbres area, for training. The Field Companies and Pioneers worked under the C.E. 2nd Corps. Our period of rest was soon over, and on 21st the 103rd Infantry Brigade took over the left sector of 49th Division front, and General Nicholson took command of the Ypres or left sector 2nd Corps front at three a.m. on that day from General Cameron, with his headquarters in the château at Lovie. The 43rd Brigade of the 14th Division, which was holding the right sector, coming under his command, and the 102nd Brigade moving up into the Siege camp area in reserve. The 30th American and 12th Belgian Divisions were on our right and left respectively.

The 103rd Brigade was relieved by the 14th Division on the night 28th/29th, the G.O.C. taking over comand of the Ypres sector. The following night the 101st Brigade, having returned from Cormettes on 28th, relieved the left brigade of the 41st Division in the Sherpenberg sector, and the 103rd Brigade moved into reserve in that sector. The right brigade, 41st

Division (124th), remained in position, and G.O.C. 34th Division assumed command of the sector, with his headquarters close to Abeele. The new sector extended for about three thousand yards, facing south-east, about midway between Kemmel Hill and Sherpenberg, and was the left sector of the 19th Corps front. The 27th American Division was on the left, and the 30th British on the right.

On 30th August Brigadier-General R. I. Rawson took over command of the 103rd Brigade from General Chaplin, who went home for six months' rest. The intention was that the 41st Division should go out and train, and then attack Kemmel Hill, and the 102nd Brigade was to be attached to it for that operation. Events, however, turned out differently.

Having taken over command at ten a.m. on 30th, General Nicholson drove round to his right-hand neighbour, General Williams, and discussed the situation with him. General Williams' news was that the patrols of the 30th Division had been advancing all day, and it struck General Nicholson so forcibly that the enemy must vacate Kemmel Hill to avoid being attacked in flank, that on his return to his head-quarters he at once issued orders for both brigades in the line to push out patrols without delay, to follow the enemy should he retire, and seize Kemmel Hill.

Both brigades lost no time in carrying out the orders, and there is dispute as to which won in the race, for General Nicholson's prediction turned out correct and the Hun stole off during the night, covered by a rear-guard which put up a certain amount of resistance. By six a.m. a patrol of the 124th Brigade had topped Kemmel Hill, and about the same time patrols of the 2/4th Queen's, 101st Brigade, reached its northern slopes. On the left the enemy held on a little longer, and it was not till noon that the 2nd Loyal North Lancs patrols were able to advance, by which time the remainder of the 101st and 124th were well east of Kemmel Hill and village. By two-thirty p.m.

the 124th Brigade was established from Donegal Farm on the south to a point some seven hundred yards south-south-west of Lindenhoek. A little later the 101st prolonged the line northwards along the old trench line known as Vierstraat Switch to the northern Divisional boundary east of La Polka, where they were in touch with the 106th American Regiment. The 124th made a further advance, and by six a.m. the Vierstraat Switch was occupied from a point one thousand seven hundred yards west of Wulverghem northwards, and the far-famed Kemmel Hill was in our hands " for the duration."

The 30th Division kept pace, and we were in touch on both flanks. The G.O.C. held a conference of brigadiers during the morning at the 124th Brigade Headquarters, which were in some dug-outs in a little valley between Sherpenberg and Reninghelst, and moved his headquarters to this place later in the day so as to be in closer touch with his troops. During the night the 103rd relieved the 124th Brigade. The night was uneventful, but the relief was not complete till seven-fifteen a.m. on 1st September. At seven a.m. information was received at Divisional Headquarters that the 30th Division had been assigned the hill north of Wulverghem as its objective. This necessitated a slight alteration in the objective which had been given to the 103rd. At nine a.m. the advance began all along the line; the objective of the 34th Division was a line running from a little east of Irish house on the right past Store Farm to the left of the 30th Division, some five hundred yards north-east of Elbow Farm.

2nd Loyal North Lancs, on the left of the 101st Brigade, advanced with its right on Suicide Road, " A " and " C " Companies being in the front line. By eleven-thirty-nine a.m. reports were received that the objective had been reached and that a patrol of the 106th American Regiment had visited " A " Company, while " C " was in touch with the

2/4th Queen's, which had a little trouble with some Huns in the Yonge Street dug-outs.

The 103rd had had a trying night. The relief had been conducted in heavy rain, and the pitchy darkness, coupled with shell holes and felled trees, made the task difficult and extremely tiring. The 8th Scottish Rifles nevertheless advanced at nine a.m., and made good progress on the left, keeping in touch with the Queen's, but the 30th Division on the right found the enemy very sticky and made slow progress. This "stickiness" extended northwards, and the Scottish Rifles' right was held up, that flank having to be thrown back in touch with the troops on their right.

At two-thirty orders were issued for the advance to the second objective, Kruisstraat Cabaret—Peckham Craters—eastern edge of Petit Bois, to commence at four-thirty p.m., but the 103rd Brigade were unable to move as neither Neuve Eglise nor Wulverghem had yet been captured. At five-thirty p.m. the signal transmitting station of the Scottish Rifles, in an old German dug-out on the slope of Kemmel Hill, suddenly blew up. Six men were killed, and all the plant destroyed. This cut off communication between the battalion and the 103rd Brigade Headquarters. At seven-thirty p.m. "Z" Company made an unsuccessful attempt to advance, but the fire from the right was too heavy.

On the left the 1/4th Royal Sussex passed through the 2nd Loyal North Lancs, pushed on with the Queen's, and reached the outskirts of Petit Bois, but at nightfall the front line was approximately : The left of the 30th Division was at Frenchman's Farm. Thence to the north the line was held as follows : Two companies Scottish Rifles to Spy Farm, two companies 2/4th Queen's thence to Beaver Huts, two companies 4th Sussex in Oak trench. In rear were from the right : Two companies echeloned to the rear, facing south, two companies King's Own

Scottish Borderers in Lindenhoek, remainder of King's Own Scottish Borderers and Argyll and Sutherland Highlanders east of Kemmel, two companies 2/4th Queen's in Vierstraat switch, and two companies 4th Sussex in the Kemmel village.

There were patrol encounters during the night, but nothing serious occurred. During the morning of the 2nd the forward area was shelled and the Royal Sussex were much troubled by machine gun fire, suffering twenty-six casualties, among them Second-Lieutenant Byrne killed.

At three p.m., after a bombardment, and preceded by a creeping barrage, the two companies of King's Own Scottish Borderers in Lindenhoek camp, " C " and " D," advanced to seize Regents dug-outs from the north, and smooth the way to advance of the Scottish Rifles to the second objective of yesterday. They were to be assisted by the guns and machine guns of the 101st Brigade group, of which the Queen's were to co-operate on the left. The attempt was a failure owing to the heavy artillery barrage and machine gun fire which enfiladed the advance. A further barrage was asked for on Peckham and Spanbroekmolen crater at eight-fifteen p.m., after which the two companies succeeded in occupying a line east of Regents dug-outs about ten p.m., and by one a.m. on 3rd the line ran from Store Farm through Regents dug-outs to Frenchman's Farm. The King's Own Scottish Borderers on left being in touch with the Queen's, and the Scottish Rifles on the right with the troops of the 30th Division.

During the night 2/3rd the 102nd Brigade took over the line from the 101st and 103rd and straightened it out, so that by four-thirty a.m. on 3rd it ran on the left from Store Farm along the road to La Cache Farm, up Kelly trench to Oak trench. The 3rd was occupied in preparing for an attack to be made the next day. The 1/7th Cheshires advanced the line during the day to the Beaver trench system, the

s

final success being achieved by the right platoon of
" B " Company, covered by its Lewis gun, seizing a
dominant position, thus allowing " A " and " D " to
occupy the system just before dark.

At five-thirty a.m. on 4th a further advance was
attempted under a creeping barrage, and a certain
amount of progress was made, and at the end of the
day the 1/7th Cheshires were just north of Ulster
Road, the line on their left being carried on by the
1/1st Herefords two hundred yards west of Peckham
crater to Oak trench. 1/4th Cheshires remained at
Store Farm.

During the night of the 4/5th the 101st Brigade
took over the right sector of the divisional front, the
1/4th Royal Sussex relieving the 1/7th Cheshires.
Patrols were active all along the front, but no further
progress was made, either that night or the next day.

The losses during the period from 1st to 8th
September were : killed, nine officers, seventy-six
other ranks; wounded, twenty-two officers, four
hundred and thirty-six other ranks; missing, one
officer and eighty-one other ranks. Slight compared
with those of earlier offensives, but sufficiently heavy
to show that the Hun was still fighting.

We now had about a fortnight of inactivity. The
103rd went to the Éperlecques area to train; the other
two brigades rang the changes in the line—there were
several petty activities and occasional bombardments.
Our gunners, who till now had been covering the
27th Division, rejoined us on 8th, setting free the
41st Divisional Artillery.

On the 20th the 103rd returned from training and
took over the Vierstraat sector from 122nd Brigade,
41st Division, and the next day this sector came under
General Nicholson's command. The sector was
immediately north of that held by the 102nd Brigade,
which was relieved by the 101st Brigade on the 22nd,
and the following day the division was transferred
from the 19th Corps to the 10th Corps. The 103rd

Brigade Headquarters moved to Frowsty House on the same day. Patrols now became very active, and there were several encounters.

On the 23rd Lieutenant P. W. Lowering, Intelligence Officer, Royal Sussex, and two men reconnoitred Spanbrockmolen crater. He entered it alone and found it occupied by a garrison of ten men, of whom he killed one and withdrew safely. On the 25th, about two p.m., Lieutenant Mason, with only five men, crawled out to a position from which the snipers defending the crater could be dealt with, and then, with much skill, he took a party to some dead ground, from which the crater was rushed with small loss, and later Peckham crater was occupied without opposition. These were valuable gains in view of the impending operations, which were to commence on the 28th and were to extend along the whole Belgian and British front, from Dixmude to the line of the Ypres-Comines Canal. The task of the 34th Division was to establish itself on the Ypres-Comines Canal, south of the bend at Hollebeke. This involved capturing the Wytschaete Ridge. To achieve this by direct assault, with only the support of the Divisional Artillery, would have been a costly business. It was therefore decided to work up as close as possible to the crest of the ridge, in order to seize it, when a turning movement of the 41st Division from the north should have sufficiently loosened the enemy's hold on it. The advance began at five-thirty a.m., 28th September, by strong patrols under cover of a smoke barrage.

On the extreme left of the division Second-Lieutenant Cairns and his platoon of the 5th King's Own Scottish Borderers, supported by Lieutenant Hyslip and his platoon, followed up the barrage into Piccadilly Farm, capturing an officer and thirty-eight men and two machine guns. This was really in the 41st Division area, and 14th Argyll and Sutherland Highlanders of that division soon turned up to take charge. The right of the King's Own Scottish

Borderers pushed on to Louwaege; on their right the Argyll and Sutherland Highlanders took Red Château by six-thirty a.m., and by ten a.m. its line ran north and south through Grand Bois. The Loyal North Lancs, on the 101st front, were equally successful, and early captured Warsaw crater and many posts, killing and capturing many Boche and a couple of machine guns.

At three-thirty p.m., good progress having been made on both flanks, the division was ordered to advance and try to get over the Wytschaete Ridge and clear up the ground to the canal, if possible before dark. The 41st Division had passed round the bend of the canal, and was then moving south-east, with its right on the canal. The 5th King's Own Scottish Borderers and Argyll and Sutherland Highlanders captured Dome House and Zero House, but were held up by machine gun fire from Wytschaete, Lieutenant McGrory of the latter battalion being killed here. The movement was continued through the night. Wytschaete was taken by "B" Company Loyal North Lancs at six-thirty a.m. on 29th by a turning movement. The night advance was very difficult and trying, but there was little or no resistance, the enemy having decided to leave. By eight-thirty a.m. the final objective had been reached, and at two-thirty p.m. the 1/7th Cheshires passed through the 101st Brigade to the canal. The turning movement of the 41st Division, and the advance of the 30th Division, brought the inner flanks of these divisions together east of the canal and north of Werwicq, thus squeezing out the 34th Division, which was accordingly assembled on and west of Wytschaete Ridge.

The night was very wet, and the troops suffered much. The rendezvous was not reached till midnight or later, and the accommodation there was of the worst. On 2nd October the division moved to an area east of the Ypres-Comines Canal about Zandvoorde (Advanced Divisional Headquarters in some old

KEMMEL & WYTSCHAETE.
31st August to 30th September. 1918.

Divisional Boundary ....
Brigade   "   ....
First Objective, 1st Sept. ....
Final   "   "   "   ....

Scale of Yards

1000   500   0   1000   2000

41st Division

30th Division

MESSINES

COMINES CANAL

YPRES

Dome House

Forester House

Piccadilly Farm

Zero House

Louwaege

Zero House

GRAND BOIS

Birkenbeck

Red Chateau

Wytschaete

Petit Bois

Wartjes Crater

La Cache Farm

Peckham

Spanbroekmolen

Croneway

Croonaert Crater

Kruisstraat

Café

Wulverghem

Elbow Farm

35

Vierstraat

26th Sept.

RAILWAY

103rd Bde.

Irish Ho.

Beaver Hut

Dugouts

Yonge St.

Regents St.

8 p.m.

Spy Fm.

Lindenhoek

31st Sept.

Frenchmans Farm

Trench

3rd

Div.

8 a.m.

4 a.m.

Observatory Farm

Hallebast

27th Div. (U.S.A.)

la Polka

Kemmel

Division

103rd Brigade

Donegal Farm

Divisional Boundary previous to 1st Sept.

la Clytte

34th Division
at 5 a.m. 31st August

124th Brigade

Bruiloze

30th Div. (British)

German dug-outs near Hollebeke). This movement was over roads in full view of the enemy's positions south of the Lys, but fortunately the Hun was fully occupied, and we only suffered one casualty. Half the 152nd Brigade, R.F.A., got blocked on the St Eloi-Hollebeke road, and spent the night there. During this day General Nicholson received orders to take over the Werwicq-Menin line from the 35th and 41st Divisions, and to be prepared to fight for it. Later the orders were repeated with the fighting omitted, and on the night of 2nd/3rd October the line was taken over, the 103rd Brigade being on the right, 102nd on the left, and the 101st in reserve about Zandvoorde. The line ran from about two thousand five hundred yards north of Werwicq to Gheluwe, a front of about three thousand five hundred yards, almost the whole area under direct observation from north and east of the Lys. The only line of supply was along a plank road, unfit for lorries, from St Eloi to the canal near Hollebeke, and thence parallel to the front. Fortunately the Hun was disorganised, and the division got in with little trouble. The enemy, however, found time in a few days to attend to this matter of our supplies, and shelled parts of the road so effectively that a new route had to be found, and this could only be used by pack animals. On the night of 5th/6th the 103rd Brigade went into reserve just east of Zandvoorde, being relieved by the 102nd, and on the same night the 101st took over the adjacent brigade front on the left from the 124th Brigade. At this time a renewal of the advance was contemplated on 7th, but it was postponed till 14th. On the 6th news arrived that the Hun had suggested an immediate armistice.

Several changes in the holding of the line took place, and by the morning of 13th the 102nd were on the right and 103rd on the left, all ready for the attack, which was fixed to start at five-twenty-five a.m. on 14th October.

The 41st Division was on the left and the 30th on the right. The line as held on the morning of the 14th ran irregularly south-west from a point roughly four hundred yards north-west of the northern end of Gheluwe, though Quack Farm to the Ypres-Gheluwe road, thence due south to the Werwicq-Gheluwe road, and thence again south-west some one hundred yards to the divisional boundary. The village of Gheluwe fell entirely within the 103rd Brigade area. The front line troops from left to right were 103rd Brigade, 5th King's Own Scottish Borderers, 8th Scottish Rifles; 102nd Brigade, 1/4th Cheshires, 1/7th Cheshires. The two battalions of 103rd were each formed in depth on a single company front; those of the 102nd on a two company front, with one in support and one in reserve. The 5th Argyll and Sutherland Highlanders were in reserve on a two company front some one thousand eight hundred yards in rear of the centre of the 103rd, and the 1/1st Herefords in rear of the 102nd Brigade. The information pointed to the area about to be attacked being held by a system of fortified posts and pill-boxes. Special arrangements were made for dealing with all of these that were known, but as the advance was to be made behind a creeping barrage it was impressed on all ranks that the leading troops must keep up with the barrage, leaving the mopping up of any post that held out to the troops following them. The village of Gheluwe was to be dealt with by the fourth companies of the King's Own Scottish Borderers and Scottish Rifles, which were to follow their leading companies, passing on either side of the village till they were abreast of the centre, and then turn inwards and mop up the village from north and south. During the first twenty-eight minutes of advance the village was to be kept under smoke and thermite barrage by the artillery and special Royal Engineer Company. About one thousand five hundred yards in advance of the jumping-off line was the Black line, on reaching which there was to be a pause of fifteen minutes for reorganisation, after which the barrage was to advance again, till it reached a line some two hundred and fifty yards beyond the Blue line, which was about one thousand five hundred yards from the Black. This Blue line on the front of the 102nd and right of the 103rd Brigade was to be the final objective, and on this part the barrage was to remain steady while specially selected points were consolidated. On the left of the 103rd Brigade the King's Own Scottish Borderers were to stand fast on the Blue line, while two companies of the Argyll and Sutherland Highlanders pushed through them and followed the barrage, pivoting on their right about Job Farm till their left reached Snooker Farm. This line was the Brown line, and was roughly parallel to, and some one thousand yards from, the railway which forms the north and north-western boundary of the turn of Menin.

Considerable adjustment was necessary to make the jumping-off line conform to the barrage line, but the troops were all in position by four-twenty-five a.m. The enemy was active with his artillery and trench mortars, and used much gas. The headquarters of the 1/4th Cheshires were hit twice, and many casualties caused. The morning was very foggy, and what with our smoke barrage round Gheluwe, the enemy's gas, and the natural fog, the advance was made in an atmosphere strongly reminiscent of a yellow London fog, which made the maintenance of direction very difficult. In parts it was impossible to see more than five yards, and officers and sergeants led with the aid of compasses; some sections advanced holding each other by the belt. Nevertheless the front posts of the enemy were overwhelmed, but most of our casualties occurred in this first stage from posts too near our line to be included in the barrage, even though the Light Trench Mortars had dealt with them.

On the 103rd front the Scottish Rifles captured

Quail Mill, taking thirty or forty prisoners and some machine guns and trench mortars. The Black line was reached up to time, and the mopping up of Gheluwe was in progress. Prisoners, mostly of the 126th and 127th Infantry Regiment, began coming in, and all seemed going well.

The advance was resumed at six-eighteen a.m. Captain Angus, 1/4th Cheshires, with "A" and "B" Companies, made a rapid advance to Coucou, where about seventy prisoners were taken, among whom was a communicative and obliging German who spoke English well and guided his captors through the Menin depot close up to Menin. Here Captain Angus left Second-Lieutenants Stafford and Rouse with some twenty men. This party held its position just north of the Menin road till about one p.m. It came under machine gun fire, and Second-Lieutenant Stafford, taking a rifle, shot two of the gunners as they were bringing their gun into action. Captain Angus continued his very adventurous tour, passing near Job Farm, and eventually returned to Battalion Headquarters near the jumping-off line, having taken some one hundred and ten prisoners and contributed towards the capture of a field gun which fell into the hands of the Scottish Rifles near Quick Farm. Later in the day this energetic officer was wounded. The 1/4th Cheshires, in addition to the above, took, during the day, a field gun and several prisoners near Query Farm and some machine guns near Quarantine Farm. The 1/7th Cheshires on the right had but a short way to go, and soon reached their objective and pushed out patrols to the outskirts of Menin.

On the extreme left the King's Own Scottish Borderers got through quickly, but near the Blue line they were held up by a machine gun, trench mortar and three field guns firing over open sights from Uniform Farm. Captain W. S. Brown, commanding "D" Company, was killed, and other casualties suffered. The farm was rushed by Second-Lieutenant

Hood and a few men, some thirty Huns bolting out at the back. At eight a.m. the fog lifted, and the little party, now reduced to seven, found itself completely isolated, no other British troops being in sight. They withdrew about seven hundred yards to a fortified farm, and the enemy re-occupied Uniform, but not for long, for " C " Company and other parties coming up, the farm was again attacked and captured by Lieutenant M. T. Dickie and Sergeant Gallacher and four men who crept close up and rushed it. By twelve-fifty p.m. the farm was finally in our hands, and by one-fifteen the Blue line was occupied.

The Scottish Rifles met with considerable resistance between the Black and Blue lines. In the dense fog the troops, fearing to lose touch of the barrage, overlooked some pill-boxes and fortified posts, which gave trouble later. Having taken Tiara Farm the Scottish Rifles had to abandon it to deal with parties of the enemy in their rear in Quaker Cottage, and then to re-take Tiara. Unction and Quadrille Farms, in the King's Own Scottish Borderers area, were not taken till ten-fifteen a.m., and Gheluwe was not entirely cleared till nine-thirty a.m. At twelve-eighteen p.m. the left company of the Scottish Rifles rushed a troublesome pill-box and attacked Job Farm, which was quickly taken, and touch established with the party of 1/4th Cheshires under Second-Lieutenant Stafford, which was relieved by the Scottish and rejoined its battalion.

The Blue line having been occupied the Argyll and Sutherland Highlanders pushed through at one-thirty p.m., a little late owing to the resistance experienced on the left flank. One of the duties of the Highlanders was to send a patrol to occupy a hillock, known as the Kidney Bean, some distance in the front of the Brown line, so as to guard the flank of the 41st Division. Fortunately the 41st had made an example of the Huns on its front, and the 20th Durham Light Infantry occupied the Kidney Bean before the Argyll and Sutherland Highlanders advanced. The enemy put up a stout resistance at Roumanian Farm, and it was six p.m. before the Brown line was fully taken. The Argyll and Sutherland Highlanders held from Snookers to Roumanian Farm, and the Scottish Rifles thence to Job. The Durham Light Infantry, on the Kidney Bean, were relieved by a platoon of the Argyll and Sutherland Highlanders about an hour later.

The approximate casualties on this very successful day were only twelve officers and two hundred and fifty other ranks, and the prisoners taken were five hundred and sixty-eight. Three field guns, many trench mortars, machine guns, and much light railway material and rolling stock were also captured.

There was intense machine gun fire all along the enemy's front during the night, which prevented the patrols we sent out entering Menin, in which many fires were seen and many explosions heard. Early on 15th patrols were pushed out. It appears that the honour of being the first through the town rests with Lieutenant Montague and a patrol of the 1/4th Cheshires, which, after overcoming some resistance, got right through the town and reached Brulee Farm by nine a.m., but the Argyll and Sutherland Highlanders were not far behind, for at nine-fifteen a.m. one of their patrols reached the Marathon bridge, which they found blown up and still burning.

Menin was quickly occupied by the 102nd, and posts established on the right bank of the Lys, at Mongrel and Marathon bridges. The 103rd carried on the line along the Wevelghem road to the east of Tent Farm. The enemy held Ripe Farm till dusk, and also the northern outskirts of Halluin. During the night of 15th/16th patrols of the 1/1st Herefords and 5th Argyll and Sutherland Highlanders crossed the river, and, meeting near the church on north-east outskirts of Halluin, captured a machine gun, which the former brought back, re-crossing by a pontoon bridge which the enemy had forgotten to destroy. The Argyll and Sutherland Highlanders patrol, under Second-Lieutenant D. Thomson, built a bridge of material salved on the bank, and by this bridge " Z " Company of the Scottish Rifles crossed at six a.m. on 16th, but they made no great progress on account of the heavy and accurate machine gun fire. The company held its position all day, suffering many casualties, and was withdrawn about seven p.m. as the bridge was nearly destroyed, and was actually broken up by a shell just after the company had recrossed.

During the night 15th/16th the 101st Brigade prolonged our line to the left, relieving the 124th Brigade, 41st Division, which, just prior to relief, had advanced the line to the northern bank of the Lys. The left of the 101st extended as far as the north-eastern outskirts of Wevelghem. The Royal Sussex and 2nd Loyal North Lancs pushed forward patrols at six a.m. on 16th, and the latter cleared Wevelghem, and by ten a.m. the north bank of the Lys was effectively held, but no crossing was made that day.

During the night of 16th/17th the 102nd Brigade was relieved by the 90th Brigade, 30th Division, and went to the neighbourhood of Johnston's Farm. Early on the 17th the Argyll and Sutherland Highlanders patrols crossed the river east of Menin and pushed boldly on, being followed by the Scottish Rifles, and by five p.m. a line had been formed along the Croisse-Kruisstraat road, in touch with the London Regiment on the right.

The Loyal North Lancs also effected a crossing near Royal Farm, " B " Company crossing one man at a time on an improvised ferry raft. A semicircular line was quickly taken up, both flanks resting on the river, and the 208th and 207th Field Companies commenced at once constructing bridges. The former company had a pontoon bridge fit to carry artillery ready by five a.m., supplementing their pontoons by trestles built out of material left behind by their opposite number in the Huns ranks. 207th Field Company built a foot-bridge close by.

" D " Company Loyal North Lancs crossed behind " B " and pushed on to Lauwe, which was occupied by two p.m., an attempt at resistance at Knokke being quickly terminated by the energetic action of the 101st Light Trench Mortar Battery. The village was occupied, and on " C " Company, Loyal North Lancs, arriving, a defensive flank was formed facing north-east between the Contrai and Aebeke roads.

The Royal Sussex crossed the Lys at dusk opposite Herebout, and prolonged the line to the left, and late in the afternoon the line extended from just south of Marcke to Kruisstraat, where touch was obtained with 30th Division. During the night the 101st Brigade extended to its left, relieving the troops of the 103rd, which went back into reserve.

On the 18th General Woodcock and the head-quarters of the 101st Brigade made a triumphant entry into Lauwe, which was the first Belgian town we had entered which was still inhabited. The inhabitants gave the General a demonstrative and enthusiastic welcome. The enemy was evidently in full retreat, and crowds of liberated civilians were met on all sides.

On the 19th the advance was resumed. The 2/4th Queen's formed the advance guard. By noon some six thousand yards had been covered, then there came a temporary check in front of Belleghem, which was occupied by the enemy, who also had machine guns in the buildings to the north. The Loyal North Lancs sent two companies round either flank of the position. The encircling took some time, and it was midnight before Courtrai road, east of Belleghem, was reached, and a company of the Queen's had passed through the village. The remainder of the division crossed the Lys, the 102nd Brigade going to St Anne's, and the 103rd Brigade to Knokke.

Capture of MENIN, 14th.–16th. October, 1918.

Advance from LYS to SCHELDT.

Scale of Miles.

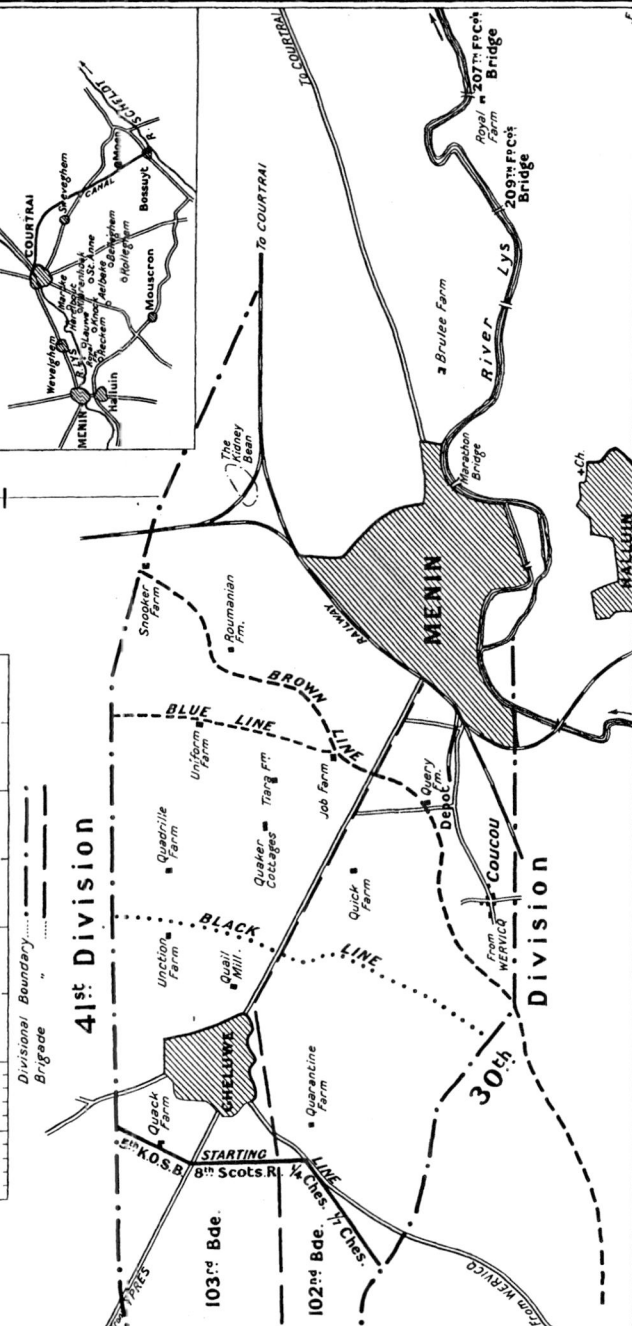

SCHELDT

Spreeghem
COURTRAI
Bossuyt
Marke CANAL
Herseaux
St. Arme
Rollegem
Moen
Helcen
Gulleghem
Mouscron
Herscamp
Deerm
Wevelghem
LYS
Halluin
MENIN

SCHELDT

To COURTRAI

To COURTRAI

The Kidney Bean

RAILWAY

MENIN

River Lys

Brulee Farm

Manebon Bridge

4 Ch.

HALLUIN

Royal Farm
207th. F.P. Co's. Bridge
209th. F.P. Co's. Bridge

Scale of Yards.

Divisional Boundary ....
Brigade ....

41st. Division

Snooker Farm

Roumanian Frm.

BROWN LINE

BLUE LINE

Uniform Farm

Trang Frm.

Job Farm

Query Depot

Quadrille Farm

Quaker Cottages

Quick Farm

COUCOU

From WERVICQ

BLACK LINE

Unction Farm

Quail Mill

SHELLUVE

Quarantine Farm

Quack Farm

8th. K.O.S.B.   STARTING
8th. Scots.Rl. ¼ Ches. LINE
½ Ches.

From PRES

103rd. Bde.

102nd. Bde.

From WERVICQ

30th. Division

From this date onwards an Army Field Artillery Brigade was attached to the division, and brigade groups were formed, each consisting of one Infantry Brigade, one Field Artillery Brigade, one company Royal Engineers, and a company 34th Machine Gun Battalion, with administrative services.

On the 20th the 30th Division passed through the 101st Brigade, which withdrew to Halbeke, the division now becoming Corps Reserve, with Divisional Headquarters in Lauwe. Here Lieutenant-Colonel A. H. Grubb took over the duties of A.A. and Q.M.G. from Major Parkin, who had been performing them most efficiently in the face of great difficulties, due to the comparatively roadless state of the country and the constant changes of position. Brigadier-General Walthall took command of the 103rd Brigade, Brigadier-General Rawson going on leave, and Lieutenant-Colonel Warburton acting as C.R.E.

On the 22nd orders were received to interpose again between the 30th and 41st Divisions and continue the advance. The 102nd Brigade, which had not been in action since the 16th, relieved the right brigade of the 41st Division in the front line. The sector occupied by the brigade faced a little north of east, six hundred yards west of, and parallel to, the Contrai-Bossuyt Canal. The left rested on the canal tunnel, part of which was held by the enemy, and right on the Scheldt, near Bossuyt.

The 1/1st Herefords were on the left, and the 1/7th Cheshires on the right, the 1/4th Cheshires in reserve. The 123rd Brigade, 41st Division, which was on the left, was to make an attack at two-fifteen a.m. on 24th, and in this the 102nd Brigade was to co-operate.

The 123rd Brigade held the line from the left of the 102nd, and almost in at right angles to it in a north-easterly direction across the canal, north of the tunnel. It was to attack in a southerly direction till its right flank was past the tunnel, and then change direction to the south-east, which would leave a gap between its right flank and the canal, which would increase as the advance progressed. The 1/1st Herefords were to close this gap, crossing the canal as soon as the 123rd had passed the tunnel. No sooner had the relief been accomplished than the support and reserve companies of the battalion had to move to the vicinity of the tunnel, their places being taken by two companies of the 1/4th Cheshires.

The attack of the 41st Division, however, did not progress far enough to render the co-operation of the 102nd necessary, and on the 24th a new scheme of attack was evolved. As a preliminary to which the 1/4th Cheshires relieved the right battalion of the 123rd Brigade, 23rd Middlesex, which held the east bank of the canal north of the northern exit of the tunnel, which was held by the enemy. Thence the 41st Division line ran south of Kwaadesstraat, and bent back to the north of Kattestraat.

The main attack was to be made in a southerly direction from this line, but a subsidiary attack was to be made by the 1/7th Cheshires in the neighbourhood of Locks 3, 4, and 5 under a heavy barrage and smoke screen put down by the 34th Divisional Artillery. It was hoped that the battalion would be able to get across the canal and meet the 1/4th Cheshires as they advanced down the east bank. The village of Moen was to be kept under a dense smoke cloud by the field howitzers from four minutes before to ninety-six minutes after zero, which it was hoped would admit of the encirclement of the village and its easy mopping up by the rear companies of the 1/4th Cheshires. The advance was to be continued on in conjunction with the 41st Division in a south-easterly direction.

The creeping barrage for the main attack was to be put down by the 41st Division Artillery, but two batteries of the 34th Division were to thicken and extend it to include the canal as far as the northern edge of Moen.

The subsidiary attack was made at three a.m., and was only partially successful. "A" and "C" Companies 1/7th Cheshires cleared Bossuyt and lined the river bank on the far side, but "B" Company was unsuccessful in its attempt at crossing at Lock 4, owing to heavy machine gun fire. The enemy at eight a.m. made a clever counter-attack under a heavy trench mortar barrage, and took three officers and twenty-two other ranks prisoners.

At nine a.m. the barrage for the main attack commenced two hundred yards in front of the jumping-off line, and moved forward at two hundred yards a minute. The 1/4th Cheshires' fighting line, under Major Morris, advanced steadily, lengthening its line to the right as the right flank of the 23rd Middlesex inclined away from the canal. By nine-thirty a.m. the 1/4th Cheshires was clear of the tunnel, over which the 1/7th Cheshires crossed and moved in support of the 1/4th Cheshires. The Cheshires easily overcame the resistance on their front, but the enemy's machine gunners farther east were more active and persistent, so that the 41st Division progress was slower.

By twelve-fifteen a.m. "B" and "D" Companies of the 1/4th Cheshires were east of Moen, and "A" was between that village and the canal. Second-Lieutenant Rouse, commanding "B," had been wounded in the thigh by shrapnel at five a.m., but he led his company till late in the afternoon, when Major Morris ordered him back.

Colonel Drage and the headquarter personnel of the 1/4th Cheshires passed through the western part of Moen, being met by some unfortunate inhabitants of that place, who were in a very unenviable position. 1/1st Herefords were close behind the 1/4th Cheshires, and rendered ready aid wherever it was needed. By one p.m. "C" Company 1/4th

Cheshires had cleared Moen of the enemy, and Colonel Drage was enabled to reorganise his battalion south of that village, preparatory to a further advance.

"'A" Company moved with its right on the canal, and " B " with its right on the Moen-Autryve road. " D " and 1/1st Herefords moved in rear of the left flank of " B," ready to ward off any attacks from that flank, as the progress of the 123rd Brigade was not known. " C " Company followed in the centre as reserve. At three p.m. Lieutenant Lokeman, of " D " Company, 1/7th Cheshires, reported to Colonel Drage having crossed the canal at Lock 4. A French civilian now came to Colonel Drage and gave him much useful information. By four p.m. " B " Company, 1/4th Cheshires, now under Second-Lieutenant Stafford, with " D," reached the northern outskirts of Autryve, and had to wait till our guns had finished bombarding it before they could enter. By eight-thirty p.m. Autryve was cleared, and all our objectives had been gained. The losses of the 1/4th Cheshires on this day were ten killed and twenty-four wounded, and they took fifty-seven prisoners and seven light machine guns. In Autryve they found many wounded civilians, to whom every attention was paid, and as many as possible were taken to hospital by the stretcher-bearers.

The 102nd Brigade's losses only totalled eighty-seven, and exactly that number of prisoners was taken.

During the night the line was organised. The left flank of the 30th Division was just west of Bossuyt, thence the 1/7th Cheshires held the line to the Moen-Bossuyt, whence the 1/4th Cheshires took up the defence to the eastern outskirts of Autryve. The 41st Division's right was at Woffelstraat, in touch with our right. The enemy withdrew across the Scheldt during the night, and we pushed our outposts to the left bank. Autryve was nearly demolished by the Huns' guns. On 26th the enemy evacuated Avelghem, which was occupied by the 41st Division.

MOEN & AUTRYVE.

Scale of Yards.

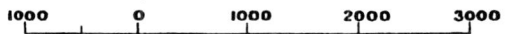

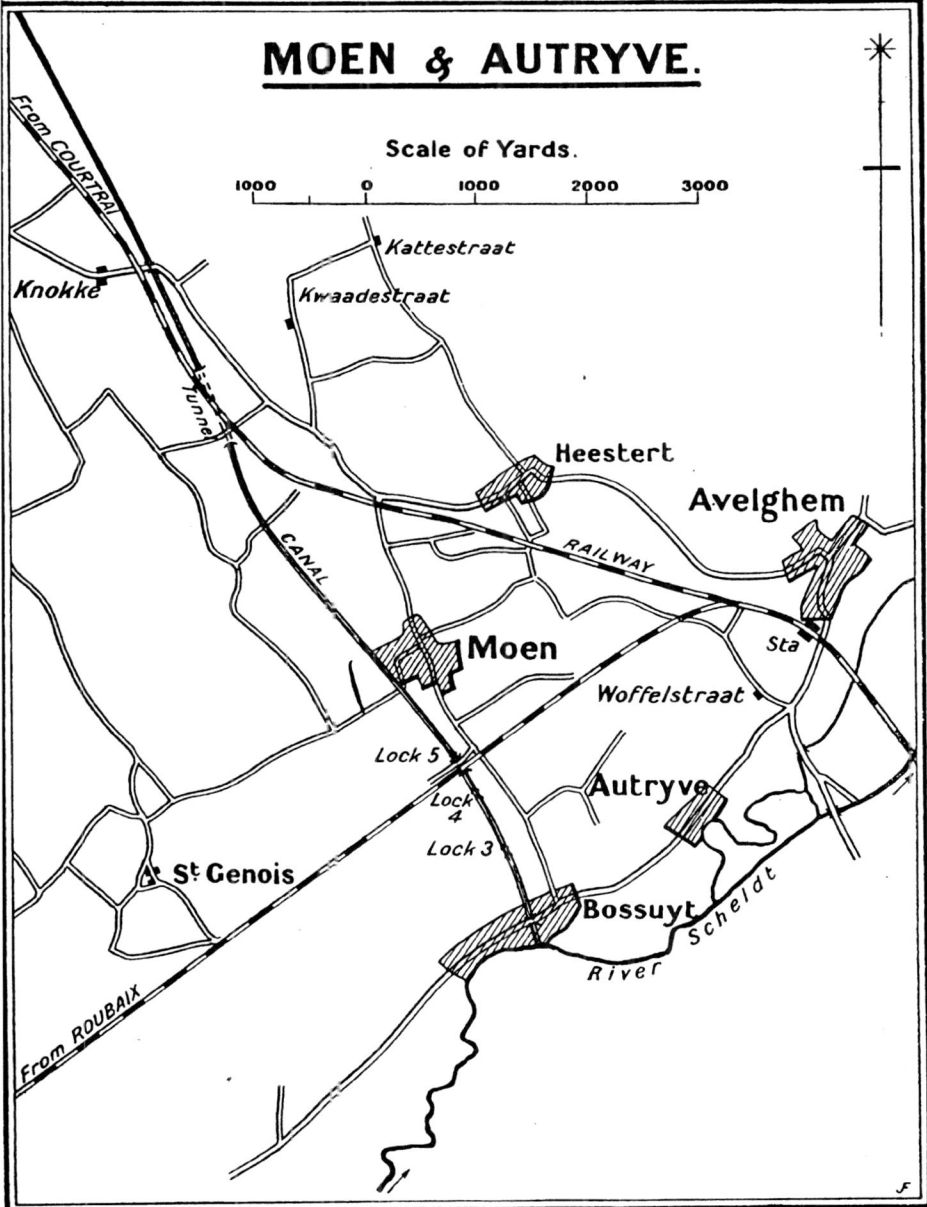

1000   0   1000   2000   3000

From COURTRAI

Kattestraat

Knokke

Kwaadestraat

Tunnel

Heestert

Avelghem

CANAL

RAILWAY

Moen

Sta

Woffelstraat

Lock 5

Autryve

Lock 4

Lock 3

St Genois

Bossuyt

Scheldt

River

From ROUBAIX

With the exception of the unfortunate episode at Lock 4 the operation had been eminently successful.

During the 25th General Nicholson received orders that the division was to be transferred to the 2nd Corps, and on 26th 101st Brigade group moved to the new area south-east of Harlebeke, and 103rd group to St Anne. During the night of 26/27th the 102nd group was relieved by the 21st Brigade, 30th Division, and concentrated in the St Anne area by midday 27th. During the same night the 101st Brigade group took over the line from Kleineberg to the railway bridge over the Krommebeek from the 108th and 109th Brigades, 36th Division, and at midday 28th General Nicholson took command of the new front. On the night of 28th/29th the 103rd Brigade group relieved the 101st in the front line, the 101st going to the Harlebeke-Deerlyck area. Divisional Headquarters were in Harlebeke, but Advanced Divisional Headquarters was "in a small convent school with some nice sisters but no windows." On 30th the final touches were put to the arrangements for a further advance on 31st, which had been in preparation for some time.

The 2nd and 19th Corps and the 7th French Corps d'Armée were taking part in the attack, and the 34th Division was to have the assistance of thirty tanks of the 12th French Tank Battalion. The 41st French Division was on our left, and the 31st British on our right.

The attack, as far as the 34th Division was concerned, was to be delivered by the 103rd Brigade, to which the 2/4th Queen's was attached. It was to be supported by the whole of the Divisional Artillery, to which were added the 51st and 113th Brigades Field Artillery and a proportion of heavies. The 34th Battalion, Machine Gun Corps (less one company), and also 1st and 4th Batteries, 1st Motor Machine Gun Brigade, were to assist in the barrage.

T

The line from which the attack of the 103rd Brigade was to be launched curved from Kleinberg slightly to the north-east as far as the railway north-east of Sterhoek, and then slightly north-west to the divisional boundary. The length of the jumping-off line was about three thousand yards, but as the lines of advance of the flank divisions converged and met at Langestraat, five thousand yards to the east, the front of the brigade was constantly contracting, and as the barrages of these flank divisions were differently timed the movements of the troops of the 103rd Brigade as they neared the apex of the triangle of their advance had to be carefully managed. The barrage put down by the 34th Artillery was to cease as soon as the advance to the second objective began, but beyond that point the 152nd Brigade, Royal Field Artillery, was to cover the advance under orders of the G.O.C. 103rd Brigade.

The first objective was a line from the eastern outskirts of Anseghem, curving south-west to the divisional boundary south of Bergstraat, about one thousand six hundred yards in length. On the right the Scottish Rifles had about one thousand two hundred yards farther to go than the left of the King's Own Scottish Borderers. There was to be a halt of two hours on the first objective.

The second objective was the line of the road east of Anseghem to Belgic Cabaret, a prolongation of the left portion of the first objective. A Liaison Company was formed under Captain R. W. Nuttall, 2/4th Queen's, composed of half a company of his battalion and half a company of 23rd French Regiment, which was on the left. This company was to keep touch between the French and British forces.

Ten tanks were allotted to each of the assaulting battalions, and ten were kept in reserve. The tanks were to form the first wave, and each tank was to be accompanied by five infantry men to " set " it at the particular strong points which were giving trouble.

Two light trench mortars were also allotted to each battalion.

The hour of assault was five-twenty-five a.m. on 31st October, and as the troops moved forward they came under the hostile barrage. On the right the King's Own Scottish Borderers and their ten tanks made rapid progress in spite of strong opposition from the enemy's front line posts. They took many prisoners and machine guns, and carefully mopped up all posts as they advanced. A thick fog aided them, and by six-forty-five a.m. they were on their objective with only twenty casualties. Tank crews and infantry were mutually happy and pleased with each other. Three of the tanks volunteered to advance and suppress obnoxious machine gun posts which were giving trouble. Two of these tanks were put out of action, their gallant crews being badly wounded.

On the left flank matters did not go so well. The 41st French Division was met by intense machine gun fire and so stout a resistance that it was unable to keep pace with the barrage, and therefore the left flank of the Scottish Rifles was exposed and the left half company was held up in Winterken by fire from the French area. The Liaison Company failed to make progress, and was also held up there. Winterken was under fire of an advanced section of seventy-seven m.m. guns north-east of Anseghem, which made all movement dangerous till they were silenced later by an advanced section of 160th Brigade, R.F.A.

This left flank continued to give anxiety all day. The 2/4th Queen's were echeloned from Winterken to Anseghem until dark. The 23rd French Regiment during the day connected with our troops in Winterken, but an attempt by them to get farther forward in the evening was frustrated.

" W " and " Y " Companies of the Scottish Rifles managed to get forward with the barrage to the neighbourhood of Anseghem. The intention had been to encircle this village from north and south and mop it up later. This was made impossible by the delay on the left, so the right of the Scottish Rifles passed to the south of the village, and reached their objective before eight a.m., forming a line from the cemetery to the left flank of the King's Own Scottish Borderers. The accompanying tanks moved through the village, but the wily Boche machine gunners remained silent and undetected till the tanks had gone away, and then became troublesome. "X" Company, Scottish Rifles, mopped up these gentry, and by ten-thirty a.m. Anseghem was cleared, but snipers and machine gunners from Kruisweg and the high ground east of it continued to be very troublesome. Three of the tanks were put out of action, and the ground in this area proved too marshy for their use. An attack was projected from Anseghem on Kruisweg by tanks and Scottish Rifles, but the idea was abandoned on account of the ground and the state of obscurity on the French front. No further progress was made on this part of the front. The King's Own Scottish Borderers moved forward at eight-thirty, and by ten-forty-five a.m. were on their final objective east of Anseghem to Belgic Cabaret. Here they came under fire of an advanced section of seventy-seven m.m. guns stationed near the church in Gyselbrechteghem and of many trench mortars and machine guns hidden in the farms near their line. Six tanks made a very gallant attempt to subdue these nuisances, but were forced to withdraw after two of them had been put out of action. At two-thirty p.m. orders were received for a further advance by the King's Own Scottish Borderers and Argyll and Sutherland Highlanders, but in view of the situation on the left, and of the fact that the Americans were reported to have reached Worteghem, which made a retirement of the enemy almost a certainty, the attack was abandoned, and instead the two battalions were directed to patrol to their fronts and try to seize the high ground about Boschkant.

In case the enemy should refuse to retire the 2nd Loyal North Lancs was placed at General Walthall's disposal and ordered up to Sterhoek, and arrangements were made for an attack in the early hours of the 1st November. This was not necessary, for the patrols met with no resistance, and before midnight "A" and "B" Companies, King's Own Scottish Borderers, "B" Company, Argyll and Sutherland Highlanders, were established from Boschkant through Gyselbrechteghem to the railway, where they were in touch with the 31st Division. As soon as this was known to the French and the Americans they advanced quickly. The Argyll and Sutherland Highlanders followed the enemy till one p.m. on 1st November, and were then withdrawn, as the 41st French and 31st British Divisions had joined hands across the 34th front at Elseghem. These two divisions advanced to the Scheldt, and the 34th Division was withdrawn in to reserve.

The Commander of the 41st Division expressed himself very warmly to General Nicholson as regards the services the 34th had rendered to the 41st on the previous day by guarding its right flank and clearing the southern end of the high ground, which facilitated its advance. The Army Commander, Sir H. C. O. Plumer, also complimented the division.

The tangible results of the day's fight were two hundred and thirteen prisoners, of whom three were officers, three field guns, thirty-three machine guns, and two Minenwerfers, and the retreat of the enemy beyond the Scheldt. Our casualties were only one hundred and fifty.

Thus ended triumphantly the battle career of the 34th Division, for on the 3rd November we marched back to the west of Courtrai.

10th November : " About nine p.m. we tapped a wireless message from German Chancellor to the effect that all Armistice conditions were accepted. This was

followed by a general discharge of lights of all sorts
from neighbouring aerodromes."

BATTLE CASUALTIES SUSTAINED DURING 1918.

Month	Killed		Wounded		Missing		Total	
	O.	O.R.	O.	O.R.	O.	O.R.	O.	O.R.
January	2	23	9	175	—	3	11	201
February	2	4	1	8	—	—	3	12
March	20	192	56	1005	62	1844	138	3041
April	31	254	135	2202	40	2397	206	4853
May	—	8	5	46	—	—	5	54
June	—	—	—	—	—	—	—	—
July	17	334	104	2451	1	162	122	2947
August	12	154	20	539	1	53	33	746
September	14	128	33	727	3	157	50	1012
October	13	186	51	1004	4	115	68	1305
November	4	34	6	97	10	15	20	146
Total ...	115	1317	420	8254	121	4746	647	14317

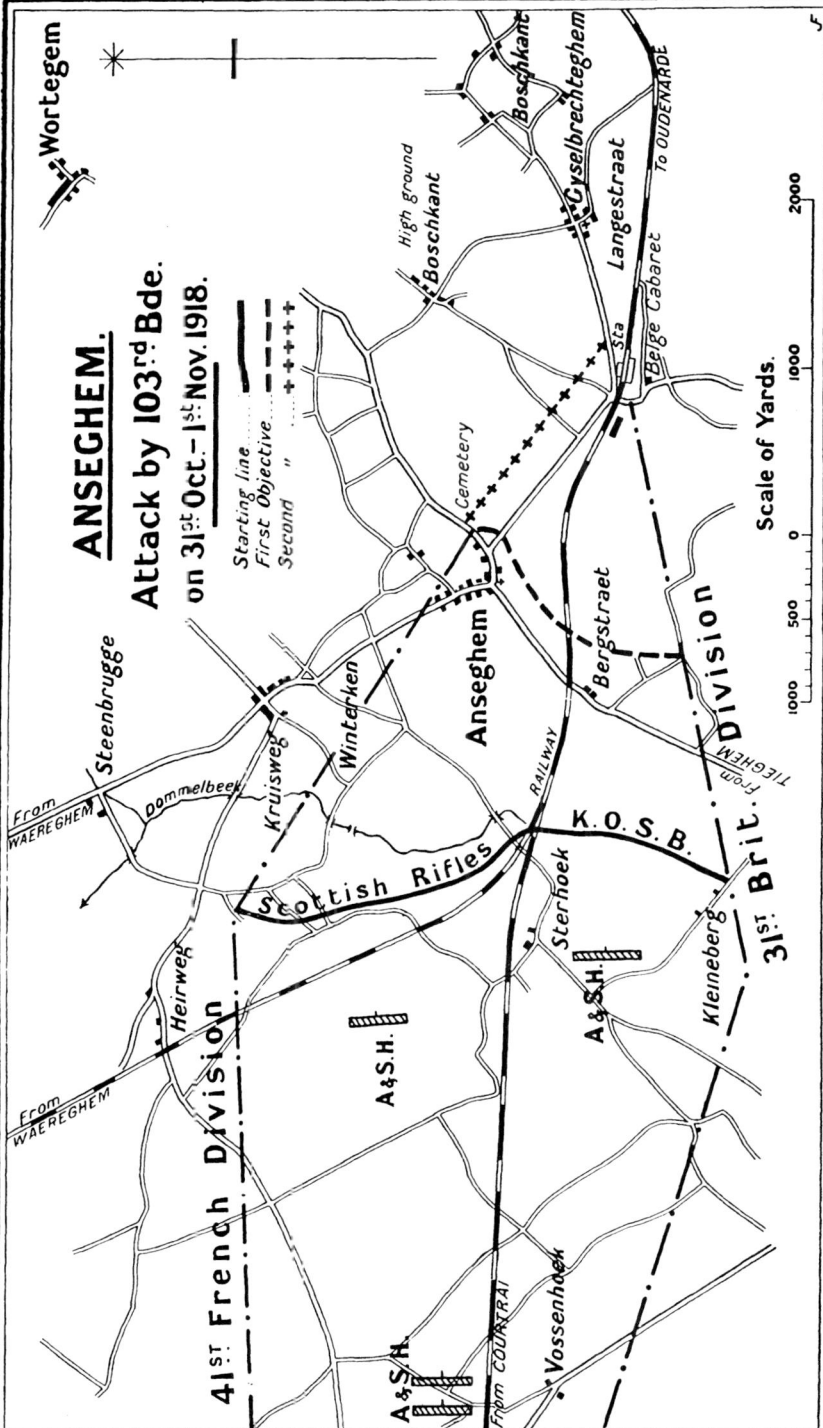

ANSEGHEM.
Attack by 103rd Bde.
on 31st Oct.–1st Nov. 1918.

Starting line ....
First Objective ....
Second " ....

Wortegem

Boschkant
Boschkant
Gyselbrechteghem
To OUDENARDE
Langestraat
High ground
Boschkant
Belge Cabaret
Sta
Cemetery
Bergstraet
Steenbrugge
Winterken
Kruisweg
Anseghem
From TIEGHEM
Dommelbeek
From
WAEREGHEM
RAILWAY
Scottish Rifles
K.O.S.B.
31st Brit. Division
Heirweg
Sterhoek
Kleineberg
A.&S.H.
A.&S.H.
41st French Division
From
WAEREGHEM
From COURTRAI
Vossenhoek
A.&S.H.

Scale of Yards.
2000   1000   0   500   1000

CHAPTER XIV

THE division was originally selected to be one of the first to march to the Rhine. This was soon cancelled, and on the 17th November it marched to an area about Lessines, arriving there on the 18th and 19th. The division was transferred to the 10th Corps, and settled down to light training and recreational training. A divisional education scheme was drawn up, but, owing to the lack of books and material, no great progress was made.

On the 12th December we were on the move again to the area in the angle formed by the Meuse and Sambre at Namur. We did not reach our destination till 19th. Except on the last day, it rained hard, and the route was over *pavé* roads and through the streets of Louviere, Charleroi, and other mining towns. Very few men fell out, though the test was a severe one. The distributions at the end of the march was as follows : Divisional Headquarters at Profondeville ; 152nd Brigade, R.F.A., Franiere ; 160th Brigade, R.F.A., Bois de Villers ; 113th Brigade, R.F.A., St Gerard ; D.A.C., Arsimont Ham ; 101st Infantry Brigade Group, Malonne ; 102nd Brigade Group, Fosse ; 103rd Brigade Group, Avelais ; Royal Engineers, Lesves and Arbres ; Pioneers, Wepion ; Machine Gun Battalion, Florette.

Here we stayed till 17th January. Training and education went on, varied by joy rides to Brussels, for which one lorry per brigade was allowed. The Chequers gave a gala performance in Brussels, and ran the annual pantomime better than ever at Malonne, Namur, and finally at Siegburg.

On 22nd December the demobilisation began, miners and pivotal men leading the way. On the 11th January group 43, teachers and students, departed, thereby upsetting our educational scheme. I wonder whether they were greatly regretted?

On 17th the move to the Rhine was commenced, by train, and was not completed until the 29th. We relieved the 2nd Canadian Division in the right sector of the Cologne Bridgehead. Divisional Headquarters was in Siegburg. One brigade held the outpost line, with its headquarters in Siegburg; the second brigade had Lohmar as it headquarters, and the third was at Whan. The artillery were at Siegburg, Wahn, and Lohmar; D.A.C. at Zandorf; Machine Gun Battalion at Troisdorf; the Field Companies at Happerschoss, Waldshelld, and Troisdorf; the Field Ambulances at Siegburg, Troisdorf, and Wahn; the train at Siegburg, Buisdorf, and Troisdorf.

The defence scheme provided for an outpost line covering the main line of resistance, which was organised in depth, and consisted of defended localities covered by field artillery and machine guns.

Every preparation was made for direct action should the enemy give any cause for it. As he did not we turned to sport. General Nicholson gave a cup for competition between the units of the division, for which there was hot rivalry. The three events in the competition were football, running, a relay race, and tug-of-war. The training, practising, and playing off of ties occupied much time in a very profitable manner. The result was a great victory for the 5th Argyll and Sutherland Highlanders, who scored the possible in all three events. The next to them were the 34th Machine Gun Battalion, with eight out of eighteen. The divisional boxing was won by the 2nd Loyal North Lancashire Regiment, which won three out of the six events.

The Cavalry Corps at Spa gave a race meeting, to which many went. Of other amusements there was no lack. Miss Lena Ashwell's ladies' concert party paid us a visit. In Cologne the opera was good and cheap. The Royal Artillery band gave a free concert at Cologne, and later at Wahn. In Cologne there were two theatres and three army cinemas, and for those who like quiet outdoor amusement there was fishing, with the added joy of being allowed to indulge in the sport without consulting the wishes of the owners of the water. This seems to have been the extent of our " frightfulness," unless insisting that the population should treat us with ordinary respect can be called by that name.

There had been several changes in the divisional staff. In December Lieutenant-Colonel Grubb left us to become A.Q.M.G., 13th Corps, and his place was taken by Major H. D. Parkin, M.C., a very popular appointment, for Major Parkin had been with us from the very commencement. In the muddy camps round Sutton Veny, and the muddier trenches of Armentières, on the Somme and round Arras and in Belgium, in times of peace and in the hottest times of war we had learnt that our D.A.Q.M.G. was a faithful friend, always to be relied on to get the very best he could for the men in the line. Therefore we congratulated ourselves when Major Parkin became A.A. and A.Q.M.G., with the rank of Lieutenant-Colonel. We also were pleased that Major Tempest, who had joined the 11th Suffolks at the beginning of the war and had been some time on the staff of the 101st Brigade, should become D.A.Q.M.G. in Lieutenant-Colonel Parkin's place.

On the 15th of March, 1919, the 34th Division died, and in its place arose the Eastern Division, which was also under command of General Nicholson, and was in many respects the old 34th under a new name. The Artillery, Engineers, Machine Gun Battalion, Train and Field Ambulances were the same, but the only infantry battalion which remained was the 1/4th Royal Sussex; all the others were replaced. The 6th and 10th Battalions Royal West Kent Regiment, and 51st, 52nd, and 53rd Battalions of the Bedfordshire and Royal Sussex Regiments took the place of the old battalions, which were either transferred to other divisions or reduced to cadre.

So ended the 34th Division, and no more fitting epitaph can be written than General Nicholson's special order published on the 4th March, 1919 :

"I cannot allow the infantry battalions, which are now leaving the division on reorganisation, to go without expressing my great appreciation of their conduct and bearing, both in and out of action, since they joined the 34th Division.

"These battalions, coming from different brigades and divisions in the east to new conditions of warfare and to commanders who were unknown to them, were almost immediately put into action with the French Army south of Soissons, in the early days of the French offensive of July, 1918.

"The conduct of all in the hard fighting and under the strenuous conditions was beyond all praise, and gained much praise from our allies.

"Subsequently, in the months of August, September, and October in Flanders and Belgium, they showed the same qualities of endurance, gallantry, and discipline in action.

"I am proud to have had such battalions under my command, and part with them with the greatest regret, and wish all ranks the best of fortune in the future.

"(Signed) C. L. NICHOLSON, *Major-General.*"

CHAPTER XV

THE tale of the 34th Division has been told, but in order to avoid interfering with the narrative much has been omitted regarding various units which formed important parts of the division. This omission I shall now make good as far as space allows me.

The 34th Divisional Train

The first Commanding Officer of the Train was Lieutenant-Colonel E. G. Evans, and his task was no light one, for the personnel of the Train was drawn from nearly every calling, and many of the men had never driven before enlisting, and several were over fifty, but under their Commanding Officer's skilful handling, assisted by the enthusiasm that pervaded the whole nation in those brave days, a high standard was reached in a wonderfully short time. The Train is a unit that those in the front line take for granted. No one bothers to think how his rations, etc., arrive, but everyone would soon realise the importance of the Train were it suddenly to go on strike, or stipulate for an eight hour day.

The conveyance of all the rations and stores for the whole division, from rail-head to refilling point, and issuing of them and accounting for them is the Train's job. The Train's work went on just the same whether the division was in the line or at rest. While

299

the risks run by the Train are not to be compared with those of a fighting unit they were not negligible. R.E. material, gas cylinders, etc., had sometimes to go to the forward area, and not infrequently the convoys came under shell fire. When this happened the drivers had to stay by their horses and pretend they liked it. The coolness and unconcern displayed on these occasions was remarkable.

The enemy's airmen were particularly attentive to the Train camps, and all horse lines. In 1917 behind Paschendale a single bomb killed seventeen horses outright, and fifteen others had to be destroyed in consequence of their wounds.

At Haute Avesnes in the spring of 1917, before the Battle of Arras, the Train had a terrible time. The camp was liquid sea of mud eighteen inches deep, and all through a spell of bad weather the horses were doing eighteen to twenty miles a day on reduced rations.

At the commencement of the final victorious advance the Train had interesting experiences with the French Army. During the summer of 1917 at Roisel the Train enjoyed a period, the only one, when conditions approached those known as "picnic," which were rudely disturbed by the enemy suddenly dropping thirty shells from a long range gun within the perimeter of the camp during refilling time. But it was the Train's day, and not a half-penny worth of damage was done to man, beast, or material.

Even under the most trying circumstances it was most unusual for a unit not to receive its rations up to time, which is surely a proof of the excellence of the supply arrangements from the base right through to the front line, and of the debt which those in front owed to those behind.

34th Divisional Salvage Company.

This unit was formed on 10th May, 1916. The personnel came from the 18th Northumberland Fusiliers. At the start its strength was Captain F. G. Wilson, Sergeant J. Walker, and twelve Privates. Full and well-considered orders were received from " Q," and the new unit showed such zeal in salving that its members had to be supplied with green brassards to save them from being arrested for looting.

The duties of the company were various :

1. Care and custody of packs of troops engaged in offensive operations.
2. Care of tents and canvas of the division.
3. The salvage of Government property, and also enemy property, wherever found.
4. The sorting of the stuff salved, and dispatch thereof to the base.

There were other tasks too varied and numerous to mention in detail. When the wounded came streaming back on the fatal 1st July, 1916, and on subsequent days, they were very grateful to the Salvage Company for meals of salved rations, cooked in salved field kitchens, and in many other ways the company gave much assistance to over-worked R.A.M.C. personnel.

The company's ration strength from early in June onwards until the division left the Somme, ranged from one hundred to one thousand two hundred, and during most of the time averaged about three hundred. Two Yeomanry Detachments, a Cylist Company, and the personnel of two Tunnelling Companies were temporarily placed under Captain Wilson's orders during this period. The detail of articles salved during the one month of July, 1916, is worth recording :

Rifles, 12,998; bayonets, 6,050; revolvers, 8; Very pistols, 28; machine guns, 51; trench mortars, 12; S.A.A. rounds, 1,580,000; bombs, 40,000; S.A.A. fired cases, 145,000; equipment, complete sets, 5,500; ground sheets, 700; steel helmets, 9,869; gas respirators, 13,280; picks and shovels, 2,000; wire cutters, 950; bully beef, 16,000 tins; bag-pipes, 6 sets, etc.

The value of this one month's collection was estimated to be about £1,500,000. On one occasion the company was able to fit out a battalion with everything except clothing, iron rations, and gas helmets.

In addition to the above, much German stuff was salved.

The sad task of removing the equipment from the dead fell to the salvage men. It was generally carried out in the early morning, before German guns began work. The company was shelled out of its billets in Albert 2nd August, 1916, and had to go into camp west of the town.

Space does not admit of giving details of the company's work during the subsequent operations, but during each offensive it was carried out with the same thoroughness. At Erquinghem at the close of 1916 the control of the reinforcement camp was given to the company. The sudden withdrawal of the division in January, 1917, from the front line system threw much work on the Salvage Company, of which Lieutenant McQuillan, 18th Northumberland Fusiliers, had just taken charge, Captain Wilson going to Divisional Headquarters as Assistant D.A.Q.M.G. In the Arras offensive the company did good work in the filling of the dumps previous to and after the attack of 9th April, 1917.

The record of the Salvage Company is one of hard work which, though it brought but little glory to those engaged in it, was very necessary, and resulted in great saving of public money, and on many occasions greatly aided the fighting units by supplying them speedily with requisites without which operations would have been delayed.

The company remained with the division until the latter was demobilised.

The R.A.M.C.

It has been impossible in this narrative to deal adequately with the work of the doctors, orderlies, and stretcher-bearers. It is to be hoped that someone more capable of doing justice to the task than the present writer will undertake it, but a few words must be said here to show that the debt owed by the fighting men to the R.A.M.C. is gratefully acknowledged.

In the very early days, when the writer was being taken round by his opposite number and instructed in what to do and what not to do, the party was held up by one of those sudden sharp shell showers that the Boche used to put down on the Armentières front. The opposite number delivered a homily on the folly of those who did not know enough "to come in out of the rain," in the middle of which a pair of individuals emerged from a dug-out opposite and proceeded without any signs of being aware of the shells down the road leading to the front line. The writer inquired whether they were to be included among the foolish ones of whom the opposite number had been speaking. "Oh no! That's the doc and his orderly; they've been asked for from the front line. Of course that's different."

Whenever I have thought of the R.A.M.C. that picture has recurred to me. Whether in a big offensive or in slight shell shower the "doc" was always ready—cool, efficient, and unwearying. From the battalion aid post up in the trenches back to the divisional rest station, a wounded or worn-out man was sure of kindly, considerate, and skilful treatment at any hour of the day or night. How they worked

those " docs " in Becourt Château and many another
such unhealthy spot all through those hot days of that
first bloody week of July, 1916, when the stream of
wounded seemed unending, and the stretcher-bearers
worked till they fell with fatigue.

Here's good luck to you all, 102nd, 103rd, and
104th Field Ambulances, and those above you, and to
you well-beloved " docs " and orderlies and stretcher-
bearers; we wish you well, even while we remember
the horrid taste you gave to our tea with your spoonfuls
of lime.

.   .   .   .

Scene, Becourt Château; time, 2nd July, 1916.
Crowds of wounded.   Few and weary Medical Officers.

First Medical Officer, bending over a stretcher :
" Now, lad, let me see what I can do for you."

Severely wounded man (pointing to second
Medical Officer) : " Noa yer don't! Yer leave me
alone; yon beggar's my Battalion doctor, no one else
touches me."

The Chaplains' Department

Throughout this story but little mention has been
made of the padres, yet they were there, doing stout
work and never shirking.   Duncan, who won an
immediate reward of the M.C. for rescuing a wounded
man in a raid, and later was killed in Arras going to
aid a man struck down by a shell.   " Puss in boots "
talking to one of his boys in the front line while the
Minnies were lobbing over as coolly as if he were at
a mothers' meeting.   Father Crotty, witty and
kindly, and ever so many more.   We take our hats
off to you all, you did us well.

When we first landed in France one battalion had
attached to it a Presbyterian and a Roman Catholic
chaplain.   They were on the best of terms, and

between them there was constant chaff. After the first night in France the Minister had a great tale of the confusion into which Father had been thrown the previous evening by the daughter of the house insisting on washing his feet when he had complained of their paining him after the long march. The Minister waxed very facetious, and there was much laughter in the mess, but in the eye of the priest, who haled from Ireland, was a dangerous twinkle. At last, being pressed by the C.O. to deny the story, His Reverence sighed and sadly admitted that he could not.

" It's true, every word of it," said he, " but the Minister has not told you that when the girl had done with my feet he asked if he could have a bath."

The Chequers

The divisional concert party was started in March, 1916. General Ingouville-Williams took great interest in the matter, and gave a handsome sum to start the show. Lieutenant Thomas, then in the 102nd Field Ambulance, who had been on the boards for six years, was given special leave to buy the necessary dresses, etc., in London town. On his return he set to work to form his company. All units were asked to send along any Henry Irvings or Dan Lenos they might have. In response fifteen individuals paraded, but alas! of these only seven or eight found favour. However, after four days rehearsing they produced a pierrot show, with the assistance of a six-reel Chaplin comedy, " Tillie's Punctual Romance." The move to the Somme a week later put a stop to the run, and the Chequers were in a state of suspended animation till August, when General Nicholson ordered its resuscitation.

Lieutenant Thomas and Corporal Brierley had been looking out for talent, and the nucleus of the Chequers troupe was collected at Franvillers. Lieutenant Thomas was producer, light comedy artist, impressionist; Corporal Brierley stage manager and scenic artist; Sergeant Pocklington, 103rd F.A., baritone; Private C. W. Moody, 10th Lincolns, pianist; Private B. Jane, dancer, and Private H. Tyler, both of 37th Division, temporarily attached. The troupe worked hard, and when the tired battalions trailed back from the mud and slaughter of Pozières and Intermediate trench they were treated to a real pierrot show, and though the member of the troupe to whom I am indebted for these notes says it was a poor show, yet it was appreciated as though it were a West End production.

At Erquinghem about Christmas, 1916, the first pantomime was produced—"Aladdin," to which reference has already been made. The Chequers, afterwards well known from the Lys to the Rhine, was first adopted at this time, and several new artistes joined the troupe, among them Jack Streets, alias "Silly Dick," from the Tyneside Scottish, and Driver Booth, R.F.A., tenor. The Chequers at this time stole the first girl from the Tyneside Scottish "Yellow Diamonds." Off the stage she was Private Harry Charles, but on it she was the best "girl" in France. The Chequers owed much to Colonel Tyler, who, by arranging for the troupe to be entertaining other folk when for any reason it could not be entertaining us, kept it always at the top of its form.

Colonel Alexander from this time watched over the troupe with fatherly interest, and besides designing the "girls'" frocks he wrote the book for the 1917 pantomime, "Dick Whittington," which, by general consent, was held to have been the best thing the Chequers ever did.

The concert party of the Divisional Supply

Column, " The Merry Tatlers," co-operated with the Chequers' troupe, to their mutual benefit, and the Chequers acknowledge that without this aid, especially that of Captain Burchell, O.C. Supply Column, and his numerous carpenters, electricians, etc., the beautiful and elaborate scenic effects, especially " The Sultan's Palace," could never have been achieved. Few who witnessed the appearance of " King Rat " through the " trap," in the prologue, realised that he had been standing in a foot of icy-cold water waiting for his cue. The stage was low, and the surface water could not be kept out of the pit which had to be dug below the " trap."

It was a great show, and the divisional band, under Sergeant Dowling, contributed considerably to its success. After a run of about two months the show was brought to a close, and on the last night about seventy actors, property-men, stage hands, electricians, etc., sat down to a " slap-up " supper provided by Colonel Tyler, who made a kind speech of thanks, which all who heard it will ever remember.

Shortly after this war broke out again, and what with running away from the Boche during March and April, after him from May till November, it was not till after the middle of the latter month that the Chequers really got to work again, and then it was at Le Gaité in Brussels, where the troupe for a week played to crowded and enthusiastic houses, though few of the audience could have understood much of the words. The Belgian charities benefited greatly by this trip.

After twelve days of strenuous rehearsing the third and last Christmas pantomime was produced— " Ali Baba," words and costumes by Colonel Alexander, scenery by Corporal Brierley, produced by Captain Thomas, musical director Sergeant Dowling. In spite of demobilisation playing havoc with the orchestra and the caste, a great success was achieved, which terminated most appropriately in Siegburg beyond the Rhine.

By the end of the run all the original Chequers had left, and Jack Streets carried on the show, and curtain was not finally rung down till Eastern Division was demobilised in Ripon in 1919.

SUMMARY OF DECORATIONS AND HONOURS WON BY OFFICERS AND MEN OF THE 34TH DIVISION

DECORATION, ETC.	1916	1917	1918	TOTAL
V.C.	—	... 3	... 1	... 4
C.B.	—	... 2	... —	... 2
C.M.G.	4	... 2	... 4	... 10
D.S.O. and Bar	20	... 24	... 28	... 72
M.C. and Bar ...	112	... 126	... 202	... 440
D.C.M. and Bar	39	... 49	... 94	... 182
M.M. and Bar ...	344	... 431	... 537	... 1312
M.S.M.	3	... 8	... 87	... 98
Bt. Colonel ...	—	... 2	... 1	... 3
Bt. Lt.-Colonel ...	2	... 2	... 3	... 7
Bt. Major ...	1	... 1	... 1	... 3
Mentions ...	123	... 135	... 115	... 373
Totals	648	... 785	... 1073	... 2506

SUMMARY OF FOREIGN DECORATIONS WON
BY OFFICERS AND MEN OF THE 34TH DIVISION

DECORATIONS	1916	1917	1918	TOTAL
FRENCH—				
Croix de Guerre	1	7	225	233
Medaille Militaire	—	4	22	26
Legion d'honneur				
Croix de Commandeur	—	—	1	1
Croix d'Officier	—	—	4	4
Croix de Chevalier	—	1	6	7
Medaille d'honneur	—	—	3	3
BELGIAN—				
Croix de Guerre	—	15	60	75
Decoration Militaire	—	2	—	2
Ordre de Napoleon, II.				
Croix de Commandeur	—	—	1	1
Croix d'Officier	—	1	—	1
RUSSIAN—				
Order of St Anne, III	1	—	—	1
Order of St George, Cl. II	1	—	—	1
Order of St George, Cl. III	2	—	—	2
Order of St George, Cl. IV	1	—	—	1
ITALIAN—				
Silver Medal	—	1	—	1
Bronze Medal	—	5	—	5
Totals	6	36	322	364

INDEX